Balancing academic rigour with relevant and reflective practitioner insights, Malik and Rowley have put together a research monograph of great quality. This highly relevant scholarship on the Indian IT industry is timely as this attempts to bridge the research-to-practice gap. This monograph is a valuable collection for researchers and HR managers working in the Indian IT industry. A unique book indeed.

S V Nathan, *Director, US-India Talent, Deloitte*

While many books have identified what makes for effective leadership, few have offered such a cohesive blend of academic and real-world findings as found here. Today's global leader will benefit greatly from the key principles found in *Business Models and People Management in the Indian IT Industry.*

Marshall Goldsmith, *author or editor of 34 books*
including the global bestsellers MOJO *and*
What Got You Here Won't Get You There

This book is in-depth and thorough and provides a good understanding of the business models and people management in the Indian IT Industry – a must read for IT industry aspirants, scholars, practitioners and policy makers alike.

Jayantee Mukherjee Saha, *Aei4eiA Pty Ltd, Australia*

Thought-provoking, the book presents a unique attempt to bridge practice-to-theory and theory-to-practice gaps through the development of a novel organising framework set against well laid-out expert content and views from both academics and practitioners actually researching and practising in the Indian IT industry.

Rowena Morais, *HR Matters*

Business Models and People Management in the Indian IT Industry

The global impact of so-called 'offshoring', including of information technology (IT) and related services, continues to be a topic of great interest to academics, practitioners and policymakers. The Indian IT industry has sustained high levels of growth in revenues and employment since the late 1980s. Even following the global financial crisis and meltdown in 2008, the industry has reported growth, albeit at a lower rate. Furthermore, the high rates of technological change and increased competition has forced businesses and managers to be innovative and create new business models.

This book examines how managers and entrepreneurs in the Indian IT industry have explored and exploited human capital opportunities at various stages of the industry's evolution to create innovative human resources (HR) practices and new business models. Based on extensive academic research and deep reflective practitioner accounts, this collection presents expert content, views and a coherent picture of the challenges and changes in the Indian IT industry and analyses how the industry has remained competitive in a constantly changing environment.

This book will appeal to researchers, students and practitioners, particularly in the fields of human resources and strategic management.

Ashish Malik is Lecturer at Newcastle Business School, University of Newcastle, Australia.

Chris Rowley is Professor at Cass Business School, City University, UK, HEAD Foundation, Singapore and Griffith Business School, Griffith University, Australia.

Working in Asia

General Editors:

Tim G. Andrews
University of Strathclyde

Keith Jackson
School of Oriental and African Studies, University of London

and

Chris Rowley
Cass Business School, City University, UK HEAD Foundation, Singapore and Griffith Business School, Griffith University, Australia

This series focuses on contemporary management issues in the Asia-Pacific region. It draws on the latest research to highlight critical factors impacting on the conduct of business in this diverse and dynamic business environment.

Our primary intention is to provide management students and practitioners with fresh dimensions to their reading of standard texts. With each book in the *Working in Asia* series, we offer a combined insider's and outsider's perspective on how managers and their organisations in the Asia-Pacific region are adapting to contemporary currents of both macro- and micro-level change.

The core of data for the texts in this series has been generated by recent interviews and discussions with established senior executives as well as newly-fledged entrepreneurs; with practising as well as aspiring middle managers; and women as well as men. Our mission has been to give voice to how change is being perceived and experienced by a broad and relevant range of people who live and work in the region. We report on how they and their organisations are managing change as the globalisation of their markets, together with their business technologies and traditions unfolds.

Drawing together the combined insights of Asian and Western scholars, and practitioners of management, we present a uniquely revealing portrait of the future of working and doing business in Asia.

Titles in the series include:

The Changing Face of Multinationals in Southeast Asia
Tim G. Andrews, Nartnalin Chompusri and Bryan J. Baldwin

The Changing Face of Japanese Management
Keith Jackson and Miyuki Tomioka

The Changing Face of Chinese Management
Jie Tang and Anthony Ward

The Changing Face of Management in South East Asia
Edited by Chris Rowley and Saaidah Abdul-Rahman

The Changing Face of Women Managers in Asia
Edited by Chris Rowley and Vimolwan Yukongdi

The Changing Face of Korean Management
Edited by Chris Rowley and Yongsun Paik

The Changing Face of People Management in India
Edited by Pawan Budhwar and Jyotsna Bhatnagar

The Changing Face of Management in Thailand
Edited by Tim G. Andrews and Sununta Siengthai

The Changing Face of Vietnamese Management
Edited by Chris Rowley and Quang Truong

The Changing Face of Management in China
Edited by Chris Rowley and Fang Lee Cooke

Business Models and People Management in the Indian IT Industry
From people to profits
Edited by Ashish Malik and Chris Rowley

Business Models and People Management in the Indian IT Industry

From people to profits

Edited by Ashish Malik and Chris Rowley

LONDON AND NEW YORK

First published 2015
by Routledge

2 Park Square, Milton Park, Abingdon, Oxon OX14 4RN
711 Third Avenue, New York, NY 10017, USA

Routledge is an imprint of the Taylor & Francis Group, an informa business

First issued in paperback 2017

British Library Cataloguing in Publication Data
A catalogue record for this book is available from the British Library

Library of Congress Cataloging in Publication Data
Business models and people management in the Indian IT industry: from
people to profits / edited by Ashish Malik and Chris Rowley.
  pages cm. – (Working in Asia)
  1. Information technology–India. 2. Information technology–India–
  Management. 3. High technology industries–India–Management. I.
  Malik, Ashish. II. Rowley, Chris
  HC440.I55B87 2015
  004.068–dc23   2014040818

ISBN: 978-1-138-78318-8 (hbk)
ISBN: 978-1-138-29533-9 (pbk)

Typeset in Times New Roman
by Wearset Ltd, Boldon, Tyne and Wear

Dedicated to my mother, Asha Malik, for her blessings, and my family, Namita, Madhav and Dhruv for their forbearance, love and encouragement.

Ashish Malik

Dedicated to my parents, Jean and Clive Rowley, their support has always been there for me.

Chris Rowley

Contents

Figures

Tables

Contributors

Stephen Blumenfeld is a Senior Lecturer and Director of the Industrial Relations Centre at Victoria University of Wellington, New Zealand.

Pawan Budhwar is Professor of International HRM and Associate Dean for Research at Aston Business School, Birmingham, UK.

Joseph A. George is partner with Workplace Catalysts LLP, Bengaluru, India.

J. Karthikeyan is a Senior Management Consultant at Mecuri Urval International, Bengaluru, India.

Ashish Malik teaches human resource management and development at the University of Newcastle, Australia.

Venkataraman Nilakant is an Associate Professor at the University of Canterbury, New Zealand.

Kapil Notra HR, HCL Great Britain Limited, London, UK.

Vijay Pereira is a Senior Lecturer of International and Strategic HRM and Leader in Knowledge Services in the Organisation Studies and HRM group at Portsmouth Business School, University of Portsmouth, UK.

Chris Rowley is Professor at Cass Business School, City University UK, HEAD Foundation, Singapore and Griffith Business School, Griffith University, Australia.

Arun Sharma is Academic Director, Johnson A. Edosomwan Leadership Institute and Professor, Marketing, School of Business Administration University of Miami, USA.

Prithvi Shergill is Head of Human Resources at HCL Technologies Ltd, NOIDA, India.

Jagdish Sheth is the Charles H. Kellstadt Chair of Marketing in the Goizueta Business School at Emory University, USA.

N.R. Srikanth is Managing Director – Human Resources, Delivery Centres for Technology Accenture, Bengaluru, India.

Amit Verma is a Senior HR Director at NVIDIA Graphics (India and South East Asia), Bengaluru, India.

Foreword

HR value creation

Dave Ulrich[1]

We live in a world of increasing change. New organizations like Amazon (founded 1994), Facebook (founded 2004), Google (founded 2005), and Wikipedia (2001) have dramatically changed both personal and professional lives. These new organizations have forced traditional organizations to focus less on hierarchy and more on agility. Organizations succeed less by rules, roles, and routines, and more by speed, learning, and change.

This dynamic volatile, uncertain, complex, and ambiguous (VUCA) world affects both the practice and theory of organizations. Business leaders have to learn to adapt and learn to stay current. They have to create organizations that anticipate rather than react and respond quickly to changing opportunities. Academics, who build theory to explain organization success, need to also evolve their thinking so that their work informs practice.

In this edited volume, Malik and Rowley try to bridge the increasing theory vs. practice gap by examining one of the most dramatic changes in the world today, the Indian IT industry (Kryscynski and Ulrich, 2014). The Indian IT industry is an outgrowth of the rapid world of change, where knowledge and ideas know no global boundaries and where insight can be quickly moved around the world. This IT industry has gone from 1% of Indian's economy in 1998 to 8% by 2012. The Indian IT industry's policy advocacy body, NASSCOM, states that there is now a diverse range of service providers, with more than 15,000 firms in operation (NASSCOM, 2014). This anthology of thoughtful writers works to show that academic theory and business practice may coexist in explaining the evolution of this industry. In particular, this work shows the role of human capital in helping shape the industry. The value of HR comes when HR practices can be used to help an individual, organization, industry, or country accomplish its goals. To deliver HR value and bridge theory and practice, let me offer three observations: (1) take an outside in perspective, (2) clarify outcomes of human capital, and (3) innovate and integrate HR practices.

1 Take an outside in perspective

Most HR professionals have an internal mindset. When we ask them "who are your customers?" they often answer, "the employees." When we ask them "what is your great work challenge?", the answers are often about finding or keeping talent, building talent, or managing compensation. To deliver real value, HR must start with the outside in. This means focusing on the context of business, including social, technological, economic, political, environmental, and demographic trends. These general trends set the environmental context in which HR works. Then, HR should deliver value to key stakeholders both inside (employees, leaders) and outside (customers, investors, communities) outside their organization. By understanding these external stakeholders, HR can align their work to meet their needs (Ulrich, Younger, Brockbank, and Ulrich, 2012). In particular, HR can tie their work to customers (Ulrich and Smallwood, 2007) and investors (Ulrich, in press).

This volume shows the external trends that affect the Indian IT industry. Some of these general trends (e.g., technology) define the industry and other trends (e.g., demographics) determine how firms within in the space.

HR professionals should have a mindset of "outside in" where they focus less on what they do and more on who gets value from what they do.

2 HR outcomes

With an outside in perspective, HR professionals offer unique information, insights, and recommendations to deliver competitive advantage. In formal and informal business discussions, each staff group brings unique insights to drive business results: finance talks about economic performance with information about revenues, costs, and financial returns; marketing discusses customers with recommendations on targeting key customers, customer response (e.g., net promoter score), and customer connection; operations makes recommendations and systems, quality, and supply chain. When HR partners in these strategy discussions, we propose that they provide insight, information, and recommendations on talent (people, workforce, human capital), capability (culture, processes, key success factors, systems), and leadership (Ulrich, 2014).

Talent. At the risk of grossly oversimplifying, let me suggest that there is actually a deceptively simple formula for talent that makes talent more productive:

Talent = Competence * Commitment * Contribution.

All three elements of this equation need to be considered and integrated to fully manage talent.

Capability. Talent is not enough. Great individuals who do not work well together as a team, or in their organization, will not be successful. Capabilities represent what the organization is known for, what it is good at doing, and how it patterns activities to deliver value. The capabilities define many of the intangibles that investors pay attention to, the firm brand to which customers can relate, and the culture that shapes employee behavior. These capabilities also become the identity of the firm, the deliverables of HR practices, and the key to implementing business strategy.

Leadership. Ultimately, leaders bring together both individuals and organizations to solve customer problems. But there is a difference between leaders and leadership. The term "leaders" refers to individuals who have unique abilities to guide the behavior of others. Leadership refers to an organization's capacity to build future leaders. An individual leader matters, but an organization's collective leadership matters more over time.

When HR professionals are both architects and anthropologists of talent, leadership, and capability, they help build organizations and people who are responsive to changing business conditions. As architects, they create blueprints and frameworks for change; they solve puzzles. As anthropologists, they identify future opportunities, often based on external context, often called mystery seeking.

In this volume, we learn about how talent, leadership, and capability were developed within the Indian IT industry. HR professionals delivered the right people, the right culture, and the right leaders so that these firms could grow.

3 Innovate and integrate HR practices

Ultimately, HR needs to offer integrated solutions to talent, leadership, and capability challenges. These integrated solutions meld together HR practices in people (staffing, training, career management), performance (appraisal, rewards), information (communication inside and out), and work (organization design, governance, physical space). When these distinct HR practices are woven together around increasing talent, leadership, and capability, they will help an organization become more than its individual talent.

Indian IT firms that survive institutionalize their success by creating these HR practices that ensure a flow of talent, leadership, and capability. HR professionals advise business leaders to make this happen.

Conclusion: academia and practice

To narrow the gap between academic and practice, let me offer some modest proposals:

*   Start with a phenomenon. Good theory, research, and practice requires a grounding in a phenomenon. Phenomenologists encourage thinkers to experience, think about, and write about what is happening that is of interest to them. The phenomenon may come from observation of an individual, leadership, or organization challenge and often is something that is a bit quirky or unusual. For example, we noticed that two firms in the same industry with similar earnings had different stock prices. This led to exploration of the intangibles in market value which lead to better understanding of how investors derive confidence in future earnings from the quality of leadership, talent, and culture within a company. To get clarity about a phenomenon, I often write (or suggest to others) one to two pages about what I am interested in and why.

- Create a point of view. With clear descriptors, it helps to try to explain why the phenomenon is happening. As noted above, figuring out why two firms in the same industry with the same earnings have different market values lead to a theory of intangibles. I find it helpful to write a page or two about why is this happening? This exercise drives a perception about the potential causes and conceptual rational for the phenomenon.
- Discover other relevant perspectives. Once the phenomenon and explanations are proposed, it is very helpful to review and systematically review what others have said. There are many theoretical perspectives which may inform and predict why things happen as they do. To unravel intangibles, I ended up reviewing economic, investor, and organization literatures. At this nexus we were able to synthesize how others had tried to make sense of this market quirk. By drawing on theoretical underpinning from others, we help position our work in the knowledge network of what others have said. We can also identify specific questions we want to explore that will expand the existing knowledge network.
- Be rigorous in your methods. Research methods and statistical approaches flow from the questions we want to answer. The methods should match the research questions. In our intangibles research, since many of the ideas were exploratory, we did extensive interviews to figure out how investors thought about the problem. This led to other research that helped address the questions we are asking. The research design and methods help offer valid answers to the questions we raise.
- Tie findings back to the problem. Once the studies have been done, it is good to close the loop and return to the original phenomenon. Have we added to the understanding of what is happening and why it is happening? Has our theory and research been able to offer new ways to think about and act on this phenomenon?
- Learn. Learning is the ability to generate and generalize ideas with impact, so it is useful to envision how our work will offer insights to multiple stakeholders. What would those experiencing the phenomenon do differently? In our investor case, what would we say to investors? If we are studying leadership, what would we say to a group of leaders about the topic we covered? What would other scholars in the academic area say? Would our theories and research methods communicate to scholars how theories need to evolve? What is missing in our work? What questions emerge or remain after answering our questions?

These steps are not always linear or explicit and can be adapted to situations. But they show how the connections across theory, research, and practice can be made. In this volume, most of the authors did a nice job by starting with the phenomenon of Indian IT industry and worked to explain this phenomenon with new and innovative theory.

HR value can be enhanced by building an outside in perspective, being clear about HR outcomes of talent, leadership, and capability, and by integrating and innovating HR. When academics start by trying to understand a phenomenon, they can use theory to guide practice and practitioners can rely on theory to do their work better. This volume offers a marvelous set of readings on this hope.

Note

1 Dave Ulrich is the Rensis Likert Professor at the Ross School of Business, University of Michigan, USA and a partner at the RBL Group, USA.

References

Kryscynski, D., and Ulrich, D. (2014). Making strategic human capital relevant: A time sensitive opportunity. *Academy of Management Perspectives*. Advance online publication. doi:10.5465/amp.2014.0127

NASSCOM. (2014). *India IT-BPM Overview*. Retrieved from www.nasscom.in/indian-itbpo-industry

Ulrich, D. (2014). The future targets or outcomes of HR work: Talent, leadership, and capability. *Human Resource Development International, 17*(1), 1–9.

Ulrich, D. (in press). *Leadership Capital Index*.

Ulrich, D., and Smallwood, N. (2007). *Leadership Brand*. Cambridge, MA: Harvard Business Press.

Ulrich, D., Younger, J., Brockbank, W., and Ulrich, M. (2012). *HR From the Outside In: Six Competencies for the Future of Human Resources*. New York, NY: McGraw-Hill.

1 Profiting from people management practices

An introduction

Ashish Malik and Chris Rowley

Introduction

The global impact of 'offshoring', including that of information technology (IT) and related services, to developing nations such as India has been a topic of great interest and debate to academics, practitioners and policymakers (Arora and Athreye, 2002; Arora and Gambardella, 2006; Arora, Arunachalam, Asundi and Fernandes, 2001; Athreye, 2004, 2005; Banerjee, 2004; Budhwar and Bhatnagar, 2009; Malik, 2009; Malik, Sinha and Blumenfeld, 2012; NASSCOM, 2014a; Thite and Russell, 2009). The high rates of technological change and increased competition have forced IT businesses and their managers to continuously reinvent their business models. It is through such constant renewal of business models and change management efforts of business leaders that the Indian IT industry has continued to sustain high levels of growth, even in a post-global financial crisis era (Malik, 2013).

From humble beginnings in the early 1970s, the Indian IT industry has come a long way. Current estimates suggest that the Indian IT industry has revenues in excess of US$118 billion and employs around three million people (NASSCOM, 2014a, b, c). Numerous metaphors have been used to portray the growth story of India's IT industry, for example, the 'horse that flew' (Vittal, 2004), the story of 'blind men and the elephant' (Rahman and Kurien, 2007) and 'from underdogs to tigers' (Arora and Gambardella, 2006) are among the most popular discourses.

Our book is different from earlier expositions on the Indian IT industry (Arora and Gambardella, 2006; Banerjee, 2004; Budhwar and Bhatnagar, 2009; Thite and Russell, 2009). While these accounts have tended to focus on the supply and demand side dynamics of human capital and related explanations of growth, our collection differentiates on a number of fronts. First, it offers an inclusive theoretical framework for examining the innovative approaches to the strategic management of human resources (HR) in the IT industry. By adopting a number of theoretical frameworks, richer explanations of business models can be uncovered. Second, it offers a much more nuanced view of how managers, entrepreneurs and consultants operating in the Indian IT industry have contributed to exploring and exploiting human capital opportunities at various stages of the industry's evolution. These diverse groups of stakeholders implemented numerous changes to business models and HR management (HRM) practices to sustain high levels of growth. Third, it presents expert content and views from academics and practitioners who are actively researching and practicing in the Indian IT industry. Thus, our book is also an unique attempt to bridge the commonly noted practice-to-theory and theory-to-practice gaps (Swanson, 1997) prevalent in the Indian IT industry. Also, following the ethos of the 'Working in Asia' series, it gives 'voice' to organisations and practitioners. Finally, it presents an evidence-based analysis of how the industry has remained competitive in a constantly changing environment. Our book will benefit practitioners, scholars and researchers of management, particularly in HRM and strategic management.

To do this, our book is split into two major parts. In Part I we cover theoretical and empirical contributions from academics highlighting the context, key theoretical approaches, research gaps and empirical contributions covering the key sectors of the Indian IT industry. Further details of Part I are provided in the upcoming sections entitled 'Context: Boundaries in a borderless world' and 'Theory: Theoretical foundations for informing practice'. In Part II we take a more practitioner-based approach with contributions that highlight in-depth experiences of HR practitioners from the Indian IT industry covering a range of topics, such as managing people in IT services and product environments, the role of coaching and organisational development interventions in exploring and exploiting human capital opportunities and how organisations can support development of large-scale generation and management of innovative approaches to business and people management. Further details of Part II are provided in the upcoming sections entitled 'Practice: Bridging the research-practice-theory-research gap', 'The critical role of leadership and change management' and 'Integrating new knowledge into a coherent assemblage'. The different emphases of these chapters suggests the need for a different chapter structure and format through which the key messages are communicated. Nevertheless, for a comparative snapshot, we provide below a summary in Table 1.1. This provides readers with a quick overview of the book's content and journey.

Business models and people management practices

From our review of the literature on strategic HRM, there is an extremely limited body of research that explicitly links HRM practices to a firm's business model and its key elements for creating and realising value (Bae and Rowley, 2003; Cascio, 2005; Clark, 2009; Hunter, 2006). This gap in the literature is rather strange, especially as there have been calls for linking HRM practices and firm performance (Buller and McEvoy, 2012). While we acknowledge there are numerous factors that create and realise value in a firm's business model (Johnson, Christensen and Kagermann, 2008; Zott, Amit and Massa, 2011), we believe there is merit in furthering our understanding of how various sets of HRM practices contribute to a firm's business model (Johnson *et al.*, 2008). By developing such an understanding one can make critical advances in the HRM–performance debate and explain how

Table 1.1 Business models and people management in the Indian IT industry

Chapters	Key emphasis
1 Profiting from people management practices	Organising framework for the book
Part 1	
2 Context and evolution of the Indian IT industry	Theoretical review focusing on context and industry evolution
3 Skills, strategy and people management in the IT industry	Theoretical foundations focusing on key HRM, strategy and HRD studies
4 HRM and firm performance: the case of Indian IT/BPO industry	Theoretical propositions for high-performance work practices paradigm
5 Orchestrating human capital in the Indian IT service market: from entrepreneurial management to professional management	Empirical findings tracking changes in managerial orientation for exploiting human capital opportunities
6 Innovative HR practices: evidence from three IT software services organisations	Empirical study highlighting key innovative HRM practices in IT services firms
7 Innovative people management approaches from three software research and product development firms	Empirical study highlighting key innovative HRM practices in product development firms
Part II	
8 Managing people in an IT software services environment	In-depth and reflective ethnographic insights on the role of skills in IT services firms
9 Managing people in an IT product and research and development environment	In-depth and reflective ethnographic insights on critical HRM and leadership practices in software and product development firms
10 Process consulting and adaptations of organisation development in the Indian IT industry	Case studies of role of organisational development interventions in the Indian IT industry
11 Senior management mentoring and coaching for exploration and exploitation	Case studies of the role of executive coaching in supporting exploration and exploitation behaviours
12 The world's largest 'ideapreneurship™': putting employees first so the customer never feels second!	Practitioner insights of how to manage innovations and new ideas in a large IT product and service environment firm
***	
13 Towards an integrated model of human capital development for business model innovation: synthesis and new knowledge	Synthesising the findings to highlight (1) the HRM practices conducive to exploration and exploitation; and (2) key HRM practices that support business model innovation

each element of a firm's business model can be supported by certain HRM practices. Through our review and analysis of the research on business models in the Indian IT industry, we map the key stages of business model evolution, shown in Figure 1.1.

Applying the resource-based view approach (Barney, 1991), it is critical to understand how firms create and realise value through unique HRM configurations and practices. Our review of business models suggests that in addition to changes in HRM practices, certain practices from organisational development, change management and HR development (HRD) are needed to gain a fuller understanding of how firms undertake business model innovations. Evolving business models require concomitant changes to an organisation's HRM practices to be able to successfully deliver new customer value propositions. Achieving this transition is never easy as firms have to undertake a number of changes not only in the way they attract their talent but also how they modify work design, HRD and retention strategies. For example, the nature of HR that were recruited and developed for the early stages of the 'body shopping' era were very different from the industry's 'Client locale to service provider locale' business model, as in the latter stage firms needed to attract and develop a very cost effective and trainable pool of technical resources, with strong programme and project management capabilities to deliver global IT services from Indian markets. Similarly, in the maturity stage of the 'anytime, anywhere' or the global service delivery business model stage, a very different set of specialised domain and business development skills and international HRM practices are needed for managing young expatriates. Finally, in the current stage of the industry's growth, 'Crowd and cloud', the management of disruptive

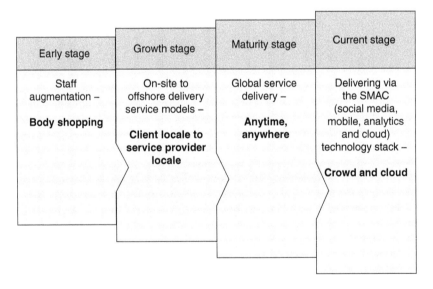

Figure 1.1 Indian IT industry: mapping business model transitions.

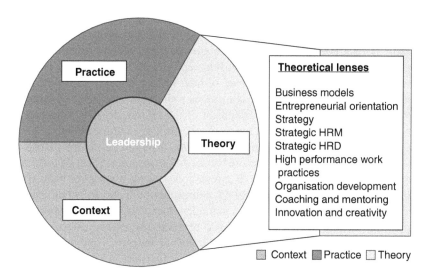

Figure 1.2 Profit through people: an organising framework.

technologies such as SMAC (social media, mobile, analytics and cloud) services poses real opportunities and challenges and requires a very different skill base for crowdsourcing of ideas and engaging in open innovation, something the industry has not been very familiar with so far (KPMG, 2013). To this end, we develop a novel organising framework for understanding the relationship and interplay between theory, context, practices and leadership for sustaining high performance through people management practices, as shown in Figure 1.2. The role and important context of country, culture and competence, for leadership in Asia is also outlined in Rowley and Ulrich (2012).

The following section briefly explains the importance of each of the four components of the framework, with specific references to the relevant contributions covered in our book.

Context: boundaries in a borderless world

The strategic choice a firm can exercise is limited by the nature of its institutional environment and the strength of its dominant coalition of stakeholders (Kochan, McKersie and Cappelli, 1984; Nilakant, 2005). The importance of context is understated in a number of theoretical models of strategic HRM that often adopt a prescriptive best-practice model approach (Huselid, 1995; Pfeffer, 1998). Others have argued for the active role of human agency in managing institutional pressures and achieving a better strategic fit (Boon, Paauwe, Boselie and Den Hartog, 2009). To this end, our collection begins by analysing the Indian IT industry's contextual environment in Chapter 2. Highlighting the importance of context and the evolution of the Indian IT industry, this chapter traces the evolution of four generations of the industry. It highlights how certain actors and institutions have facilitated dealing with the contextual barriers and institutional pressures faced by the industry. These actors, or the human agency, created opportunities for developing an expansive environment, which provided much needed leeway for industry leaders to develop and expand their strategic choice options. The chapter presents an account of how India's resource endowments, institutional dynamics and deliberate choices, as well as the confluence of certain happy accidents, all shaped the development of the IT industry. The change in the landscape in a post-2008 global financial crisis is also examined briefly.

Building on the role of human agency in an institutional environment is Chapter 5, covering the role of entrepreneurial and managerial talent in orchestrating human capital opportunities. It draws upon a long association with the senior executive boards of successful IT companies in India, traveling often between customer locations in the USA and talent locations in India. It provides a longitudinal account of how strategic HRM practices, its drivers, choice-points and possible errors all variously affected the Indian IT industry's ability to create global impact. It notes the role played by senior leadership and entrepreneurial talent as critical in the evolution of the industry and provides examples of how the leadership successfully orchestrated the exploration and exploiting of human capital. It discusses how the industry's managerial talent conceived opportunities for growth, as well as shaped the way for strategic HRM in support to the industry.

Theory: theoretical foundations for informing practice

Studies of strategic HRM have provided support for the relationship between HRM practices, competitive strategy and firm performance (Becker, Ulrich and Huselid, 2001; Becker and Huselid, 2006; Delery and Doty, 1996; Huselid, 1995; Paauwe, 2004; Pfeffer, 1998; Schuler and Jackson, 1987; Wright, Dunford and Snell, 2001). These studies have emphasised various aspects of the classic performance equation (Performance $=f$ ability, motivation and opportunity), often employing numerous theoretical underpinnings for explaining the relationship between HRM and performance. Notable among the key theoretical perspectives include: human capital theory, the resource-based view, transaction-cost theory and numerous versions of high performance work systems (HPWS) models, including adopting a quality management-oriented HPWS bundle (Barney, 1991; Becker, 1964; Malik, 2009; Williamson, 1975; Wright *et al.*, 2001). Acknowledging the multidisciplinary lens needed in explaining the HRM and performance link, Chapter 3 presents the relationships between skills, strategy and HRM in the IT industry. An inclusive framework is used to analyse the key theoretical propositions relevant for the born-global, high-technology professional services IT industry. A case is made for adopting a multidisciplinary approach wherein human capital exploration and exploitation opportunities can be better understood by examining a firm's business development, operations and human capital management functions. Such an approach allows for a rich and holistic understanding of skills and capability development, critical in the exploration and exploitation of human capital opportunities in business-to-business contexts.

In a similar vein, Chapter 4 highlights the importance of high performance work systems in the Indian IT industry. This chapter is concerned with the contribution HRM and human capital management makes to high performance work systems in Indian IT organisations. It discusses the relationship between theories of transaction costs economics (Williamson, 1975), human capital (Becker, 1962), resource-based view (Barney, 1991) and its impact on HRM and the HPWS paradigm. Indian IT organisations offer knowledge intensive services which are dependent on HR for delivery. Although technology underpins the delivery of such services and processes, employees are central to organisational resources and represent a cornerstone for value creation. The management of HR is, therefore, central to overall performance and success. This chapter discusses the bundles of HPWS leading to strategies adopted and adapted by high performing, successful Indian IT organisations and concludes with several future research propositions.

Practice: bridging the research-practice-theory-research gap

There is an ongoing need to address the gaps between theory and practice and how, through the rigorous application of theory, researchers can bridge the issues of rigour and relevance in research and practice, respectively (Gulati, 2007; Ritchie, Lewis, Nicholls and Ormston, 2013; Swanson, 1997). In an attempt to deal with such gaps, our book integrates research that informs practice and vice versa. To this end, we offer a combination of research undertaken by academics and practitioners on various aspects of exploring and exploiting human capital opportunities in the Indian IT industry. As identified in Chapter 2, the Indian IT industry can be broadly sub-grouped into IT software services and IT products and that both these product and service environments require very different approaches in managing their HR. Understanding innovative HRM practices adopted by each sub-sector of this industry is the focus of four chapters (6, 7, 8 and 9), two each for each of the sub-sectors from both academic and practitioner experiences.

Chapter 6 provides evidence of innovative HRM practices from three IT software services organisations in India. Employing a qualitative case study research strategy, empirical evidence is presented of how firms operating in an IT services environment organise their HRM architecture to explore and/or exploit human capital and market opportunities. The role of strategic choice and investment in certain capabilities demonstrates how some firms' HR practices are better aligned than others to explore than exploit human capital opportunities. Chapter 7 highlights the innovative HRM approaches from three software research and product development firms. This argues that although the Indian labour market has rich pools of talent and expertise that are suited for operational and execution excellence, operating in a product development environment requires a different mindset and calibre of human capital. While the current

Indian educational system and a hardwired service mindset may explain the sector's talent ecosystem, certain work design, learning and HRM approaches have been instrumental in developing a human capital base necessary for exploration. Employing a qualitative case based research strategy, this chapter presents empirical evidence of how firms operating in an IT product environment organise their HRM architecture to explore and or exploit the human capital and market opportunities that are available.

Chapter 8 provides a reflective ethnographic practitioner account, sharing deep insights of his experiences of managing people in an IT software services environment. This highlights that skills development is an integral part of the Indian IT services providers' strategy and that firms have not only looked at it as a tool for selection, motivation and retention, but also as a way to manage the pipeline of talent and cost of bench. While entry level training programmes have been largely industrialised, organisations have brought in innovation in training delivery and output evaluation processes. These innovative methods have also optimised the cost of training. The learning options further to the initial entry level training have been viewed opportunistically and at different points in time have been used as a tool for career advancement, motivation and retention, and performance management or the lack of the same.

Chapter 9 distils the experiences of more than two decades of managing people in medium and large IT product and R&D environment firms. It suggests that managing people in a product development requires significant investments in building a comprehensive long-term human capability mindset that transcends product definition, development, productionisation and post-product development support. The Indian labour market has historically focused on building near term competencies and lacks a human capital ecosystem for exploiting market opportunities. This chapter provides an overview of the HRM challenges faced by IT product firms and prescribes a set of appropriate HRM practices and leadership approaches for product development firms in the Indian IT market to continue to deliver high levels of innovative activity.

The critical role of leadership and change management

Firms operating in the IT industry are often confronted with technological-, employee- and client-induced changes. Often such changes have an impact on modifying a firm's existing business model. Depending on the nature and scale of the change management programme, firms undertake a range of interventions, such as organisational development interventions at individual, group, process and/or strategic leadership levels. Application of organisational development approaches have been dominant in managing change in medium- to large-scale IT organisations operating in India (Gurjar, 2009). Further, the role of leadership in supporting exploration and exploitation of learning has been widely acknowledged in studies of innovation and organisational ambidexterity (Smith and Tushman, 2005; O'Reilly and Tushman, 2007; Jansen, George, Van den Bosch and Volberda, 2008). Acknowledging the importance of organisational development and innovation, our book presents some in-depth practitioner accounts focusing on process consulting and adaptations of organisation development in the IT industry (Chapter 10), senior executive coaching (Chapter 11) and managing innovation through a supporting HRM framework (Chapter 12).

Chapter 10 elaborates on organisational development interventions in the Indian IT industry and how these helped in supporting exploration and exploitation of human capital opportunities. It suggests that the values of professional practice and economic surplus have been richly explored in the literature. In the IT industry's evolution in India, pragmatism resulted in many 'firsts' for management and employees in the creation of 'open' climates and 'enabling' workspaces. Employee stock options, liberal pay packages, the five-day work week and employee friendly benefits such as crèches and gymnasiums, all became telltale signs of the industry. However, with scale-based growth, organisations were facing challenges due to increased work complexity and a strain on role and work relationships. Drawing upon practitioner insights in facilitating organisational learning and development, this chapter uses the lens of covert processes to trace unconscious tendencies that are likely to be stressful to the longevity of the industry and the resilience of its workforce. It traces individual-, group- and organisation-level dilemmas that need tending to in the Indian IT industry's context.

Noting the critical role played by leadership in fostering innovation, Chapter 11 provides case studies of nine senior management coaching experiences for developing behaviours that are conducive to exploration and exploitation of human capital opportunities. This chapter highlights the role of executive coaching and mentoring in IT software services and product development teams for building both personal effectiveness and innovation and exploitation capabilities. The chapter draws upon extensive consulting, coaching and mentoring experiences of senior executives. Through active involvement the author helped executives confront business and people management issues affecting efficiencies, creativity and lateral thinking within the senior management teams.

Chapter 12 builds on HCL Technologies' *Employee First, Customer Second* (EFCS) approach, which resulted in a book by the ex-CEO of HCL Technologies. It discusses Version 2.0 of the EFCS proposition. It argues that the unique differentiator of the EFCS proposition was in the insight that true value lies in the interaction zone between the employee and the customer – the value zone – and that the role of management is to enthuse, enable and empower the value zone. This chapter reflects on the journey that HCL Technologies took in the development of product, processes and practices that not only contributed to empowering the value zone, but enabled the paradigm shift in the company to truly invert the pyramid. These innovations have reinforced beliefs and led to behaviours that have in turn led to a culture that is employee driven and management embraced, making HCL one of the largest ... in the world.

Integrating new knowledge into a coherent assemblage

Finally, through the concluding chapter, we provide a meta-analysis of the key themes emanating from the above contributions as well as our own reviews of recent work on the Indian IT industry to analyse the key learning implications for policymakers, academics and practising managers. The final chapter also summarises the challenges faced at an industry level. As a result, we present an integrated model for analysing HRM practices needed for exploration and exploitation and how such practices supports a firm's business model and its elements. The genesis of our model is based on the academic and practitioner insights covered in our collection. Finally, we discuss the ways in which scholar-practitioners and researchers can deploy the framework for their research and practice.

Conclusion

To summarise, this chapter provided a novel organising framework for studying the dynamics of people management in the Indian IT industry. This chapter also introduced how different elements of our framework interact with each other. This interaction is uniquely captured through the work of several contributing authors in this book and as such our novel approach adds value to our understanding of business models and managing people and HRM in the Indian IT industry.

References

Arora, A., and Athreye, S. (2002). The software industry and India's economic development. *Information Economics and Policy*, *14*(2), 253–273.

Arora, A., and Gambardella, A. (Eds.) (2006). *From underdogs to tigers? The rise and growth of the software industry in Brazil, China, India, Ireland, and Israel*. Oxford: Oxford University Press.

Arora, A., Arunachalam, V.S., Asundi, J.V., and Fernandes, R. (2001). The Indian software services industry. *Research Policy*, *30*(8), 1267–1287.

Athreye, A. (2004). The role of transnational corporations in the evolution of a high-tech industry: The case of India's software industry – A comment. *World Development*, *32*(3), 555–560.

Athreye, A. (2005). The Indian software industry and its evolving service capability. *Industrial and Corporate Change*, *14*(3), 393–418.

Bae, J., and Rowley, C. (2003). Changes and continuities in South Korean HRM. *Asia Pacific Business Review*, *9*(4), 76–105.

Banerjee, P. (2004). *The Indian software industry: Business strategy and dynamic coordination*. New Delhi: Palgrave Macmillan.

Barney, J. (1991). Firm resources and sustained competitive advantage. *Journal of Management*, *17*(1), 99–120.

Becker, B.E., and Huselid, M.A. (2006). Strategic human resources management: Where do we go from here? *Journal of Management*, *32*(6), 898–925.

Becker, B.E., Ulrich, D., and Huselid, M.A. (2001). *The HR scorecard: Linking people, strategy, and performance*. Boston, MA: Harvard Business School Press.

Becker, G. (1962). Investment in human capital: A theoretical analysis Part 2 – Investment in human beings. *Journal of Political Economy, 70*(5), 9–49.

Becker, G. (1964). *Human capital: A theoretical and empirical analysis.* Princeton, NJ: Princeton University Press.

Boon, C., Paauwe, J., Boselie, P., and Den Hartog, D. (2009). Institutional pressures and HRM: Developing institutional fit, *Personnel Review, 38*(5), 492–508.

Budhwar, P., and Bhatnagar, J. (2009). *The changing face of people management in India.* Abingdon: Routledge.

Buller, P.F., and McEvoy, G.M. (2012). Strategy, human resource management and performance: Sharpening line of sight. *Human Resource Management Review, 22*(1), 43–56.

Cascio, W.F. (2005). From business partner to driving business success: The next step in the evolution of HR management. *Human Resource Management, 44*(2), 159–163.

Clark, I. (2009). The private equity business model and associated strategies for HRM: Evidence and implications? *The International Journal of Human Resource Management, 20*(10), 2030–2048.

Delery, J.E., and Doty, D.H. (1996). Modes of theorizing in strategic human resource management: Tests of universalistic, contingency, and configurations. performance predictions. *Academy of Management Journal, 39*(4), 802–835.

Gulati, R. (2007). Tent poles, tribalism, and boundary spanning: The rigor-relevance debate in management research. *Academy of Management Journal, 50*(4), 775–782.

Gurjar, N. (2009). A practitioner's perspective on the Indian info-services industry. In M. Thite and R. Russell (Eds.). *The next available operator: Managing human resources in Indian business process outsourcing* industry (115–144). New Delhi: Sage.

Hunter, L. (2006). Low cost airlines: Business model and employment relations. *European Management Journal, 24*(5), 315–321.

Huselid, M. (1995). The impact of human resource management practices on turnover, productivity, and corporate financial performance. *Academy of Management Journal, 38*(3), 635–672.

Jansen, J.P.J., George, G., Van den Bosch, F.A.J., and Volberda, H.W. (2008). Senior team attributes and organizational ambidexterity: The moderating role of transformational leadership. *Journal of Management Studies, 45*(5), 982–1007.

Johnson, M.W., Christensen, C.C., and Kagermann, H. (2008). Reinventing your business model. *Harvard Business Review, 86*(12), 50–59.

Kochan, T.A., McKersie, R.B., and Cappelli, P. (1984). Strategic choice and industrial relations theory, *Industrial Relations: A Journal of Economy and Society, 23*(1), 16–39.

KPMG (2013). *The SMAC code: Embracing new technologies for future business.* Bangalore: Author. Retrieved from www.kpmg.com/IN/en/IssuesAndInsights/ArticlesPublications/Documents/The-SMAC-code-Embracing-new-technologies-for-future-business.pdf

Malik, A. (2009). Training drivers, competitive strategy, and clients' needs: Case studies of three business process outsourcing companies. *Journal of European Industrial Training, 33*(2/3), 160–177. doi:10.1108/03090590910939058

Malik, A. (2013). Post-GFC people management challenges: A study of India's information technology sector. *Asia Pacific Business Review, 19*(2), 230–246. doi:10.1080/136 02381.2013.767638

Malik, A., Sinha, A., and Blumenfeld, S. (2012). Role of quality management capabilities in developing market-based organisational learning capabilities: Case study evidence from four Indian business process outsourcing firms. *Industrial Marketing Management, 41*(4), 639–648.

NASSCOM (2014a). *The IT-BPM sector in India – Strategic Review 2014.* New Delhi: NASSCOM.

NASSCOM (2014b). India IT-BPM Overview. Retrieved from www.nasscom.in/indian-itbpo-industry

NASSCOM (2014c). Knowledge Professionals. Retrieved from www.nasscom.in/knowledge-professionals

Nilakant, V. (2005, August). *Institutional dynamics in the evolution of the Indian software industry.* Paper presented at the Academy of Management Conference, Hawaii, USA.

O'Reilly, C.A., and Tushman, M.L. (2007). *Ambidexterity as a Dynamic Capability: Resolving the Innovator's Dilemma.* Working Paper No. 07-088. Cambridge, MA: Harvard Business School.

Paauwe, J. (2004). *HRM and performance: Achieving long-term viability.* Oxford: Oxford University Press on Demand.

Pfeffer, J. (1998). *The human equation: Building profits by putting people first.* Boston, MA: Harvard Business School Press.

Rahman, W., and Kurien, P. (2007). *Blind men and the elephant: Demystifying the global IT services industry.* New Delhi: Sage Publications.

Ritchie, J., Lewis, J., Nicholls, C.M., and Ormston, R. (Eds.). (2013). *Qualitative research practice: A guide for social science students and researchers.* Los Angeles, CA: Sage Publications.

Rowley, C., and Ulrich, D. (2012). Lessons learned and insights derived for leadership in Asia. *Asia Pacific Business Review, 18*(4), 675–681.

Schuler, R.S., and Jackson, S.E. (1987). Linking competitive strategies with human resource management practices. *Academy of Management Executive, 1*(3), 207–219.

Smith, W.K., and Tushman, M.L. (2005). Managing strategic contradictions: A top management model for managing innovation streams. *Organization Science, 16*(5), 522–536.

Swanson, R.A. (1997). HRD research: Don't go to work without it. In R. Swanson and E. Holton (Eds). *Human resource development research handbook: Linking research and practice.* San Francisco, CA: Berrett-Koehler Publishers.

Thite, M., and Russell, R. (2009). *The next available operator: Managing human resources in Indian business process outsourcing industry.* New Delhi: Sage.

Vittal, N. (2004). The horse that flew. In *India: Technology and a vision for the future* (Chapter 24). Hyderabad: ICFAI Press.

Williamson, O.E. (1975). *Markets and hierarchies: Analysis and antitrust implications.* New York, NY: Free Press.

Wright, P.M., Dunford, B.B., and Snell, S.A. (2001). Human resources and the resource based view of the firm. *Journal of Management, 27*(6), 701–721.

Zott, C., Amit, R., and Massa, L. (2011). The business model: Recent developments and future research. *Journal of Management, 37*(4), 1019–1042.

Part I

Human capital issues in the Indian IT industry

2 Context and evolution of the Indian IT industry

Ashish Malik and Venkataraman Nilakant

Introduction

This chapter discusses the role of different institutional actors and strategic choices exercised by entrepreneurs in developing and improving existing business models of Indian IT firms. The remarkable and sustained level of growth posted by the Indian IT industry is one of the reasons that it continues to attract practitioner and academic interest towards this industry. While there are numerous stories of the success of large Indian IT companies and how they might have benefited from the diffusion of transnational firms' business and management practices, some researchers have noted how large multinationals report growth in productivity through the application of unique innovative human resource management (HRM) and management approaches and an increased incidence of reverse diffusion from India to the developed markets (Cappelli, Singh, Singh and Useem, 2010; Govindarajan and Trimble, 2012; Kumar and Puranam, 2012; Radjou, Prabhu and Ahuja, 2012). The Indian IT industry is a significant contributor to the nation's gross domestic product (approximately 8%) and employs in excess of three million people.

This chapter begins with a brief overview of India's socio-economic composition and its demographic details. It then discusses the evolution of its IT sector in light of the global development and expansion of the IT sector. Alternative explanations surrounding the role of skills development, organisational capabilities and learning, which are core aspects of a firm's ability to explore and exploit opportunities and sustaining organisational growth, are also discussed. The chapter concludes with the challenges faced by the sector, including those arising in a post-global financial crisis era.

India: key demographics

Understanding how the sector evolved and how it continues to demonstrate growth enables a better understanding of the contextual environment in which firms organise their skills and capability development activities. Rao (2004) argues that, to frame a nation's human resource development (HRD) needs at a macro level, it is important to understand its human resource endowments, the structure of its economy, its culture and its demographic characteristics. In this regard, India is the second most populous country and the largest democracy in the world. With an estimated population of 1.23 billion (World Bank, 2013), India is a country of 34 geographical units, 18 official languages, and numerous religious beliefs and social caste hierarchy systems (Rao, 2004). Its economy is predominantly agricultural, with a literacy rate of about 61% and about 29% of its people living below the poverty line (World Bank, 2013). Socio-cultural beliefs in India, though, reflect a strong orientation towards education: a typical middle-class family would desire their child to become a doctor or an engineer.

With a workforce of close to 440 million people and a significant majority (close to 50%) of its population less than 25 years of age (Rao and Varghese, 2009), India also has one of the largest pools of technically qualified and English-speaking graduates, working in a range of industries. Although India has 651 universities and about 27,000 higher education colleges producing 5.3 million graduates each year in various disciplines, of which about 30% are technical and science graduates (Chaturvedi and Sachitanand, 2013; NASSCOM, 2014c), the issue of their immediate employability in today's globalised economy is still a significant concern (NASSCOM-KPMG, 2004; NASSCOM, 2010). Despite the fact that India boasts one of the oldest technical colleges in the world, the School of Survey in Chennai, established in 1794, there is an ongoing need to increase industry–academia collaboration to keep up with the growing demands of the IT sector (NASSCOM-KPMG, 2004; NTITSD, 2003).

Economic development

Before the government of India introduced its economic liberalisation programme of the 1990s, the dominant logic was *import substitution* and *self-reliance*. Although this led to well-developed primary, secondary and tertiary sectors, it also created the *licence-Raj* system, which regulated the number of industrialists and their outputs by issuing licenses and regulating quotas. During this period, the education infrastructure expanded to ensure a constant supply of skilled people for these industry sectors. Whereas most service and manufacturing sectors have been in existence for more than a century (for example, banking, finance, power, insurance, railways and petroleum refineries), their growth gained further momentum immediately after India became a republic in 1947. Centralised planning took over to meet the twin national goals of *import substitution* and *self-reliance*. The result was the development of knowledge, experience and skills in a range of industry sectors and a well-developed labour market, ensuring a gradual but steady growth of industries. However, numerous deterrents to full-scale economic development existed in the *licence-Raj* era, such as corruption, bureaucracy, 'red-tapism' and the monopolistic participation of state-owned enterprises in key industry sectors. Foreign investment and ownership was both limited and regulated, leading to limited inflow of foreign exchange and technological knowledge.

The following section provides an overview of the nature and structure of India's IT sector. When one considers the poor and backward country image that India had and its protected and technologically underdeveloped economy, which teetered on the brink of bankruptcy, in the recent past, the success of India's IT sector and how that was achieved merits further exploration. This is particularly relevant, given the mixed bag of media response to the recent growth of India's IT sector.

Overview of India's IT sector

Revenues, employment and structure

Although the Indian IT industry has existed since the mid-1970s, albeit initially in a very rudimentary form, it is only in the last two decades that the sector has witnessed a steady growth in revenue and employee numbers. The sector grew at an average compounded annual rate of 50% between 1989 and 2000. Only recently has the annual growth rate stabilised between 20% and 25% per annum (NASSCOM, 2007, 2010). Its revenue has increased from US$175 million in 1989–1990 to US$118 billion in 2014, of which exports, are primarily to the US and European markets, comprise 73% of the total IT-BPO exports revenue and the sector contributes to 8.1% of India's GDP (NASSCOM, 2014a, b). The sector offers direct employment to 3.1 million people and indirectly employs 8.9 million people (NASSCOM, 2014c).

Broadly, the sector can be classified into three sub-sectors: IT hardware manufacturing (ITHM); IT software services (ITSS), including software product development; and IT-enabled services (ITeS), which includes business processes outsourcing (BPO) services. Within ITSS, there are numerous areas of specialisation and service lines. The sector caters to a range of industries (commonly called 'verticals'). Within these industries, it caters to a range of specialisations (commonly called 'domains' or 'horizontals'). The sector also caters to a number of global industries, such as banking, financial services and insurance (BFSI), high-technology sector, telecom, manufacturing, health, energy, cars, media and publishing, airlines and transport, and public utilities. It is important to note here that these global industries have also been in operation for a long time in India, some (for example, BFSI, oil and gas, construction and utilities, education) for more than a century. This would suggest that the country's labour market has skilled and experienced human resources to be tapped by the ITSS and ITeS/BPO sectors, although these human resources are not typically servicing the cutting edge of the high-end technology market.

The waterfall model of the software development life cycle comprises requirements analysis, higher and lower level design, coding, testing, and post-production maintenance and support. Other services in ITSS include IT consulting, infrastructure management, networking services, product development, and embedded software design and development. Firms may provide services for the entire software development cycle, which is typical in a *product development*

environment, or it may provide services for various stages of software development, for example, coding, testing, application maintenance and support, typical
of firms operating in a *project environment*. To this end, it would be fair to say
that the ITSS sector in India provides services that are typical of a software
development life cycle, as depicted in Figure 2.1.

In short, ITSS mainly includes firms operating in either a *project environment*, offering a range of services in the software development cycle, or a
product environment, or both. Typical software product firms develop and sell
software packages, such as Microsoft's MS Office or SAP's SAP-ERP. A closer
examination of the Indian ITSS sector reveals that the share of product development work relative to IT services (or projects) has historically been extremely
low, for instance sitting at only 5% in 1990. Only recently has product development and R&D work in the sector increased, moving from about 8% of software
exports in 1999, the year that the Indian government made changes to the country's foreign ownership rules, intellectual property protection and venture capital
(Dossani, 2005; Heeks, 1996, 1998), to 27% of ITSS exports in 2010
(NASSCOM, 2010). Further examination of the revenues of key players in the
sector reveals that less than 1% of all of the firms in the sector – about 4,000 in
total – account for almost 60% of the export revenue (Athreye, 2005; Ethiraj,
Kale, Krishnan and Singh, 2005; NASSCOM, 2007). This would suggest that a
small number of firms have grown at higher than average rate for the sector and
that there are distinctions in organisational performance between the larger and
small and medium-sized firms in the sector.

A notable point here is that most of these firms rely on software services
rather than on software products as their main source of revenue, notwithstanding popular belief that the development of a software brand/product is

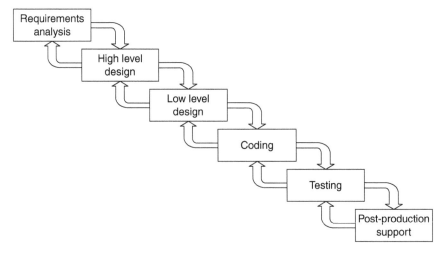

Figure 2.1 The waterfall model: software development life cycle (adapted from Arora
and Asundi, 1999, p. 27, Figure 1).

essential for sustained competitive advantage. While product superiority and leadership is a characteristic of large brands such as Microsoft, Oracle, Adobe and SAP, the *services* market is nevertheless much larger than the *product* market (Banerjee, 2004). Product development requires higher level investment and capabilities in R&D, marketing and promotion, which most Indian firms did not possess, at least not in the early stages of their development. In this regard, product superiority is said to arise from a manufacturing mindset, ensuring that the product will continue to be perceived as superior. On the other hand, while perceived as risky and less rewarding, projects offer some advantages over the product environment (Banerjee, 2004). That is, for instance, the same programming code can be deployed over a number of projects, and projects require limited upfront investment in R&D and marketing. Additionally, while the revenue is generally much higher in product environments, owing to global reach, their profitability is similar to that of firms in the IT services sector (Arora, 2006). Finally, even in a product environment, there will always be a need for project service firms to support and maintain, and undertake coding, testing or even collaborative product development for product firms.

This is the marketspace where the Indian software services firms have carved a niche for themselves, and they are gradually moving up the value chain of research and software product development. What remains to be seen is whether any Indian firms are able to develop and register significant patents for their products. There are, nonetheless, early indications that there is reason for these Indian firms in the software services industry to be confident of their future success (Arora, 2006).

The ITeS/BPO services sub-sector on the other hand can be broadly classified into voice and non-voice services. An example of the former is customer care/call centres; an example of the latter is back-office business process outsourcing. The latter typically attract a medium to high dollar rate compared to the former. Examples of high-end non-voice services include market analytics, market research, HR outsourcing and legal services. There is in this regard essentially a price and added-value continuum for this sub-sector, as depicted in Figure 2.2.

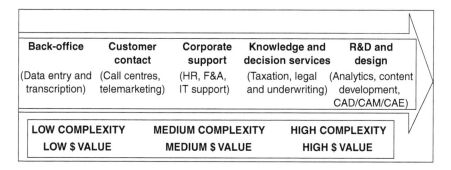

Figure 2.2 Continuum of ITeS/BPO services (adapted from NASSCOM and KPMG, 2004).

Moreover, extant research in the ITeS/BPO sector has identified market-based organisational learning and quality management capabilities as a key source for sustained competitive advantage in that sub-sector (Malik and Blumenfeld, 2012; Malik, Sinha and Blumenfeld, 2012).

Business models and nature of contracts

At present, there are a range of business models in operation India's IT sector, the foundations of which can be traced back to the early stages of development of the sector. Firms in the sector include domestic firms and multinational corporations (MNCs), with collaboration between the two throughout the sector. Firms in the sector typically operate as third-party service providers, most of which are large domestic firms; captive operators, which are commonly referred to as wholly-owned subsidiaries of MNCs; or joint venture business partnerships, such as third-party service providers which set up a shop for MNCs on either a build, operate and transfer (BOT) or a build, operate, lease and transfer (BOLT) basis.

For MNC captives, the business model employed has always been based on a simple cost plus a mark-up margin. For domestic firms, though, 'time-and-materials' (T&M) contracts were previously the norm. Yet, because they lacked credibility to undertake fixed price (FP) projects successfully, the only way that a client firm could get a better deal through service providers was to negotiate a tough (low) dollar rate, to cover any time and material overruns. That is, in the early stages of development, business contracts for third-party service providers were mainly T&M contracts, under which projects are undertaken on the basis of billable time and materials (labour and infrastructure) supplied for clients' projects. While T&M contracts are still prevalent, improvements to organisational capabilities, changes to environmental conditions and enhanced competencies of domestic firms have led to the emergence of FP contracts (Athreye, 2005).

Global growth of high-tech clusters and India's IT sector

The rapid growth of high-tech clusters around the world has attracted academic interest and produced a burgeoning body of literature offering explanations of the various factors that have led to their emergence (Arora, Gambardella and Torrisi, 2001; Arora and Gambardella, 2004; Arora and Athreye, 2002; Bresnahan, Gambardella and Saxenian, 2001; Finegold, 1999; Saxenian, 1994, 2001). While the extant literature offers useful insights about the roles of human capital agglomeration, interdependence and cooperation, and their externality-inducing effects on clusters of high-tech firms, in the context of India's IT sector, these explanations are not generalizable to the firm level. There are a number of reasons for this.

First, the literature offers a partial explanation as to why only one high-tech cluster – the IT sector – evolved and other high-tech sectors in India, such as the pharmaceuticals and engineering hardware sectors, did not perform well (Athreye, 2005; Subramanian, 1992). In addition, with reference to the geographical ecologists' model, Indian IT clusters were not concentrated in any one city and did not follow a set pattern. For example, they started in Mumbai and then became established in New Delhi, Pune and finally Bangalore and Hyderabad, which are now referred to collectively as India's Silicon Valley (SV) (Arora, Gambardella and Torrisi, 2001). The catalysts for change in India were also quite different from those in Silicon Valley. To this end, the state played an indifferent role in India and did not encourage private entrepreneurial activity in the IT sector (Dossani, 2005).

Another reason insights from the academic literature are not generalizable to the Indian case is that domestic firms in India did not have adequate access to the same technical, managerial and financial resources as did firms in other countries. This affected Indian IT firms' service credibility in the overseas markets (Arora, Gambardella and Torrisi, 2001; Athreye, 2005). Furthermore, collaboration between industry and academia was virtually non-existent in India during the early stages of the sector's development and evolution. Finally, there was generally an unsupportive entrepreneurial climate for private investment, such that entrepreneurs had to find a 'way around' the Indian government's reasoning which led to development of state-owned enterprises in the high-technology sectors (Dossani, 2005). These limitations should be kept in mind when considering the theoretical literature describing the evolution of the Indian IT sector in Chapter 3 of this book.

The evolution of India's IT sector

The theoretical literature describing the development and growth of India's IT sector can be broadly grouped into three main strands:

- human capital agglomeration (economics), comparative advantage and the role of transnational corporations (TNCs) (Giarrantana, Pagano and Torrisi, 2004; Patibandla and Petersen, 2002; Athreye, 2004, 2005)
- public policy, institutional dynamics, and evolving service capability (Athreye, 2005; Arora, 2006; Arora, Arunachalam, Asundi and Fernandes, 2001; Dossani, 2005; Nilakant, 2005)
- strategy, resources, organisational capabilities, and dynamic coordination (Athreye, 2005; Banerjee, 2004; Ethiraj *et al.*, 2005)

Each of these three diverse theoretical strands is critically reviewed, and limitations to the use of organisational level analysis to assess the development and growth of India's IT sector are discussed in this chapter.

Human capital accumulation, comparative advantage and the role of TNCs

The presence of certain factor endowments such as low cost, English-speaking technical human resources (Heeks, 1996), and geographical and time advantages have favoured the development of India's IT sector (Arora, Arunachalam *et al.*, 2001; Arora and Athreye, 2002). Patibandla and Petersen (2002) and Giarratana *et al.* (2004), for example, argue that initial factor endowments and related arbitrage opportunities led to the entry of TNCs in India. This had a cumulative impact on the overall stock of human capital, as a consequence of knowledge spillovers from TNCs to domestic firms. Giarratana et al. (2004) advance three ways that such knowledge spills over to domestic firms. These include:

1   demonstration effects and imitation through working closely with clients and learning their standard operating procedures (Gorg and Strobl, 2002a);
2   labour turnover from multinational companies to domestic firms when *experienced* employees leave (Banerjee, 2004; Gorg and Strobl, 2002b); and
3   increased competition, which compels domestic firms to increase their efficiency (Caves, 1974).

This theoretical explanation has its detractors, nevertheless (Athreye, 2004, 2005; Subramanian, 1992; Nilakant, 2005). In particular, the evidence suggests that there was, in fact, little competition in the country's software industry, as there was no planned effort by the Indian government to invest in human capital (Dossani, 2005). Instead, it was the hardware industry that caught the government's attention and was the focus of its investment planning (Subramanian, 1992). Further, if human capital agglomeration was the case, why did firms in other sectors, such as pharmaceutical sector, not mirror the performance of the IT sector (Athreye, 2004; 2005)? This question is partly answered by the changing role of the state, institutional dynamics and the evolving organisational capabilities of domestic IT firms. More recently, however, owing to the complexity of the Indian institutional environment, large global firms have started setting up country-specific HR headquarters in India for providing full autonomy in HR-specific matters (Budhwar, 2012) and also the development of global HR roles for managing complex diffusion of reverse innovation from emerging market multinationals to their overseas subsidiaries (Thite, Budhwar and Wilkinson, 2014).

Public policy, institutional dynamics and evolving service capability

Although Dossani (2005) argues that the state played an indifferent and sometimes even hostile role in the promotion and support of the IT sector, Nilakant (2005) contends that the Indian government did, in fact, play an active role in this regard, and that certain key actors and institutional dynamics actually promoted development of the sector. Using the institutional dynamics framework developed by Scott, Ruef, Mendel and Caronna (2000) and Davis, McAdam, Scott and Zald (2005), Nilakant (2005) argues that the growth of the sector can be broadly attributed to the role certain key actors played in influencing the dominant logic of government at that time, which was to adapt governance structures to deal with the industry's development and growth needs. Prior to the government's liberalisation programmes, centralised planning, import substitution and self-reliance had dominated the Indian government's thinking. Despite this, there were certain key actors who, at various stages of the evolution and growth of the sector, convinced the government to change its dominant logic and governance structures.

While he acknowledges the initial role of agglomeration economies in human capital in the entry of TNCs and the consequent benefits that the sector derived from TNCs' entry, Athreye (2004) contends that these efforts were insufficient to sustain the increasing competitive pressures from tight labour markets due to foreign competition. In that as well as a later paper, Athreye (2004, 2005) argues that the growth and expansion of the IT sector in India was the outcome of enhanced and unique organisational capabilities developed by domestic IT firms through their continuous improvement on the existing business model of TNCs. With the increasing competition in factor markets for both domestic firms and TNCs and the declining billing rates for offshore software services (Singh, 2003), how did domestic firms continue to demonstrate increases in productivity, albeit of a nominal nature (see Table 2.1 for details)?

In the later of these two papers, Athreye (2005) argues that, because firms in India's IT sector were competing with TNCs in the factor markets only and had no competition from them in the product markets, either locally or globally, at least in the early stages of their development, domestic firms grew and increased their productivity by improvising their organisational capabilities and refining the business model originally developed by the TNCs.

Furthermore, it was this ability of domestic firms to transform and recombine engineers' basic skills and knowledge acquired from factor markets into better organisational capabilities that allowed such sustained growth. Those organisational capabilities include tighter project management and the development of standardised and proprietary tools for efficient deployment of resources

Table 2.1 India's rising productivity for software revenue per employee

Year	Employees	Avg. rev/employee ($)[1]
1993–1994	90,000	6,198
1994–1995	118,000	6,998
1995–1996	140,000	8,924
1996–1997	160,000	11,036
1997–1998	180,000	15,000
1998–1999	250,000	15,600
2000	284,000	32,635
2004	n/a	35,362
2014[2]	3,132,000	37,675

Source: Arora, Arunachalam *et al.*, 2001; Dossani, 2005.

Notes
1 Avg. rev/employee data for 2000 and 2004 is from Dossani, 2005.
2 Author's compilation based on revenues and employment figures (NASSCOM, 2014a).

(Athreye, 2005). This capability evolved over time through four distinct phases. At each phase, domestic organisations were compelled to improve upon the basic business model, not only to differentiate themselves from their competition, but also to increase their productivity. It is further argued that, given the generic nature of some of those capabilities, external spillovers allowed for the development of small firms in the sector.

Developing a temporal classification

Nilakant's (2005) theorised phases of growth juxtapose with Athreye's (2005) four phases of evolving capabilities of domestic firms of India's IT sector. Taken together, Nilakant's (2005) institutional dynamics framework and Athreye's (2005) insights into the development and evolution of IT capabilities provide a clearer picture of how the sector has come of age. This underscores the need for theorists and researchers to consider evolving contextual factors that drive investment in training and development at an enterprise level.

Hence, rather than considering these as two separate accounts, it is suggested that a single integrated and coherent account of the sector's evolution and growth be put forth. This single account should reflect the temporal nature of organisational and human capabilities and of skills developed, in particular as these evolved at different stages of the IT sector's development. With this integrated approach in mind, Nilakant's (2005) institutional dynamics model and Athreye's (2005) stages of evolving organisational capabilities and development are considered further in the following section. We contribute by marking these periods with key changes as well as by identifying a new period (2005 onwards) not previously identified in the literature

To 1984

Prior to 1984, the Indian government's dominant logic was import substitution and self-reliance (Nilakant, 2005). This was a period of excessive regulation of the country's IT sector, in which the government's focus was exclusively on the development of the hardware sector and supporting state-owned enterprises for IT services (Dossani, 2005). Because of the government's regulatory policies, for instance, IBM had to exit from the Indian market, doing so in 1978 because the government's Foreign Exchange Regulation Act (FERA) required the multinational firm to dilute its equity (Nilakant, 2005; Athreye, 2005). With IBM's departure, there was a void in the market for servicing the mainframes and legacy systems it had installed in the domestic market. Following this, 1,200 ex-IBM engineers were employed by a newly formed state-owned enterprise, Computer Maintenance Corporation (CMC), to service the void in the market, and domestic Indian firms were barred from operating in this area. As a result, CMC dominated this niche.

Despite this effort to shield CMC from competition, in the medium term, some knowledge spillovers helped domestic firms to develop capability for local and overseas markets for IBM mainframes installed globally. This capability proved to be extremely beneficial for dealing with legacy systems and migratory projects in the second phase of growth (Nilakant, 2005). This was also the period when there was a move from mainframes to workstations and in which the development of software could be undertaken independently of hardware platforms (Dossani, 2005). This, however, fostered red-tapism and corruption in government channels. Domestic firms faced cumbersome regulations and procedures for small hardware and related equipment imports. Red-tapism reduced domestic firms' ability to compete and further damaged their already poor credibility. During this phase, software exports from India were negligible, although some firms were beginning to secure business from overseas.

1985–1991

Between 1985 and 1991, the worldwide crash of hardware prices and a move away from mainframes to client server systems led the demand for customised software applications development to increase dramatically. The end of this phase coincided with the Indian government's 1991 reforms and liberalisation programme (Athreye, 2005). Change to the dominant institutional logic was also required to enable further development of the country's IT sector. This change was particularly needed to reduce the high tariffs for importing hardware (Nilakant, 2005). Certain key actors in the government, including the then Prime Minister Rajiv Gandhi, were influential in changing the dominant logic, which was required if India was to implement liberalised policies in order to meet the sector's hardware and software needs. During this period, Tata Consultancy Services (TCS), one of India's largest domestic ITSS firms, under the leadership of F.C. Kohli, pioneered the 'on-site' business model, described by some as 'body-shopping' (Nilakant, 2005). TCS won two large contracts in the United States, one with American Express Incorporated and the other with Institutional Group & Information Co. (IGIC). The nature of those contracts was T&M, as TCS's reputation in the overseas markets at that time was poor.

The on-site business model involves firms sending programmers to clients' sites for projects, where most learning is 'learning by doing' and representatives of the IT company work closely with clients at the client's worksite, which enables company representatives to better understand the client's business model and their unique cultural environment. Use of this model helped the 1985–1991 period helped to fill the credibility gap, as working directly with and in such close proximity to clients improved communication between IT firms and their clients and helped resolve any conflicts between the two in much less time than under previous business models. During this phase of development, long-term software services contracts secured by large players in the IT sector, as well as their capability to deliver cost-effective and quality services, increased India's credibility as a global destination for ITSS.

Despite these successes, towards the end of this period, viability of the on-site model was challenged by external forces, mainly by legislative changes in the

United States. In particular, the US government enforced tighter H1B visa quotas and more stringent qualification norms, and it imposed market rate salaries for programmers from India (Nilakant, 2005). This created a need to seek out alternative business models as well as a need to change the Indian government's dominant logic. Proposals to establish tax-free software technology parks and export-processing zones with satellite communications infrastructure were mooted by some in government who were attracted to the idea of establishing large TNCs, such as Texas Instruments (TIs) and Citicorp Overseas Limited (COSL). These firms were allowed to use dedicated satellite links, which had previously been the exclusive domain of India's Department of Defence and Atomic Energy Commission. Cheaper infrastructure and satellite communications allowed faster development and, given the 12-hour time difference between India and the US, efficiency increased and turnaround times reduced. Domestic firms were given access to additional satellite communications capacities from TI, which helped those Indian firms to grow as well.

1992–1999

The period between 1992 and 1999 was a time of full financial liberalisation and large-scale imitative entry of TNCs. By this time, not only were on-site contracts on the decline, but the new model of offshore development centres (ODCs), using dedicated satellite communication links, took hold in India's IT sector and quickly gained momentum (Athreye, 2005; Nilakant, 2005). During this era, competition in the sector intensified, especially for domestic firms who were competing with TNCs in the factor markets and who had limited finances with which to establish their own satellite facilities. As a result of their limited resources, domestic IT firms in India had to improvise on the ODC and on-site models.

One such strategy was to use 'quality signalling' by adopting quality management frameworks, such as the capability maturity model (CMM) developed by Carnegie Mellon University's Software Engineering Institute (SEI). The SEI-CMM quality framework has five functional levels and is focused on improving process maturity for software development, as well as on developing better organisational and management capabilities. It resulted in a redefined ODC model and productivity improvements across the sector. With enhanced organisational capabilities and credibility signalling through use of quality certifications, domestic Indian IT firms began to undertake risky but more lucrative FP contracts.

2000–2004

Since 2000, consolidation and shifts in global software demand have taken place. This is reflected in the dotcom crash and shakeouts in the industry. During this phase of development of the IT sector, most large domestic firms have established their credibility, have increased their internal capabilities in software development and process control, and have moved up the value chain of the software development lifecycle. This has particularly been true of Indian firms in the high-end software services industry, including product design, development and embedded software services.

Also during this period, India's telecommunications sector, including its Internet services, was deregulated (Athreye, 2005). Private investment in telecommunications has led to an enhanced telecommunications infrastructure and bandwidth. As a result, there has been a huge expansion in the ITeS/BPO services, such as call centres and business process outsourcing centres, since 2000. The number of new players in the sector increased significantly, and even existing ITSS players added ITeS/BPO service lines for servicing existing and new clients.

As some large firms in the sector have begun to explore and demonstrate the 'Babbage effect', wherein firms are able to split tasks into high and low end and pay workers according to the complexity of the task, the offshore business model has yielded substantial productivity gains. High-end tasks are assigned to highly qualified and experienced staff, with routine, low-end tasks being given to less-qualified staff (Athreye, 2005). Grouping and streaming of such tasks requires the development of certain organisational capabilities to pack and unpack resources.

Since 2005

Further to this, in the last decade from the mid-2000s, the need to manage rising costs and employee turnover has led to the adoption of certain HRM practices and process management strategies in India's IT sector. Such practices include investing in corporate training and education, use of proprietary tools, knowledge diffusion, adoption of quality standards, the recombination of resources and implementation of innovative reward systems.

Overall, the focus of developing organisational capabilities in the sector has been focused primarily on software process control and large-scale labour management practices (Athreye, 2005). Yet, despite the fact that there is general agreement on the role of evolving capabilities and the supportive role of the state in the later stages of their evolution, little is known of how firms develop such capabilities. More specifically, what are these capabilities, where do they come from, and why do they matter? Research (Banerjee, 2004; Ethiraj *et al.*, 2005) has shed some light on this.

Strategy, resources, organisational capabilities and dynamic coordination

The notion of capabilities is debated and understood differently in different theoretical orientations and focuses on aspects of capability development, including organisational, economic, individual, human and dynamic capabilities (Barney, 1991; Bryson and O'Neil, 2008; Eisenhardt and Martin, 2000; Teece,

Pisano and Shuen, 1997; Winter, 2003). Some researchers argue that capability is the ability to deploy resources (Amit and Schoemaker, 1993). On the other hand, Ethiraj et al. (2005) contend that capabilities reflect assets that can generate rent for the organisation. These authors point to capabilities as quasi-rents, as they are an outcome of assets embedded in the organisational context. They further argue that the optimal use of such assets is dependent on the presence of other assets, such as managerial capital, appropriate culture and technology, or the ability to utilise a bundle of these organisational assets.

Having analysed project-level data of a large Indian ITSS organisation, Ethiraj et al. (2005) conclude that firms develop certain capabilities best through 'learning by doing' and that organisational capabilities, like individual capabilities, evolve over an extended period of time. Such capabilities are unique and heterogeneous in nature and cannot be acquired by other firms in factor markets. Thus, they generate rent for the organisation, and each organisation has the choice of developing certain capabilities, as different capabilities generate different rents. The decision to invest in a particular capability is also partly informed by the demand for, and supply of, software services in the market. The demand for software services, as we know, exists on a continuum, from low-end to high-end.

Moreover, corresponding service capability requirements have also changed (Athreye, 2005). Hence, on the supply side, the nature of the software contract (T&M and FP) and the delivery model need consideration. Ethiraj et al. (2005) argue that on-site delivery generally has resulted in the development of client-specific capabilities, which occur as a result of repeated interactions with the client and as a consequence of better understanding of a client's unique requirements. Changes are then made to ensure that these requirements are met.

In the case of the offshore delivery model, tight project management capabilities are needed to ensure delivery is on schedule in terms of time, cost and client specifications. On the question of whether the nature of the contract was T&M or FP, Ethiraj et al. (2005) argue that the former led to the development of tighter project management and strong client-specific capabilities, whereas the latter led to the development of strong project management and generic people management capabilities.

In a similar vein, Banerjee (2004) argues that, while resources, skills and knowledge are important, how a firm combines and recombines its resources and competencies to generate higher-level competencies for achieving competitive advantage is crucial. To that end, Banerjee classifies competencies into three groups: first order, second order and core competency. First-order competencies are available from factor markets, and every firm can easily acquire them. Second-order competencies are those that are generated by recombining first-order competency with other resources and organisational rules.

Using data from small domestic IT start-up firms, Banerjee (2004) argues that the core competency of an IT firm is its higher level competency, which is a decision capability, as it allows switching from a project to product environment and vice versa. In explaining the growth of India's IT industry, Banerjee (2004,

2006) advances two key points: a job-switching thesis and the importance of dynamic coordination for information-in-expectation to yield a novelty or surprise profit. The job-switching thesis suggests that human resources with medium to high experience in a given domain can provide novel information that is of value to the hiring firm and may provide an opportunity for growth. These human resources are carriers as well as generators of such information-in-expectation. In Schumpeterian terms, these human resources bring surprise profit to the firm.

Banerjee (2004) further asserts that domestic software firms in India are opportunity-seeking and look for dynamic coordination between client firms and suppliers. This opportunistic behaviour, wherein the financial reserves of software firms are invested in highly liquid money market instruments, offers the firm a cadre of buffer employees ('employees on bench time') waiting to be deployed for a new project. This will lead a software firm to seek coordination among software-writing firms and the users of its software through strategic demand management of services, and is accomplished by influencing the client organisations' strategic environment. Such a firm will seek to align its strategy to its clients' strategic milieu. Then, by working closely with those clients, the firm can influence and change the strategic environment of it client base. Eventually, service provider firms will modify their own strategic environment to service the clients' needs, sometimes using their higher-level switching competence and product-service-product competence.

While the above accounts have provided us with an understanding of how the sector has evolved over the last three decades, there is scope for further differentiation within the period from 2000 onwards. In particular, despite the recent changes it has witnessed in the revenue composition of ITSS (projects and products) and an emerging value chain in the ITeS/BPO sub-sector, this has heretofore generally been assumed to be a homogeneous period in the evolution of the sector (Dossani, 2005; Arora, 2006). Nevertheless, it should be acknowledged that the diversity of business models followed in this period have resulted in increasing capabilities to undertake high-end work, in particular since 2003.

Furthermore, international and domestic competition has not only intensified in factor markets, but has also been quite intense in product markets in more than a decade. Since 2000, the Indian economy has been posting strong GDP growth rates, in the range of 8%–9% per annum, which puts pressure on the overall infrastructure and resources. Although India currently spends about 3.8% (US$8.3 billion) of its GDP on its education and training infrastructure (http://education.nic.in), NASSCOM-McKinsey projections for 2012 that the Indian IT sector was poised to post a sales turnover in excess of the US$85 billion and would generate direct and indirect employment for about 4.5 million people proved to be overly optimistic (NASSCOM, 2006a; MIT, 2002).

Despite the quantitative expansion of institutions since 1947, there needs to be significant investment and collaboration among all the key players in the system, including employers, employees and government, to meet the projected growth rates. In this race for greater productivity and profits, success or failure rests primarily on the quality of human resources, and this is where the greatest attention needs to be focused (MHRD, 2007; NASSCOM-KPMG, 2004; NTITSD, 2003).

The problem of sustainability was further compounded in 2008 and 2009 by the appreciation of the Indian rupee, which rose by around 15% against the US dollar in that time. Medium- to long-term foreign exchange hedging contracts will provide some respite, but are not sufficient. A stronger rupee will have an impact on the profitability of domestic firms and TNCs, although that impact is likely to be felt mostly by domestic ITSS firms than by TNCs, and greater still by ITeS/BPO firms, which cater to the lower end of the market.

There have been some attempts to better understand the development of organisational capabilities, but these have focused either on extremely large and high-growth domestic firms (Ethiraj *et al.*, 2005) or small ITSS start-ups (Banerjee, 2004). Furthermore, while there is general agreement that training and development plays an important role in the expansion and growth of organisational capabilities, further research which investigates the internal and external factors that drive a firm's decision to invest in training is needed. This can be accomplished by looking at organisations' competitive strategy and organisation of work (Ashton and Sung, 2006; Boxall, 2003). More specifically, the influence of external factors in firms operating in a dynamic outsourcing and offshoring environment need to be studied using a case-study theory-building approach (Eisenhardt, 1989).

Conclusion

Themes from the foregoing discussion are intended to inform the development of a broader theoretical framework in Chapter 3. To this end, despite limitations in the existing literature, some key conclusions can be drawn from this discussion concerning the development and evolution of India's IT sector.

One conclusion to be drawn from the literature and this discussion is that Indian IT firms have demonstrated significant diversity in their international profile and performance, in the business models they employ, in the services they provide, in their product markets and specialisations, and in their mode of service delivery (Heeks, 1998; Dossani, 2005, Athreye, 2005; Ethiraj *et al.*, 2005). These distinguishing characteristics are important to this discussion as they shed light on the environment in which a firm operates and, in turn, its competitive strategy and the nature and extent of its capability development (Boxall, 2003).

In addition, most Indian IT firms report high levels of employee turnover. In particular, employees with extensive experience and skill in a given domain are seen as a source of profit by less-established firms, who are willing to pay more in order to attract such employees (Banerjee, 2004; Gorg and Strobl, 2002b). For this reason, high employee turnover is an important human resource management issue and, more specifically, affects training and human resource development decisions made by firms in the sector.

A third conclusion is that there is a high degree of coordination, cooperation and interdependence among and, for those working on various projects, within Indian IT firms. This is important from a learning perspective, as much of the learning that takes place in the sector is through a skills web and utilises 'learning by doing' and 'learning from experience' approaches. In addition, participants in this learning-sharing process include IT firms' clients and suppliers (Banerjee, 2004; Ethiraj et al., 2005).

Additionally, with the evolving capabilities of domestic firms, there appears to be a temporal dimension to skills development and training (Athreye, 2005). To this end, Ethiraj et al. (2005) and Banerjee (2004) have identified certain key capabilities and competencies that firms in the sector develop, including client-specific and project management capabilities. More recent studies, though, have considered how capabilities such as market-based organisational learning capabilities are developed and the role quality management capabilities plays in the success of IT/BPO firms (Malik and Blumenfeld, 2012; Malik et al., 2012).

Finally, given the rising productivity of human resources in the sector, Indian IT firms are now capable of implementing large-scale people management practices. With intensifying competition in both product and factor markets, those organisations have had to confront the 'make-or-buy' training dilemma. Given this, it is important that firms in the sector give greater consideration to the HR strategies they utilise and, in particular, their strategic decisions regarding the level of skills they desire to recruit, including entry level (graduate) and lateral (experienced) recruiting.

In this regard, a closer examination of these organisations' HRM practices, their linkages to the overall strategy of the organisation, and their skills and innovation capability development is needed. That is to say, whether firms employ a 'make' or a 'buy' strategy in developing their human resources can be a key differentiator in an increasingly competitive environment and tough economic times. One example of research in this area is Malik's (2013) study of Indian IT/BPO firms in the post-GFC era, which found that differences in strategic orientation affect both people management and capability development in those firms.

This chapter has presented an overview of India's socio-economic and demographic features, followed by an account of how the IT sector of India developed and evolved. In the next chapter, we offer a review of the literature which takes into account the unique cultural and contextual factors discussed in this chapter. That literature review is situated within the wider arena of human resource development and management (HRD/M) and proposes a novel framework for analysing the role of HRD/M in exploring and exploiting product and factor market opportunities available to Indian IT firms.

References

Amit, R., and Schoemaker, P.J.H. (1993). Strategic assets and organizational rent. *Strategic Management Journal, 14*(1), 33–46.

Arora, A. (2006). *The Indian software industry and its prospects.* Working Paper No. 23. Pittsburgh, PA: The Heinz School of Public Policy and Management, Carnegie Mellon University.

Arora, A., and Athreye, S. (2002). The software industry and India's economic development. *Information Economics and Policy, 14*(2), 253–273.

Arora, A., and Gambardella, A. (2004). *The globalization of the software industry: perspectives and opportunities for developed and developing countries.* NBER Working Paper No. 10538. Cambridge, MA: National Bureau of Economic Research.

Arora, A., Arunachalam, V.S., Asundi, J.V., and Fernandes, R. (2001). The Indian software services industry. *Research Policy, 30*(8), 1267–1287.

Arora, A., Gambardella, A., and Torrisi, S. (2001a). *In the footsteps of the Silicon Valley? Indian and Irish software in the international division of labour.* Discussion Paper No. 00-41. Stanford, CA: Stanford Institute for Economic Policy Research.

Ashton, D., and Sung, J. (2006). *How competitive strategy matters? Understanding the drivers of training, learning and performance at the firm level.* Research Paper No. 66. Oxford: Oxford and Warwick Universities, Centre for Skills, Knowledge and Organisational Performance.

Arora, A., and Asundi, J. (1999). *Quality Certification and the Economics of Contract Software Development A Study of the Indian Software Industry.* Paper No. w7260. Cambridge, MA: National Bureau of Economic Research.

Athreye, A. (2004). 'The role of transnational corporations in the evolution of a high-tech industry: The case of India's software industry' – A comment. *World Development, 32*(3), 555–560.

Athreye, A. (2005). The Indian software industry and its evolving service capability. *Industrial and Corporate Change, 14*(3), 393–418.

Audretsch, D.B., and Feldman, M.P. (1996). Knowledge spillovers and the geography of innovation and production. *American Economic Review, 86*(3), 630–640.

Banerjee, P. (2004). *The Indian software industry: Business strategy and dynamic co-ordination.* New Delhi: Palgrave Macmillan.

Banerjee, P. (2006). Strategies of outsourcing: From de-risking to outsourcing. In H.S. Kehal and V.P. Singh (Eds.). *Outsourcing and offshoring in the 21st century: A socio-economic perspective.* London: Idea Group.

Barney, J. (1991). Firm resources and sustained competitive advantage. *Journal of Management, 17*(1), 99–120.

Boxall, P. (2003). HR strategy and competitive advantage in the service sector. *Human Resource Management Journal, 13*(3), 5–20.

Bresnahan, T., Gambardella, A., and Saxenian, A. (2001). 'Old economy' inputs for 'new economy' outcomes: Cluster formation in the new silicon valleys. *Industrial and Corporate Change, 10*(4), 835–860.

Bryson, J., and O'Neil, P. (2008, May). *Developing human capability: Employment institutions, organisations and individuals.* Discussion Paper. Wellington: Industrial Relations Centre, Victoria University of Wellington.

Budhwar, P. (2012). Management of human resources in foreign firms operating in India: the role of HR in country-specific headquarters. *The International Journal of Human Resource Management, 23*(12), 2514–2531.

Cappelli, P., Singh, H., Singh, J., and Useem, M. (2010). *The India way: How India's top leaders are revolutionizing management.* Boston, MA: Harvard Business School.

Caves, R.E. (1974). Multinational firms, competition and productivity in host-country markets. *Economica, 41*(162), 176–193.

Chaturvedi, A., and Sachitanand, R. (2013, 18 June). A million engineers in India struggling to get placed in an extremely challenging market. *The Economic Times*. Retrieved from http://articles.economictimes.indiatimes.com/2013-06-18/news/40049243_1_engineers-iit-bombay-batch-size

Davis, G.F., McAdam, D., Scott, W.R., and Zald, M.N. (Eds.). (2005). *Social movements and organization theory*, New York, NY: Cambridge University Press.

Dossani, R. (2005). *Origins and growth of the software industry in India*. Working paper. Palo Alto, CA: Stanford University, Asia-Pacific Research Center.

Eisenhardt, K.M. (1989). Building theories from case study research. *Academy of Management Review*, *14*(4), 532–550.

Eisenhardt, K.M., and Martin, J.A. (2000). Dynamic capabilities: What are they? *Strategic Management Journal*, *21*(10/11), 1504–1511.

Ethiraj, S.E., Kale, P., Krishnan, M.S., and Singh, J.V. (2005). Where do capabilities come from and how do they matter? A study in the software services industry. *Strategic Management Journal*, *26*(1), 25–45.

Finegold, D. (1999). Creating self-sustaining, high-skill ecosystems. *Oxford Review of Economic Policy*, *15*(1), 60–72.

Giarratana, M., Pagano, A., and Torrisi, S. (2004). The role of multinational firms in the evolution of the software industry in India, Ireland, and Israel. In A. Arora and A. Gambardella (Eds.). *From Underdogs to Tigers: Bridging the Gap* (pp. 207–235). New York, NY: Oxford University Press.

Gorg, H., and Strobl, E. (2002a). Multinational companies and indigenous development: An empirical analysis. *European Economic Review*, *46*(7), 1305–1322.

Gorg, H., and Strobl, E. (2002b). *Spillovers from foreign firms through worker mobility: An empirical analysis*, Discussion Paper No. 591. Bonn: IZA.

Govindarajan, V., and Trimble, C. (2012). *Reverse innovation: Create far from home, win everywhere*. Boston, MA: Harvard Business Press.

Heeks, R. (1996). *Indian software industry: State policy, liberalisation and industrial development*. New Delhi: Sage.

Heeks, R. (1998, October). *The uneven profile of Indian software exports*. Development Infomatics Working Paper No. 3. Manchester, England: University of Manchester, IDPM. Retrieved from www.seed.manchester.ac.uk/subjects/idpm/research/publications/wp/di/di-wp3/

Kumar, N., and Puranam, P. (2012). *Inside India: The emerging innovation challenge to the West.* Boston, MA: Harvard Business Review Press.

Malik, A. (2013). Post-GFC people management challenges: A study of India's information technology sector. *Asia Pacific Business Review*, *19*(2), 230–246.

Malik, A., and Blumenfeld, S. (2012). Six Sigma, quality management systems and the development of organisational learning capability: Evidence from four business process outsourcing organisations in India. *International Journal of Quality & Reliability Management*, *29*(1), 71–91.

Malik, A., Sinha, A., and Blumenfeld, S. (2012). Role of quality management capabilities in developing market-based organisational learning capability: Case study evidence from four business process outsourcing firms. *Industrial Marketing Management*, *41*(4), 639–648.

MHRD. (2007). *Selected educational statistics – 2004–05*. New Delhi: Ministry of Human Resource Development, Department of Higher Education, Statistics Division.

MIT. (2002). *Study team report on human resource development for 10th Five Year Plan – 2002–2007*. New Delhi: Ministry of Information Technology.

NASSCOM. (2006a). *Why India?* Retrieved from www.nasscom.org.

NASSCOM. (2006b). *Knowledge professionals.* Retrieved from www.nasscom.org.

NASSCOM. (2007, August). *IT industry factsheet.* Retrieved from www.nasscom.org.

NASSCOM. (2010). *The IT-BPO sector in India: Strategic review 2010* New Delhi: Author.

NASSCOM. (2014a). *India IT – BPM overview.* New Delhi: Author.

NASSCOM. (2014b). *India IT – BPM exports.* New Delhi: Author.

NASSCOM. (2014c). *Knowledge professionals.* New Delhi: Author.

NASSCOM, and KPMG. (2004). *Strengthening the human resource foundations of the Indian IT enabled services/IT Industry.* New Delhi: NASSCOM.

Nilakant, V. (2005, August). *Institutional dynamics in the evolution of the Indian software industry.* Paper presented at the Academy of Management Conference, Hawaii, USA.

NTITSD. (2003). *Task force on meeting the human resource challenge for IT and IT enabled services: Report and recommendations.* New Delhi: Department of Information Technology, Ministry of Communication and Information Technology, Government of India.

Patibandla, M., and Petersen, B. (2002). Role of transnational corporations in the evolution of a high-tech industry: The case of India's software industry. *World Development, 30*(9), 1561–1577.

Radjou, N., Prabhu, J., and Ahuja, S. (2012). *Jugaad Innovation: Think frugal, be flexible, generate breakthrough growth.* San Francisco, CA: Jossey-Bass.

Rao, T.V. (2004). Human resource development as national policy in India. *Advances in Developing Human Resources, 6*(3), 288–296.

Rao, T.V., and Varghese, S. (2009). Trends and challenges of developing human capital in India. *Human Resource Development International, 12*(1), 15–34.

Saxenian, A. (1994). *Regional advantage, culture and competition in Silicon Valley and Route 128.* Cambridge, MA: Harvard University Press.

Saxenian, A. (2001). *Bangalore: The Silicon Valley of Asia?* Working Paper No. 91. Palo Alto, CA: Stanford University, Center for Research on Economic Development and Policy Reform.

Scott, W.R., Ruef, M., Mendel, P.J., and Caronna, C.A. (2000). *Institutional change and healthcare organizations: From professional dominance to managed care.* Chicago, IL: University of Chicago Press.

Singh, S. (2003, November 10). Infotec: Home run. *Business World.* Retrieved from www.businessworldindia.com/Nov1003/coverstory01.asp

Subramanian, C.R. (1992). *India and the computer: A study of planned development.* New Delhi: Oxford University Press.

Teece, D.J., Pisano, G., and Shuen, A. (1997). Dynamic capabilities and strategic management. *Strategic Management Journal, 18*(7), 509–533.

Thite, M., Budhwar, P., and Wilkinson, A. (2014). Global HR Roles and Factors Influencing their Development: Evidence from Emerging Indian IT Services Multinationals. *Human Resource Management, 53*(6), 921–946.

Winter, S.G. (2003). Understanding dynamic capabilities. *Strategic Management Journal, 24*(10), 991–995.

World Bank. (2013). *India: Data and statistics.* Retrieved from www.worldbank.org.in.

3 Skills, strategy and people management in the Indian IT industry

Ashish Malik and Stephen Blumenfeld

Introduction

Chapter 3 offers a critical review of the theoretical and empirical literature on the development and evolution of India's information technology (IT) sector. The themes emerging from that discussion have implications for skills development in Indian IT firms, particularly in light of the IT services market's disjointed development and unbalanced profile (Heeks, 1998). One conclusion drawn from that assessment is that differing levels of skills development exist across the sector and, hence, that different types of organisational capabilities, such as client-specific and project management capabilities, are being developed for sustained high performance (Ethiraj, Kale, Krishnan and Singh, 2005).

Another suggestion flowing from the extant literature is that human capital agglomeration across the sector has had an impact on skills development (Patibandla and Petersen, 2002). In addition, quality accreditation has been critical to both market sensing and Indian IT firms' operational capabilities (Arora, Arunachalam, Asundi and Fernandes, 2000; Kumar, 2001; Asundi and Arora, 2002; Malik, Sinha and Blumenfeld, 2012). Finally, the literature points to the conclusion that there are two broad types or categories of business strategies employed by Indian IT firms: product development strategies and software services project strategies (Banerjee, 2004).

The chapter reviews the literature from academic paradigms critical to understanding the business model of firms in the Indian IT sector and to those firms' sustained performance. The first section of this chapter considers the role of skills development in the Indian IT sector, which is critical to firms in the sector maintaining the right mix of skills. This is considered here in the broader context of human resource development (HRD). That discussion is followed in the second section by a review of the means by which Indian IT firms deliver high quality, affordable software services through high performance work systems (HPWS) and quality management (QM), both of which have proven critical to service scalability and quality control in the sector. In the third and final section of this chapter, we offer an assessment of how these firms use critical information about their clients' latent and expressed needs to enhance skills development, organisational learning and output quality.

A theoretical framework of HRD in Indian IT companies

In light of the diversity of strategies employed by organisations operating in the sector and the multiplicity of observations advanced in the literature to explain the generally successful development and expansion of India's IT sector, there is a need for a more detailed exploration and discussion of the theoretical underpinnings of these various observations. More also needs to be said, for instance, of the interaction between strategy, skills development and people management practices, with a view towards providing more focused insights into how and why these contribute to a firm's business model, particularly in the context of India's IT sector.

With these objectives in mind, this chapter begins with a brief overview of the multidisciplinary foundations of human resource development (HRD) and the business models which derive from these theoretical and empirical foundations. Swanson's (2007) approach to developing theoretical frameworks in applied disciplines, which offers a framework for understanding specific factors identified in the literature as being correlated with the provision of training and employee development, is then discussed. This is followed by a review of the various theoretical perspectives of a firm's decision to invest in training and development. The concluding section of this chapter concerns a number of unresolved issues in the literature, especially in the context of India's IT sector; that discussion forms the basis of future research propositions.

A consideration of the predictions of human capital theory (HCT) and their implications for HRD in IT firms is followed by an account of the mediating role of technology in enhancing skills development and increasing productivity in IT firms, as characterized in neo-human capital theories (NHCT). Then, owing to the complexity of organisational decision-making, the impact of competitive and HRM strategies in shaping the nature and extent of training is discussed. Following this, we consider how quality management approaches have been shown in most studies of high performance work practices (HPWPs) to play a role in sustained competitive advantage and in the organisation's production function and training provision (Morgan and Piercy, 1996; Reed, Lemak and Mero, 2000; Ridoutt, Dutneall, Hummel and Smith, 2002; Smith, Oczkowski, Noble and Macklin, 2004).

Keeping in mind the dynamic nature of coordination that exists between clients and service provider firms (Banerjee, 2004), this chapter also considers Sinkula, Baker and Noordeweir's (1997) market-based organisational learning framework for understanding how certain organisational values drive organisations' behaviours and actions. Inclusion of this approach in this analysis allows for understanding of the context and learning culture in which IT organisations promote the development of certain knowledge-questioning values and knowledge-producing behaviours, as well as their relationship with other organisational capabilities (Morgan and Piercy, 1996; Day, 1994).

Innovation and change in the business model for Indian IT companies

The term 'business model' is defined in numerous ways (Zott, Amit and Massa, 2011), although the creation and capturing of value from the customer's point of view is a common thread running through most attempts in the literature to define this concept. Johnson, Christensen and Kagermann (2008), for instance, delineate four components to a business model. These include customer value, a profit formula, key resources and an underpinning set of processes which support the first two components. This emphasis on customer value suggests that a firm should respond effectively to its customers' needs, which may emanate from problems associated with wealth, access, skill and time. The latter three of these sources of customer needs are particularly relevant to the development and evolution of the business model employed by leading Indian IT firms. That is, critical problems facing these firms in their early development were access to large pools of highly qualified and relatively cheap human resources, lack of a strong skills infrastructure, and time-zone differences.

Leading firms, such as Tata Consultancy Services, Infosys Technologies and Wipro, attended to each of these problems at various stages of their development (Arora, Arunachalam, Asundi and Fernandes, 2001; Arora and Athreye, 2002). These firms first employed cheap yet highly qualified human resources, through what has been described as 'body-shopping'. On-site software development at overseas client sites and offshore delivery centres were techniques employed by these firms in their next stage of development. This business model subsequently evolved into a global delivery business model, operating across and serving multiple locations around the world. More recently, with the introduction of disruptive technologies, such as open source, virtualisation and cloud platforms, a new hybrid form of global delivery model became the mainstream business model of many of the larger IT firms established in India (NASSCOM, 2010).

In implementing this business model, large global IT firms paid careful attention to the key components of business models, profit formula, resource mix and strong underpinning processes (Johnson et al., 2008). Careful management of these determined the success of top IT firms, as well as that of subsequent small- and medium-sized entrants into the global IT market. A critical lever of this business model for IT firms was the presence of effective and efficient skilled human resources, the development of which required significant investment by IT firms in their skills infrastructure to produce low cost yet highly skilled employees. Furthermore, investment in strong quality management frameworks helped deliver project specifications on time and a level of service often exceeding clients' expectations.

To secure sustained business from its clients, an IT firm must also develop its ability to understand its clients' latent and expressed needs and to ensure that these needs are disseminated and translated objectively into actionable tasks to development teams within the organisation. In other words, IT firms need keen market-sensing and quality management capabilities to ensure that the client-specific information is best understood and acted upon in the most efficient and effective manner (Malik and Blumenfeld, 2012; Malik *et al.*, 2012). Meeting these requirements ensures that the firm is able both to explore and to exploit its resources simultaneously in order to deliver a high and sustained level of value to its customers.

Formulating a theory of HRD in Indian IT firms

Because HRD is often considered an aspect of HRM, the relationship between the two concepts has never been clearly articulated, either in the academic literature or in practice. One reason for this is that both HRD and HRM are concerned primarily with the role of a firm's human resources in organisational performance (Mankin, 2001). To this end, management scholars often emphasise the training–performance paradigm, where a bundle of HRM practices, including training-based strategies, is posited as the key to measurable business performance improvements (Purcell, Kinnie, Hutchinson, Rayton and Swart, 2003). Others, though, have borrowed from other academic disciplines in an effort to develop a distinct theoretical and practical basis for HRD.

Swanson (2001), for instance, incorporates the concepts of scarce and sustainable resources and human capital from the field of economics, behavioural and cognitive development theories from psychology, and systems, chaos and futures theories from sociology in an effort to formulate a comprehensive theory of HRD. He contends that a firm's mission, strategy, structure and technology interact with the economic, political and cultural milieus within which it operates. HRD is described in this formulation as a process for enhancing the quality of the organisation's human resources and, in turn, organisational performance. Within this conceptualisation of HRD, the firm is assumed to be a purposive, economic entity that operates to achieve a financial surplus.

As applied fields of study, though, HRD and adult education are concerned with human beings within the organisational context and with managing learning, performance and change. Yang (2004) argues that these three phenomena are interrelated, with the first being the common thread that runs through the latter two. In this sense, he contends, it is not possible for improvements in performance to be realised or for changes to be implemented in the absence of learning.

To better understand how skill formation, strategy, operations and people management practices form critical elements of a successful IT firm's business model, we incorporate a multiplicity of theories in our conceptualisation of HRD from both an inward- and outward-looking perspective. The availability of highly skilled and cost effective resources requires an understanding of a variety of theoretical perspectives, including theories of human capital development, neo-human capital, HRM, high performance work practices (HPWPs) and organisational learning. We make no attempt, however, to address perspectives of HRD based on the sociology of adult education, which is concerned with individual, rather than organisational, learning.

The approach adopted here is a pragmatic one. Theoretical explanations from a variety of disciplines are offered to enhance contextual relevance and further our understanding of Indian IT firms' decisions to invest in human capital in order to exploit its opportunities to serve their clients and evolving business model. To demonstrate how an IT firm can develop knowledge of its clients' expressed and latent needs and embed such knowledge in its daily routines, we borrow concepts from marketing and management. This assumes, of course, that the organisation desires to utilise its resources efficiently in order to deliver outputs as per its clients' specifications in a timely manner.

One conclusion flowing from this assumption is that a business model incorporating total quality management practices can yield project management capabilities that enable a firm to service its clients better (Dean and Snell, 1991; Snell and Dean, 1992; Reed, Lemak and Montgomery, 1996; Reed *et al.*, 2000). In particular, the theories of market orientation (Kohli and Jaworski, 1990; Kohli, Jaworski and Kumar, 1993; Narver and Slater, 1990) and learning orientation (Argyris and Schön, 1978; Senge, 1990), both key elements of the market-based organisational learning framework espoused by Sinkula et al. (1997), can offer insights into how IT firms can develop unique customer value propositions as part of the business model they utilise.

Human capital theory and its application to HRD in Indian IT firms

Since the 1960s, human capital theorists have emphasised the importance of education and training as a means of increasing employee productivity (Abramovitz and Paul, 1996; Becker, 1962, 1964). As first set forth by Nobel laureate G.S. Becker (1962, 1964), it has long been noted that the availability of high-end skills in an economy's human capital base is essential to competitiveness and overall well-being. The basic thrust of human capital theory (HCT) is that continuous investment in education and training and improved learning results in increased productivity and, in turn, higher earnings for both individual employees and the organisations that employ them. To this effect, employer-sponsored training has been shown in the empirical literature to result in both higher productivity and increased wages (e.g. Acemoglu and Pischke, 1998a, b; Bartel, 2000).

One conclusion drawn from this literature is that firms are more likely to invest in firm-specific human capital than in developing generic skills (Becker, 1964). The former is concerned with the individual's immediate job requirements and is, in most cases, not transferable to other organisations. As a consequence, any investment in firm-specific training can be recouped by the employer during the employee's tenure with that organisation. As it recoups its investment in firm-specific training, the organisation can increase the employee's wages over time.

Furthermore, since firm-specific skills are not transferable to other organisations, the employee's skills are of significantly greater value to his or her current employer than to any other potential employee. This provides an additional incentive for the employee to remain with the organisation which made that investment in his or her training and skills development. That is, organisations investing in firm-specific training will render their employees relatively less attractive to other organisations. On the other hand, because they are of the similar value to other employers, the benefits of generic training and skill development are transferable to other organisations, which can increase employee turnover. Most organisations, therefore, desire to transfer the cost of general training to employees.

Not surprisingly, the question of whether or not firms should invest in generic versus firm-specific training has been intensely debated in the literature. In particular, because elements of generic and firm-specific training are likely to be present in any HRD initiative, the distinction between firm-specific human capital and generic human capital is often blurred (Maglen, 1990). A related methodological problem encountered in HCT is that it is difficult to measure the gains in productivity accruing from such investments. Also, given the business complexity and rapid technological change in many skills-intensive industries, it is hard to establish when one type of training becomes the other.

Despite these methodological problems, various studies have confirmed that firms using HPWPs, such as lean production, total quality management, team working, learning organisation, job rotation and business process reengineering, seem to invest a good deal in both technical and firm-specific training, as well as in generic and transferable training (Ridoutt *et al.*, 2002; Smith *et al.*, 2004). For instance, research from India's IT/BPO industry suggests that, owing to its dynamism and the skill inadequacies that exist in India's external labour market and wider institutional environment, firms in this sector are more likely to invest in both generic and firm-specific training (Malik, 2009; Malik and Nilakant, 2011). This gives rise to the proposition that Indian IT firms undergoing high levels of business model and technological change will invest in both generic and firm-specific training.

A neo-human capital approach to HRD in Indian IT firms

HCT portrays a worker's skill set as capital in which the worker invests time and money to develop (Acemoglu and Pischke, 1998a, 1998b; Bartel, 2000). Becker's HCT is based in part on the neoclassical economic premise that, in a competitive labour market, the wage rate equals the marginal product of labour. Two implications of this are (1) that a worker receives all returns from general training and (2) that firms will not pay the cost of general training. Neo-human capital theory (NHCT) – which arose during the 1980s, a period in which many sectors in developed economies were undergoing high levels of technological change, as has the Indian IT sector over the past 30 years – challenges the orthodoxy of HCT.

The NHCT approach is based on the premise that new technology is a means of improving productivity and that firms will develop their employees in order to gain greater flexibility in response to innovation and technological change. One conclusion drawn from this is that highly trained and educated employees are more likely to adopt to technological change than are less-educated, less-skilled employees (Wozniak, 1984, 1987; Bartel and Lichtenberg, 1987). This would suggest that the demand for highly educated workers will decline with the organisation's experience with a particular technology, a conclusion supported by findings from a number of recent studies.

Following the introduction of new technologies, skill requirements initially increase but later decline, as mechanisation increases (Nelson, Peck and Kalacheck, 1967). New production methods are frequently broken down into simpler tasks and jobs are often deskilled in a stark division of labour. Because demand for their skills typically declines as plant and equipment depreciate in value, better educated workers generally have a comparative advantage over their less-educated counterparts with respect to their adaptability to new technologies (Bartel and Lichtenberg, 1987). This comparative advantage is even more pronounced in R&D-intensive sectors, where transition to new technologies is typically slow and new production methods are ill-defined, at least initially.

The extant literature also indicates that, in practice, organisations are often willing to share in the cost of general training, contrary to the predictions of HCT. Acemoglu and Pischke (1998a, b) explain this paradox as an artefact of information asymmetries or market imperfections created by the inability of organisations to observe the true abilities of workers. Nonetheless, while this may hold true for most IT product development firms, because of the dynamism in the services it provides its clients and the typical make-up of its labour market, the application of this explanation to the Indian IT industry's services segment is questionable. Rather, evidence from the India's IT/BPO sector points to the increasing influence of client specifications on the provision of general skills training (Malik, 2009; Malik and Nilakant, 2011). This would mean that Indian IT firms will invest more in generic and transferable skills training, not as a consequence of information asymmetries, but rather of the dynamic nature of clients' project requirements.

Several large IT firms operating in India employ vast numbers of highly skilled workers with little or no work experience but with knowledge in a narrow technical domain (Malik *et al.*, 2012). These organisations make significant investments in training and development of these workers, usually in a range of areas (Malik, 2009). Given the inadequacies of the national engineering curriculum, firms in this sector invest significantly in technology and soft skills training to meet client specifications, and they develop training plans based on forecasts of their future skill requirements. While a strategic underpinning to this practice seems obvious, the focus of these firms is more on delivering a cost effective business model (Malik, 2009).

Human resource management, business strategy and training

Schuler and Jackson's (1987) typology suggests firms may pursue one of three of competitive strategies, each with its own consequent training demands. Under a cost-reduction strategy, for instance, training and skills development are not high on the organisation's list of strategic priorities. Such organisations will, therefore, not invest much if anything in developing their employees and will prefer to hire employees with qualifications and skills already in hand. Organisations that alternatively pursue either an innovation or a quality-enhancement strategy, though, typically adhere to HRM practices aimed at attracting and maintaining highly qualified, skilled, creative and flexible employees and involve their employees in key decisions. These organisations generally invest heavily in both R&D and training and development. Organisations with an innovation strategy will do this in order to keep their core staff satisfied and reduce turnover; organisations that follow a quality-enhancement strategy will elect to do this to gain cooperation and achieve continuous improvement.

Building on Schuler and Jackson's (1987) strategic typology, Boxall (2003) offers a framework for understanding the relationship between market characteristics, competitive dynamics and HR strategy, with a specific focus on firms in the service sector. He develops a typology of three kinds of markets that firms can get into, and he identifies the nature and basis of competition and work organisation for each. Boxall identifies three types of markets, mass-service markets, high value-added market types, and differentiated markets. Between these archetypical markets, the nature of knowledge content, work design, competitive dynamics and HRM strategy will vary. Significantly, Boxall's (2003) typology suggests there are opportunities to implement high performance, high involvement and high commitment work systems (HPWPs) in both differentiated markets and markets where there is higher value-added economic benefit available.

Research on HPWS focuses on improving performance through a bundle of universally applicable HR practices (Pfeffer, 1994, 1998). These work systems are said to lead to low employee turnover, high quality HR service delivery, improved skills capability, strategic integration, and improved attitudes and behaviours. These key performance indicators (KPIs) are considered instrumental to increasing productivity, as is the role of line managers in implementing such practices (Purcell et al. 2003). Despite this, given the high level of complexity and the need to accommodate an organisation's contextual factors and employee voice in developing any HR practices, critics of best-practice models challenge the claims espoused by these models (Lloyd and Payne, 2004, 2005; Marchington and Grugulis, 2000). In addition, in light of the high cost of implementing such practices, application of such models may be feasible only in large, diversified organisations.

Boxall (2003) argues, though, that the skills that firms should possess for implementation of HPWPs need not be high, so long as there is an economic justification for implementing HPWPs. Nevertheless, large and diverse organisations are likely to be operating in all the three market types, concomitantly offering vastly different products and services. What is also not clear is the nature of the specific HR practices that an organisation may adopt under any particular market scenario. Importantly, whether an organisation invests relatively more or less in training and development, and the type of knowledge and skills developed, remains unclear.

Importantly, empirical evidence does not support the need for organisations in differentiated product markets to take a high skills road (Mason, 2005). In particular, differentiated product markets are not associated with the employment of a highly skilled labour force (Sung and Ashton, 2005). For instance, with specific regard to the differentiated Indian IT sector, both firms involved primarily in project work and those focused primarily on developing software products and R&D operate, in practice, somewhere along a continuum ranging across Boxall's (2003) typology of service markets. That is, firms in the sector may develop skills in-house or, instead, deliver high-end services by employing a strict Taylorist work design.

Banerjee (2004) notes that the particular dynamics of the Indian IT sector reflect a Marshallian adjustment processes, characterised by localised production of a single commodity. To this end, Indian IT firms operate in regional markets and form strategic alliances and use strategic demand management to achieve their strategic business planning objectives. Indian IT firms typically have a fluid structure and employ a business strategy that integrates business units into common production and delivery processes. Successful implementation of this strategy is, of course, dependent upon the strength of the organisation's capabilities, which is consistent with a resource-based view of the firm (Barney, 1991).

The resource-based view suggests HRM is critical to the development of certain competencies necessary for it to achieve sustained competitive advantage (Barney, 1991; Leonard, 1998; Wernerfelt, 1984; Wright, McMahan and McWilliams, 1994). Hamel and Prahalad (1990) developed the concept of core competencies, which describes learned attributes that provide a firm with its competitive advantage. For an organisation's resources to deliver sustained competitive advantage, those resources must add value to the firm, and be unique or rare and, hence, incapable of being substituted with other resources or provided by competing firms (Barney, 1991). This necessitates development of organisational practices that support training and skills development, employee retention and focused recruitment, as well as management of the tacit and explicit knowledge critical to the achievement of sustained competitive advantage.

Most knowledge and physical resources of IT firms can be procured from the market and, hence, an organisation's unique path dependencies often can be transferred to other organisations through job switching and competitors' market information-sensing capabilities (Sinkula et al., 1997). For this reason, neither tacit nor explicit knowledge is a viable source of competitive advantage. If knowledge is explicit and codified, then it is transferable to other organisations and, unless protected by patents, is effectively a market good. As Banerjee (2004) elaborates, even where knowledge is difficult to imitate, if tacit knowledge exists and resides in the minds of the individuals, it can arguably be transmitted by virtue of job switching to rival firms which can potentially profit from that knowledge.

Banerjee (2004) offers a typology which differentiates knowledge relevant to a firm's business model and strategic objectives into three categories: knowledge as a factor of production; knowledge as a source of competitive advantage; and knowledge as organisational wealth. All three types of knowledge are strategic, yet none is a pure asset which can be procured from the market. Rather, each type of knowledge proffers a decision rule allowing a firm to 'switch' from one market (e.g. product) to another (services) in response to its strategic needs. Given the two principal divisions in India's IT sector (product environment and project or services environment), and depending on its strategic milieu and make-up, a firm's knowledge assets and need to develop higher-level competencies will vary. Further, the firm's ability to switch from product to project environment and vice versa is a core competency and can be a source of competitive advantage. This competency is developed through investments in strategic knowledge, which determines the ease with which the organisation is able to switch from one environment to the other.

One conclusion drawn from the extant literature in this area is that organisation change – either technical or structural change – has a profound impact on skill formation. Findings from the earliest attempts to explain the role of training and HRM in strategic change suggest that training is triggered by either technical product market changes, resulting in gaps in skill requirement (Sparrow and Pettigrew, 1985; Pettigrew, Sparrow and Hendry, 1988). Skill demand itself is said to be associated with technical change (Mason, 2005; Sung and Ashton, 2005) and with the introduction of new products or services (Kitchin and Blackburn, 2002). Additionally, workplace reorganisation, investment in quality, new technology and enterprise size are known to be significant drivers of training (Hayton et al., 1996; Smith and Hayton, 1999), as are new products or process technologies, organisational change and technological innovation (Ridoutt et al. 2002). Changes to a firm's strategy are, therefore, also said to have a significant impact on its skills requirements and, as a consequence, on its training provision.

Some consider new management practices (NMPs) or HPWS vehicles for the high levels of skills development required in a knowledge economy and have identified linkages between HPWPs and demand for investment in skills (Ashton and Sung, 2002; Felstead and Ashton, 2000). Smith et al. (2003, 2004), for instance, find support for a positive association between various NMPs and training provision. The recipe is a model of certain practices which, if implemented, are likely to take organisations on a path of high skills development and consequently high performance and growth.

One conclusion drawn from the forgoing is that, where the focus of NMPs or HPWPs is on employee control and cost reduction, only technical skills will be valued and developed. However, where such HPWPs allow for empowerment, employee discretion and autonomy, the focus of skills development will include both technical and behavioural skills (Ashton and Sung, 2002; Smith et al., 2004).

Two further conclusions can be drawn from this. First, owing to the fact that highly complex projects and services with a control-oriented work design, Indian IT firms are likely to invest more in high levels of technical skills training. Moreover, given their highly complex projects and services and empowerment-oriented work design, IT firms in India will invest more in high levels of behavioural skills training.

Other research has found that business strategy and skills utilisation is inextricably linked. Boxall (2003), for instance, argues that the ability to invest in high quality work systems is dependent on an organisation's competitive strategy. It is more likely that firms operating in differentiated and highly differentiated product and services markets will invest in quality management systems. Similarly, Ashton and Sung (2006) argue that an organisation's business strategy determines the nature and extent of its skills demand.

Ashton and Sung (2006) observe that organisations that produce standardised products or services and that compete on price typically adopt a 'product-centred' product market strategy. These organisations use a mass production technology and task-focused interpersonal relations, a Fordist strategy that relies on unskilled labour and low-cost production efficiency and which is not compatible with employee development, high performance work practices, innovation and discretionary work effort. More importantly such organisations are less likely to invest in a broad range of skill sets. This suggests that Indian IT firms with a cost leadership strategy will invest less in training and quality management systems.

On the other hand, organisations that produce differentiated products or services and compete on the basis of quality will use batch or customised technologies. In these organisations, interpersonal relations and employee development are seen as an integral part of their competitive advantage, and the level of skills utilisation by these organisations is high. Organisations with a differentiated production function and with a people-development focus in their social and interpersonal work relations are more likely to invest in a range of skills (Ashton and Sung, 2006). It follows that Indian IT firms which service differentiated markets will invest more in training and quality management systems than will firms servicing mass markets.

Quality management in IT

Having considered the relationship between a firm's business model and its investment in human capital and human resource development, we now turn to the role of quality management in skills development. Quality management is adopted by organisations as part of their business strategy and is directed at achieving and maintaining a high level of performance. It includes creating and implementing quality planning, quality assurance, quality control and quality improvement.

A quality management philosophy focused on customer satisfaction and continuous improvement and which reflects a view of the organisation as a total system is referred to as total quality management or simply TQM (Dean and Snell,

1991; Prajogo and Brown, 2004; Sitkin, Sutcliffe and Schroeder, 1994; Snell and Dean, 1992). TQM has a customer satisfaction focus and is characterised by teamwork, cost reduction, continuous improvement, commitment from top management, an emphasis on training and education, and a work culture that reflects these values (Reed et al. 1996, 2000). These values can be encapsulated into three broad categories: a commitment to information sharing; continuous improvement; and team working (Prajogo and McDermott, 2006).

Quality management practices have established an important place in the services and manufacturing sectors, where such practices have been shown to improve organisational performance and serve as a source of sustained competitive advantage (Morgan and Piercy, 1996; Reed *et al.*, 2000). Quality management practices employed in these sectors are typically focused on minimising any variance from a pre-established norm and make use of a range of statistical techniques for monitoring the quality of the product or service delivery. This suggests that, while TQM content, the key features of which are market advantage, product design efficiency, process efficiency and product reliability, may be a source of competitive advantage to firms, it is *how* organisations deploy their TQM practices that has the potential to create sustained competitive advantage (Reed et al., 2000).

Morgan and Piercy (1996) express the view that quality management approaches support both differentiation and cost leadership strategies. Other research has found that the effect of differentiation strategy on quality is moderated by cost leadership strategy; that is, the stronger the cost leadership strategy, the greater the effect. That same research provides an explanation for the linkages between product and service quality, cost leadership, and differentiation strategies. Firms have also been found in that research to pursue both differentiation and cost leadership strategies (Prajogo, 2007). Moreover, differentiation can be achieved by focusing on external dimensions of quality, such as customer satisfaction and innovation. Similarly, a low-cost strategy can be serviced by focusing on internal aspects of quality, such as process improvement and both waste and cost reduction. This suggests IT firms can select quality management frameworks for delivering various strategic initiatives, including cost leadership and differentiation, as well as operational outcomes, including cost and waste reduction, functional integration, capability development, customer satisfaction and process improvement.

There are numerous quality management systems adopted by firms in the IT sector. These include ISO 9000, the Capability Maturity Model index (CMMi), the Baldrige criteria for performance excellence, lean production, and six sigma. Most of these standards focus on aspects of process maturity and employee capability development (Kumar, 2001; NASSCOM, 2005). According to the Indian IT industry association NASSCOM (2006), by December 2005, over 400 Indian companies had acquired quality certifications, including 82 firms certified at CMM Level 5, more than any other country. TQM, Six Sigma, Lean Production, ISO 9000 and CMM mandate specific types of training for employees at various levels.

For organisations in the Indian IT sector to remain competitive, they must continually develop and deliver quality products/services on time and at low cost. Also, organisational capability is dependent on *how* the organisation implements both internal and external dimensions of its quality management approach. For example, high level of process maturity is a commonly used quality standard in information technology support services, in which high product quality and development effort are key competitive factors. A key issue in this regard is whether high levels of quality can be achieved without diversely impacting cycle time and effort. Research has shown that quality improvement, faster cycle time and effort reduction can all be achieved by reducing defects and rework; the net effect of process maturity has been found to be reduced cycle time and development effort (Harter, Krishnan and Slaughter, 2000).

The CMM model, which was originally used by the US Department of Defense to assess contractors' capabilities, typically categorises process maturity at five levels. The essence of this approach is first to observe and capture the processes employed by the firm and then to simplify and standardise by developing metrics for those processes, with the objective of reducing or, ideally, eliminating variance in performance (Royce, 1970). The highest of the five levels of maturity is achieved over a period of time through sustained investment in quality management resources, assessments and training. Therefore, over-investment in quality management can be counterproductive.

Recognition that achievement of the highest level of process maturity requires movement through lower levels of achievement, and requires long-term investment is critical to IT firms' business models. For organisations to survive in the Indian IT sector, they must continually develop and deliver products/services on time and at low cost. Their ability to do so depends on the achievement of high levels of process maturity, which are associated with high product quality and increased development effort (Harter *et al.*, 2000).

In addition, quality accreditation is known to have a positive effect on both sales revenue and overall firm performance. For instance, in a study of 95 Indian software firms and 12 of their US-based clients, quality certification was found to be an important signalling tool for potential customers. Quality certification provides the software vendors with the ability to deliver sophisticated, high value-added services with a high per unit output cost, thereby enabling them to undertake complex projects. Quality certification also affords the software services firm a better understanding of its clients' needs during negotiations, before any contract with those clients is signed (Arora and Asundi, 2002).

Successful implementation of TQM, as Parzinger (1997) suggests, is dependent on the organisation progressing through stages of the product/process life cycle. Other research points to the need for significant investment in both quality processes and human resource development. This investment must take place during the early stages of the product/service or process life cycle and in accordance with clients' expectations, with the overall expectation that productivity will improve (Krishnan, Kriebel, Kekre and Mukhopadhyay, 2000). This dual emphasis may explain some of the conflicting findings in the extant literature, in particular why

TQM has been shown to be successful and have a positive impact on the formalisation of training in some organisations, but not in others. This anomaly points to the existence of a temporal dimension to adoption and deployment of quality management systems and that quality management may impact both the organisations' training and its production function.

These considerations give rise to the proposition that well-developed quality management systems play a role in shaping the nature and extent of training provision needed to service an organisation's business model. Extant literature suggests that for an organisation to develop distinctive capabilities, it should demonstrate a commitment to developing a learning culture, open-mindedness for new learning, and a shared vision (Senge, 1990). Further, in the context of globalisation and outsourcing, there is a high level of interdependence and dynamic coordination in knowledge transfer from the client to the service provider (Banerjee, 2004). This requires an understanding of *how* organisations develop client-specific capabilities and other learning necessary to meet their clients' needs.

A market-based organisational learning framework

In their conceptualisation of a market-based organisational learning process, Sinkula et al. (1997) suggest that the process of organisational learning, as previously elaborated by Fiol and Lyles (1985) and Huber (1991), is facilitated by three elements: organisational values that promote learning; the organisation's market-information processing behaviours; and organisational actions. An organisation's learning orientation involves three sets of organisational values associated with the organisation's tendency to learn: commitment to learning; open-mindedness; and a shared vision to influence the organisation's ability to create and use knowledge (Argyris and Schön, 1978; Senge, 1990). Owing their tacit, covert and unobservable nature, interpretation and organisational memory are excluded from this model.

Commitment to learning is an organisational value that fosters learning through ongoing training and development of the organisation's employees and allocates resources for such development. Open-mindedness requires an organisation to challenge its current thinking and to be open to any new information it receives and to any new trend. Moreover, an organisation's shared vision encompasses its ability to communicate and disseminate any knowledge and competencies. These values can be implemented partly by direct investment in training and partly by fostering a culture of supporting and sharing new learning and skills development at all levels. In this respect, an organisation's learning orientation influences the degree to which it is satisfied with its current thinking and, hence, the degree to which proactive learning occurs (Senge, 1990; Sinkula et al., 1997).

The influence of client needs on the creation of new knowledge, a critical input for any training provision, is best understood in the context of market information processing, the means by which external market information is transformed into knowledge (Sinkula, 1994). Market information processing involves sensing and disseminating information from the external market across the organisation. Information dissemination is the ability to diffuse the information generated, vertically and horizontally (Argyris and Schön, 1978). Because it involves capturing precise and critical information about a customer's needs and the external competitive environment, though, information sensing or generation is perhaps of even greater importance. In particular, if information acquisition is done well, disseminating that information across the relevant parts of the organisation and then framing a response is relatively easy.

Market information processing is developed from a key marketing construct, market orientation: 'the organization-wide generation of market intelligence pertaining to current and future needs of customers, dissemination of information horizontally and vertically within the organization, and the organization-wide action or responsiveness to market intelligence' (Kohli et al. 1993, p. 467). While the concept was developed with the intent of meeting an organisation's strategic marketing needs, the information acquired and disseminated through market orientation has direct relevance for developing various operational, marketing and training responses. From a client perspective, an organisation's market orientation's linkage with its learning orientation is critical to strengthening the organisation's relationship with its training and development efforts, as well as with its marketing outcomes. Such linkages are possible by creating an organisational culture that supports behaviours for creating superior customer value. Market orientation is one such knowledge-producing behaviour (Sinkula et al., 1997).

A firm's market orientation consists of three components: information sensing or acquisition both from its customers and from its competitors; horizontal and vertical dissemination of that information within the organisation; and framing appropriate organisational responses to that information via inter-functional coordination (Kohli et al., 1993; Narver and Slater, 1990). As it enables the organisation to keep itself informed about its customers and competitors, information generation is critical to a firm's market orientation. However, if its information dissemination and response-framing ability are inefficient and ineffective, changes to its business model will be limited. Moreover, the firm's ability to store, process and interpret new information may either enhance or hinder the utility of that information before any response is framed.

Sinkula et al. (1997) were the first to test the interrelationships between organisational learning, a values-based construct that formally connects organisational values, as described by Argyris and Schön (1978) and Senge (1990), to the organisation's market information processing behaviours, as characterised by Kohli et al. (1993) and Narver and Slater (1990), and organisational actions. On the assumption that values drive behaviours and subsequent actions, Sinkula et al. (1997) confirmed the following three hypotheses:

1   that the extent to which an organisation engages in market information behaviour is a function of its learning orientation;
2   that an organisation's dissemination of market information is a direct and indirect function of its learning orientation, such that the indirect effect of

learning orientation on information dissemination is dependent on its information generation; and

3   that the frequency with which an organisation disseminates its marketing programmes (organisational response) is a function of the extent to which it disseminates the information.

Learning orientation, a values-based construct, is characterised by increased market information generation and dissemination, a knowledge-based construct. The availability and use of market information, in turn, affects the degree to which the organisation makes changes to its strategies, a behavioural construct (Sinkula *et al.*, 1997). Organisations with high levels of learning orientation are more likely to question their current theory-in-use, to challenge basic assumptions and to be receptive to new ideas and knowledge. While new knowledge is procured through an organisation's market orientation abilities, it can be refined, redefined and challenged through its learning orientation, depending on the extent to which this is developed. Organisations may thus utilise adaptive, generative or transformational learning processes.

A learning orientation induces knowledge questioning values to refine the information acquired and disseminated through a firm's market orientation. High learning orientation is likely to enhance the market-orientated behaviours, because a learning orientation constantly challenges the assumptions of the information and an organisation's theory-in-use. In terms of adaptability of a new product or service, it is likely that a market orientation will result in faster product development, especially if learning orientation is low. As a result, firms with low learning and high market orientations are more likely to focus on product, service and process enhancements or incremental changes rather than on new products or radical innovations (Baker and Sinkula, 1999a, 1999b).

Because it challenges the clients' assumptions and it relies on a range of additional information sources, including market intelligence processing, to make informed decisions regarding what the firm's customers want, a strong learning orientation may not necessarily result in new product development. Although there is limited understanding of how market and learning orientations can be developed (Malik and Blumenfeld, 2012), one recent study found strong support for the role of quality management capabilities in developing market-based organisational learning capabilities (Malik *et al.*, 2012). This finding supports Day's (1994) case for utilising TQM to implement market orientation programmes. One conclusion from this is that, in a high technology services environment, high levels of market and learning orientation require significant investment in technical and general skills training to enhance understanding customer's latent and expressed needs.

Conclusion

This chapter provides a detailed review and critique of the dominant theories, frameworks and empirical research aimed at explaining a firm's decision to invest in skills development. This discussion has identified how training, quality management, HRM practices and market-sensing capabilities are critical elements of Indian IT firms' business models. As noted here, an organisation's business model is aimed at aligning its intangible information- and knowledge-based assets with value-generating processes and its strategic objectives. For Indian IT firms, in particular, this implies that what the organisation has to offer its customers is knowledge and skills that complement its customers' knowledge, resources and equipment (Prahalad and Ramaswamy, 2000).

This chapter has also considered the implications of the growth and development of knowledge work for human capital theory, the basic thrust of which is that continuous investment in education and training and improved learning results in increased productivity and, in turn, higher earnings for both individual employees and the organisations that employ them. Importantly, as value created in its customers' value-generating processes is considered pivotal to the firm's sustainable competitive advantage, the knowledge and skills possessed by its human resources are crucial determinants of the firm's competitive advantage. It is, therefore, in the interest of all organisations in rapidly changing knowledge sectors, such as the market for IT services, to invest in lifelong learning of those whose careers are dependent on continual skills enhancement and to share in the development of human capital.

As further elaborated here, there are two key elements to business strategy. The first is product market strategy, which determines the market type in which the firm seeks to compete. In this regard, a firm may elect to compete in a high value-added market and produce differentiated products or services, or it may prefer to compete in a low-valued added market, in which it sells standardised products or services. A firm that elects to produce high volumes of a standardised product or service will opt for a form of mass production or, its service sector equivalent, a call-centre technology. Use of mass production technology enables the firm to contain its costs through the employment of unskilled or semiskilled, unqualified or low qualified labour. Alternatively, a firm that seeks to produce complex products or services will opt for a system of small batch or one-off customised production tailored to its customers' requirements. Typically, this requires highly skilled, highly qualified labour with the technical knowledge and ability to tailor the product or service to the unique specification of the customer.

The second element of business strategy is competitive strategy, which expounds the means by which an organisation proposes to gain competitive advantage in its chosen market. As suggested by Ashton and Sung (2006) in their 'strategic skills' model, a firm's business strategy is shaped by competitive pressures and the regulatory environment within which the firm operates. Various means by which Indian IT firms may choose to compete in their rapidly changing environment include developing unique products or services, continually improving the quality of its products or services, or producing relatively low cost products or services. If it elects to compete on the basis of quality or the uniqueness of its products or services, skill and skill development become central to the firm's competitive strategy. Alternatively, if it elects to produce inexpensive products or services, the firm will seek to reducing the skill content of its output and thereby its labour costs by minimising its reliance on skilled labour.

What the foregoing implies is that there is a range of business strategies at which skills contribute more or less to the firm's competitive advantage. In this regard, an organisation's competitive strategy is associated with its interpersonal or social relations, which determine how the organisation utilises skills and, in particular, how its employees function and are mobilised to operate the technology employed in the production process. A people-focused strategy, for instance, will include human resource management practices associated with high performance working systems (HPWSs), including the development of skills associated with the delivery of customised solutions to a company's IT requirements, or personal wealth management. Moreover, a people-oriented skills strategy typically necessitates development of skills beyond the immediate requirements implied by the firm's technical relations.

On the other hand, the firm may elect to pursue a product market strategy aimed at developing and utilising task-oriented skills akin to a Fordist (or neo-Fordist) system of production and division of labour, as associated with assembly lines or call centres. If the firm is to shift from mass production to more differentiated products, though, it will need to increase its employees' technical knowledge and enable greater skills utilisation, which require that the firm target its competitive strategy and change its interpersonal relations. This implies that, within the constraints imposed by its technical relations, the organisation's interpersonal relations determine how the skills of its labour force are put to use by the firm and how these contribute to organisational performance (Ashton and Sung, 2006).

Through this analysis, several propositions with regard to Indian IT firms have been delineated:

Proposition 1 Indian IT firms undergoing high levels of technological change will utilize a business model which emphasizes increased investment in both generic and firm-specific training.

Proposition 2 Indian IT firms will employ a business model that stresses investment in generic and transferable skills training, not due to information asymmetry, but rather due to servicing clients' project needs.

Proposition 3 The demand for large numbers of highly skilled workers will decline as firms gain more experience experience in a given technology domain, which will affect a shift in the organisation's business model.

Proposition 4 Highly complex projects and services require business model aimed at making high levels of investment in training.

Proposition 5 Firms with a business model focused on cost leadership will invest less in training and quality management systems.

Proposition 6 Firms servicing slightly and highly differentiated service markets will invest more in training and quality management systems as part of their business model than will firms servicing mass service markets.

Proposition 7 The strength of an organisation's quality management systems helps in shaping the nature and extent of training provision needed to service its business model.

Proposition 8 In a high-technology services environment, high levels of market and learning orientation will require a business model which emphasizes higher levels of investment in technical and general skills training for understanding customers latent and expressed needs.

These eight propositions reflect the posited relationships between training, strategy, operations and people management practices and how these contribute to an Indian IT firm's business model.

References

Abramovitz, M., and Paul, A.D. (1996). Technological change and the rise of intangible investments: The U.S. economy's growth-path in the twentieth century. In OECD, *Employment and growth in the knowledge-based economy* (pp. 35–60). Paris: Author.

Acemoglu, D., and Pischke, J.-S. (1998a). Why do firms train? Theory and evidence. *Quarterly Journal of Economics, 113*(1), 79–119.

Acemoglu, D., and Pischke, J.-S. (1998b). Beyond Becker: Training in imperfect markets. *The Economic Journal, 109*(453), 112–142.

Argyris, C., and Schön, D.A. (1978). *Organizational learning: A theory of action perspective*. Reading, MA: Addison-Wesley.

Arora, A., and Athreye, S. (2002). The software industry and India's economic development. *Information Economics and Policy, 14*(2), 253–273.

Arora, A., Arunachalam, V.S., Asundi, J.V., and Fernandes, R. (2001). The Indian software services industry. *Research Policy, 30*(8), 1267–1287.

Arora, A., and Asundi, J. (2002). *Quality certification and the economics of contract software development: A study of the Indian software industry*. NBER Working Paper No. 7260. Pittsburgh, PA: H. John Heinz III School of Public Policy and Management and Carnegie Mellon University.

Ashton, D., and Sung, J. (2002). *Supporting workplace learning for high performance working*. Geneva: ILO.

Ashton, D., and Sung, J. (2006). *How competitive strategy matters? Understanding the drivers of training, learning and performance at the firm level*. Research Paper No. 66. Oxford: Oxford and Warwick Universities, Centre for Skills, Knowledge and Organisational Performance.

Asundi, J., and Arora, A. (2002, December). *Quality certification and the economics of contract software development: A study of the Indian software industry*. NBER Working Paper No. 7260. Pittsburgh, PA: H. John Heinz III School of Public Policy and Management and Carnegie Mellon University.

Baker, W.E., and Sinkula, J.M. (1999a). Learning orientation, market orientation, and innovation: Integrating and extending models of organisational performance. *Journal of Market-Focussed Management, 4*(4), 295–307.

Baker, W.E., and Sinkula, J.M. (1999b). The synergistic effects of market orientation and learning orientation on organisational performance. *Journal of the Academy of Marketing Science, 27*(4), 411–427.

Banerjee, P. (2004). *The Indian software industry: Business strategy and dynamic coordination.* New Delhi: Palgrave Macmillan.

Barney, J. (1991). Firm resources and sustained competitive advantage. *Journal of Management, 17*(1), 99–120.

Bartel, A.P. (2000). Measuring the employer's return on investments in training: Evidence from the literature. *Industrial Relations, 39*(3), 502–524.

Bartel, A.P., and Lichtenberg, F.R. (1987). The comparative advantage of educated workers in implementing new technology. *The Review of Economics and Statistics, 69*(1), 1–11.

Becker, G. (1962). Investment in human capital: A theoretical analysis Part 2 – Investment in human beings. *Journal of Political Economy, 70*(5), 9–49.

Becker, G. (1964). *Human capital: A theoretical and empirical analysis* Princeton, NJ: Princeton University Press.

Boxall, P. (2003). HR strategy and competitive advantage in the service sector. *Human Resource Management Journal, 13*(3), 5–20.

Day, G.S. (1994). The capabilities of market-driven organizations. *Journal of Marketing, 58*(4), 37–52.

Dean, J.W., Jr., and Snell, S.A. (1991). Integrated manufacturing and job design: Moderating effects of organisational inertia. *Academy of Management Journal, 34*(4), 776–804.

Ethiraj, S.E., Kale, P., Krishnan, M.S., and Singh, J.V. (2005). Where do capabilities come from and how do they matter? A study in the software services industry. *Strategic Management Journal, 26*(1), 25–45.

Felstead, A., and Ashton, D. (2000). Tracing the link: Organisational structures and skill demands. *Human Resource Management Journal, 10*(3), 5–21.

Fiol, C.M., and Lyles, M.A. (1985). Organisational learning. *Academy of Management Review, 10*(4), 656–670.

Hamel, G., and Prahalad, C K. (1990). The core competences of the corporation. *Harvard Business Review, 68*(3), 79–91.

Harter, D.E., Krishnan, M.S., and Slaughter, S.A. (2000). Effects of process maturity on quality, cycle time and effort in software development. *Management Science, 46*(4), 451–467.

Hayton, G., McIntyre, J., Sweet, R., McDonald, R., Noble, C., Smith, A., and Roberts. P. (1996). *Final report: Enterprise training in Australia,* Melbourne: Office of Training and Further Education.

Heeks, R. (1998). *The uneven profile of Indian software exports.* Development Informatics Paper No. 3. Manchester, England: University of Manchester, IDPM. Retrieved from www.sed.manchester.ac.uk/idpm/research/publications/wp/di/ di_wp03.htm

Huber, G.P. (1991, February). Organizational learning: The contributing processes and the literatures. *Organization Science, 2*(1), 88–115.

Johnson, M.W., Christensen, C.C., and Kagermann, H. (2008). Reinventing your business model. *Harvard Business Review, 86*(12), 50–59.

Kitchin, J., and Blackburn, R. (2002). *The nature of training and motivation to train in small firms.* Research Report No. RR330. Nottingham: Department for Education and Skills.

Kohli, A.K., and Jaworski, B.J. (1990). Market orientation: The construct, research propositions, and managerial implications. *Journal of Marketing, 54*(2), 1–18.

Kohli, A.K., Jaworski, B.J., and Kumar, A. (1993). MARKOR: A measure of market orientation. *Journal of Marketing Research, 30*(4), 467–477.

Krishnan, M.S., Kriebel, C.H., Kekre, S., and Mukhopadhyay, T. (2000). An empirical analysis of productivity and quality in software products. *Management Science, 46*(6), 745–759.

Kumar, N. (2001). Developing countries in international division of labour in software and service industry: Lessons from the Indian experience. *World employment report 2001: Life at work in the information economy* [CD-ROM]. Geneva: ILO.

Leonard, D. (1998). *Wellsprings of knowledge: Building and sustaining sources of innovation.* Boston, MA: Harvard Business School Press.

Lloyd, C., and Payne, J. (2004). *Just another bandwagon? A critical look at the role of the high performance workplace as a vehicle for the UK high skills project.* SKOPE Working Paper No. 49. Oxford: Oxford and Warwick Universities, SKOPE.

Lloyd, C., and Payne, J. (2005). *High performance work organisation: A driver for the high skills vision?* SKOPE Issues Paper No. 6. Oxford: Oxford and Warwick Universities, SKOPE.

Maglen, L. (1990). Challenging the human capital orthodoxy: The education-productivity link re-examined. *The Economic Record, 66*(4), 281–294.

Malik, A. (2009). Training drivers, competitive strategy and clients' needs: Case studies of three business process outsourcing organisations. *Journal of European Industrial Training, 33*(2), 160–177.

Malik A., and Nilakant, V. (2011). Extending the 'size matters' debate: Drivers of training in three business process outsourcing SMEs in India. *Management Research Review, 34*(1), 111–132.

Malik, A., and Blumenfeld, S. (2012). Six Sigma, quality management systems and the development of organisational learning capability: Evidence from four business process outsourcing organisations in India. *International Journal of Quality & Reliability Management, 29*(1), 71–91.

Malik, A., Sinha, A., and Blumenfeld, S. (2012). Role of quality management capabilities in developing market-based organisational learning capabilities: Case study evidence from four Indian business process outsourcing firms. *Industrial Marketing Management, 41*(4), 639–648.

Mankin, D. (2001). A model for human resource development. *Human Resource Development International, 4*(1), 65–86.

Marchington, M., and Grugulis, I. (2000). 'Best practice' human resource management: Perfect opportunity or dangerous illusion? *International Journal of Human Resource Management, 11*(6), 1104–1124.

Mason, G. (2005, May). *In search of high value added production: How important are skills?* Research Report No. 663. Nottingham: Department for Education and Skills.

Morgan, N.A., and Piercy, N.F. (1996). Competitive advantage, quality strategy, and the role of marketing. *British Journal of Management, 7*(3), 231–245.

NASSCOM. (2005). *Key statistics: IT sector.* Retrieved from www.nasscom.org.

NASSCOM. (2006). *Why India?* Retrieved from www.nasscom.org.

NASSCOM. (2010). *The IT-BPO sector in India: Strategic review 2010.* New Delhi: NASSCOM.

Narver, J.C., and Slater, S.F. (1990). The effect of a market orientation on business profitability. *Journal of Marketing, 54*(4), 20–35.

Nelson, R., Peck, M., and Kalacheck, E. (1967). *Technology, economic growth, and public policy.* Washington, DC: Brookings.

Parzinger, M. (1997). A stage-wise application of total quality management through the product life cycle. *Industrial Management & Data Systems, 97*(3), 125–130.

Patibandla, M., and Petersen, B. (2002). Role of transnational corporations in the evolution of a high-tech industry: The case of India's software industry. *World Development, 30*(9), 1561–1577.

Pettigrew, A., Sparrow, P., and Hendry, C. (1988). The forces that trigger training. *Personnel Management, 20*(12), 28–32.

Pfeffer, J. (1994). *Competitive advantage through people: Unleashing the power of the workforce.* Boston, MA: Harvard Business School Press.

Pfeffer, J. (1998). *The human equation: Building profits by putting people first.* Boston, MA: Harvard Business School Press.

Prahalad, C.K., and Ramaswamy, V. (2000). Co-opting customer competence. *Harvard Business Review, 78*(1), 79–90.

Prajogo, D.I. (2007). The relationship between competitive strategies and product quality. *Industrial Management & Data Systems, 107*(1), 69–83.

Prajogo, D.I., and Brown, A. (2004). The relationship between TQM practices and quality performance and the role of formal TQM programs: An Australian empirical study. *The Quality Management Journal, 11*(4), 31–42.

Prajogo, D.I., and McDermott, C.M. (2006). The relationship between total quality management and organizational culture. *International Journal of Operations & Production Management, 25*(11), 1101–1122.

Purcell, J., Kinnie, N., Hutchinson, S., Rayton, B., and Swart, J. (2003). *Understanding the people and performance link: Unlocking the black box.* London: CIPD.

Reed, R., Lemak, D.J., and Mero, N.P. (2000). Total quality management and sustainable competitive advantage. *Journal of Quality Management, 5*(1), 5–26.

Reed, R., Lemak, D.J., and Montgomery, J.C. (1996). Beyond process: TQM content and firm performance. *Academy of Management Review, 21*(1), 173–202.

Ridoutt, L., Dutneall, R., Hummel, K., and Smith, C.S. (2002). *Factors influencing training and learning in the workplace.* Leabrook, SA: NCVER.

Royce, W. (1970). Managing the development of large software systems, *Proceedings of IEEE WESCON, 26*(August), p. 1–9.

Schuler, R.S., and Jackson, S.E. (1987). Linking competitive strategies with human resource management practices. *Academy of Management Executive, 1*(3), 209–213.

Senge, P.M. (1990). *The fifth discipline: The art and practice of learning organisation.* New York, NY: Doubleday.

Sinkula, J.M. (1994). Market information processing and organisational learning. *Journal of Marketing, 58*(1), 46–55.

Sinkula, J.M., Baker, W.E., and Noordeweir, T. (1997). A framework for market-based organisational learning: Linking values, knowledge, and behaviour. *Journal of the Academy of Marketing Science, 25*(4), 305–318.

Sitkin, S.B., Sutcliffe, K.M., and Schroeder, R.G. (1994). Distinguishing control from learning in total quality management: A contingency perspective. *Academy of Management Review, 19*(3), 537–564.

Smith, A., and Hayton, G. (1999). What drives enterprise training? Evidence from Australia. *The International Journal of Human Resource Management, 10*(2), 251272.

Smith, A., Oczkowski, E., Noble, C., and Macklin, R. (2003). Organisational change and management of training in Australian enterprises. *International Journal of Training and Development, 7*(1), 94–110.

Smith, A., Oczkowski, E., Noble, C., and Macklin, R. (2004). The impact of organisational change on the nature and extent of training in Australian enterprises. *International Journal of Training and Development, 8*(2), 2–15.

Snell, S.A., and Dean, J.W. (1992). Integrated manufacturing and human resource management: A human capital perspective. *Academy of Management Journal, 35*(3), 467–504.

Sparrow, J., and Pettigrew, A. (1985). Britain's training problems: The search for a strategic HRM approach. *Human Resource Management, 26*(1), 109–127.

Sung, J., and Ashton, D. (2005). *Achieving best practice in your business: High performance work practices: Linking strategy and skills to performance outcomes.* London: DTI.

Swanson, R.A. (2001). Human resource development and its underlying theory. *Human Resource Development International, 4*(3), 299–312.

Swanson, R.A. (2007). Theory framework for applied disciplines: Boundaries, contributing, core, useful, novel, and irrelevant components. *Human Resource Development Review, 6*(3), 321–339.

Wernerfelt, B. (1984). A resource-based view of the firm. *Strategic Management Journal, 5*(2), 795–815.

Wright, P.M., McMahan, G.C., and McWilliams, A. (1994). Human resources and sustained competitive advantage: A resource-based perspective. *The International Journal of Human Resource Management, 5*(2), 301–326.

Wozniak, G. (1984). The adoption of interrelated innovations: a human capital approach. *The Review of Economics and Statistics, 66*(1), 70–79.

Wozniak, G. (1987). Human capital formation and early adoption of technology. *Journal of Human Resources, 22*(1), 101–112.

Yang, B. (2004). Can adult learning theory provide a foundation for human resource development? *Advances in Developing Human Resources, 6*(2), 129–145.

Zott, C., Amit, R., and Massa, L. (2011). The business model: recent developments and future research. *Journal of Management, 37*(4), 1019–1042.

4 HRM and firm performance

The case of the Indian IT/BPO industry

Vijay Pereira and Pawan Budhwar

Introduction

This chapter examines the contribution of human resources (HR) towards high performance work systems (HPWS) in India-based information technology (IT) and business process offshoring (IT/BPO) organisations. It aims to add to the evolving body of literature on human resources management (HRM) in India in general and into the IT/BPO sector in particular. It thus contributes to the debate about the theoretical basis of IT/BPO strategies with implications for strategic level decision-makers, and examines the extent to which transaction cost economics (TCE), human capital (HC) and the resource-based view (RBV) explanations of HR practices are evident in the analysis context. The argument developed here is that HR practices in Indian IT/BPO organisations show evidence of longer-term developmental activities appropriate for organisations that are developing, or have the potential to develop, synergistic IT/BPO relationships contributing to resource complementarities with clients. This idiosyncratic approach highlights the role of both individual employees (as units of human capital) and the broader HRM system. This chapter therefore highlights the lack of research into HPWS in Indian IT/BPO organisations, as compared to the vast body of HPWS literature and hence we propose areas for future research.

Globalisation has transformed the way business and work are conducted. The increased use of offshore outsourcing or 'offshoring' has meant stakeholders are affected by work being carried out in geographically different global locations. This trend has changed global employment patterns with management implications and consequences. In recent years, India has become a major hub for IT/ BPO and 'information technology enabled services' (ITeS) work, attracting both relatively low-skill transactional work, and highly skilled 'professional' work. There is increased interest in the phenomenon from academics, researchers and practitioners who want to understand these new trends and their implications. Relatively little research on offshoring and outsourcing has investigated the phenomenon's consequences and implications for HRM strategies and practices, particularly for the firms supplying these services. As mentioned above, this chapter thus identifies gaps in research on HPWS in this pivotal industry and proposes areas for future research.

Rationale for this topic

The growth of the Indian economy, especially the growth in Indian firms and their resources are salient issues in the current environment (Budhwar and Varma, 2011b; Cappelli, Singh, Singh and Useem, 2010; Kumar, Mohapatra and Chandrasekhar, 2009). Arguably the greatest area of growth in this respect is in the IT/BPO industry which was worth $69.4 billion in 2009. In 2012 it accounted for almost 7.5% of India's GDP and employed close to 2.2 million people (NASSCOM, 2012). However, for established firms, the outsourcing of business processes carries a number of potential risks (Earl, 1996; Aron and Singh, 2005; Aubert, Patry and Rivard, 1998; Hoecht and Trott, 2006). These include unsuccessful outsourcing experiences in which suppliers fail to meet expected service levels and/or deliver the expected cost savings. Therefore, for younger Indian IT/BPO firms the development of sustainability is a key issue in order to compete with more established firms, particularly those originating in or associated with countries that have a more established reputation in IT/BPO service delivery and grow their success at an international level. Several Indian organisations are now well-known globally and hence it is an imperative for them to sustain this and remain competitive.

As a prime destination for outsourced work, India is a critical case for research into IT/BPO sector. Lahiri, Kedia and Mukherjee (2012) state several reasons for investigating the Indian IT/BPO industry. First, India remains the top choice among various offshoring destinations for Western client firms (Luo, Zheng and Jayaraman, 2010; Zaheer, Lamin and Subramani, 2009). Second, the Indian IT/BPO industry has evolved from low value-added services (e.g. call centres) to high value-added knowledge-based services (Raman, Budhwar and Balasubramanian, 2007). Finally, as one of the world's largest and most dynamic economies, India-based studies add value to the overall understanding of the global business environment. It is in this context then, that the nature of the Indian IT/BPO sector is an ideal research area, with its challenges of servicing rapid growth, building long-term sustainability, advancing up the value-chain of provided services and coping with skills shortages, attrition and the considerable fluidity in the global business models being pursued by firms.

In terms of HRM research, some studies of Indian call centres and IT/BPO organisations have highlighted the prevalence of formal, structured and rationalised HRM systems (Budhwar, Luthar and Bhatnagar, 2006; Budhwar, Varma, Singh and Dhar, 2006), with some evidence of innovative practices in 'high-end' services (Raman *et al.*, 2007). The rapid growth of the outsourcing industry has resulted in both high turnover and skill shortages, as employers compete for a restricted segment of the labour force and have been forced to consider new types of response (Kuruvilla and Ranganathan, 2010). Moreover, according to Budhwar (2012, p. 2515), there are Indian 'country specific headquarters (CSHQs) (also called India headquarters or India centres)' which have complete HR departments dedicated mainly to their Indian operations. Budhwar asserts that these HR departments have complete autonomy from their organisational and country headquarters, not because they are capable of being 'centres of excellence', but because of the differentiations, complexities and uniqueness of the nature of Indian business operations. Such findings and situations raise particularly interesting questions about the nature of these HRM practices within those firms that seek to offer remote services to external clients. Not many studies have enquired into what 'bundles' of high performance work systems (HPWS) strategies (e.g. Huselid and Becker, 2011) these organisations adapt in order to be competitive and sustainable businesses.

Similarly, the literature informing people management practices in multinational enterprises (MNEs) in different national contexts has been well documented (Dowling, Festing and Engle, 2013), both from the US (Briscoe, Schuler and Tarique, 2012) as well as the European perspective (Dickmann, Brewster and Sparrow, 2008; Brewster, Sparrow and Harris. 2005). Emerging economies, such as Brazil, Russia, India and China (collectively known as the BRIC economies), have been at the centre of research and their MNEs are being investigated through theoretical lenses encompassing strategy, location choice, market entry mode, marketing strategies, internationalisation process, etc. (e.g. Wright, Gardner, Moynihan and Allen, 2005; Buckley *et al.*, 2007; Demirbag, Tatoglub, and Glaistera, 2009; Luo and Tung, 2007; and Mathews, 2006). However, there is insufficient knowledge of the HRM practices surrounding these new challengers and a 'need for a broader geographical base to our understanding of IHRM' (Brewster, Carey, Grobler, Warnisch and Holland, 2008, p. 206). As a feature of sustained performance, emerging market MNE HRM policies and practices play crucial roles in helping facilitate reverse knowledge transfer to emerging market multinationals' other subsidiaries and in the success of the firm in diverse cultural environments (Thite, Budhwar and Wilkinson, 2014).

In terms of the HRM–firm performance link, HPWS literature and research focuses mostly on manufacturing, with less on the service sector (Huselid and Becker, 2011). Scant attention has been paid to HPWS especially in the knowledge industry, such as the IT/BPO sector. In addition, most research on HPWS has been 'UK and US centric' (Delbridge, Hauptmeier and Sengupta, 2011, p. 488) and most studies of HPWS are quantitative, statistical and involve large industry-wide surveys, with a continued call for qualitative in-depth case studies (e.g. Becker and Gerhart, 1996; Guest, 2011). The research literature also lacks 'longitudinal' evidence (e.g. Luthans and Slocum, 2011, p. 405; Guest, 2011, p. 9). Little is known about the triggers for HPWS; the role of HR and HR professionals in implementation of HPWP (Glover and Butler, 2011) and the role/influence of senior management/leadership/line in HPWP/S. In future we propose that research on these identified areas needs to be undertaken in the Indian IT/BPO sector.

The Indian IT/BPO industry context

India is regarded as the world's second largest growing economy after China (Budhwar and Varma, 2010, 2011b). This section introduces key features of the

Indian IT/BPO industry, which have aided in its economic growth. In India, information and communication technology (ICT) is the fastest growing segment of the economy, both in terms of production and exports. With complete delicensing of the electronics industry (with the exception of aerospace and defence electronics), and liberalisation of foreign investment and export-import policies, this sector attracts significant attention from international companies, who see it not only as an enormous market but also as a potential production base. The Indian IT sector has also been relatively resilient during the current global financial downturn. In 2012, the overall Indian IT/BPO aggregate revenues exceeded US$100 billion, with exports in 2014 expected to cross US$84–87 billion (NASSCOM, 2014a). The Indian industry's performance was marked by sustained revenue growth, steady expansion into newer services, increased geographic penetration and an unprecedented rise in investments by MNCs, despite growing concerns about gaps in talent and infrastructure impacting cost competitiveness. NASSCOM (2014b) further reported that as a proportion of national GDP, the sector revenues have grown from 1.2% in financial year 1998 to over 8.1% in 2014. Thus, the Indian IT/BPO sector has shown itself to be building a strong reputation in terms of high standards of service quality and information security. The industry also continues to portray its drive to set global benchmarks in quality and information security through a combination of provider and industry-level initiatives and, in strengthening the overall frameworks, creating greater awareness and facilitating wider adoption of standards and best practices. Within the broad-based industry structure, IT is led by large Indian firms and IT/BPO by a mix of Indian and MNC third-party providers and captives, and this reflects the supply-base. Whilst the larger players continue to lead growth, gradually increasing their share in the industry aggregate; several high-performing small and medium enterprises (SMEs) also stand out. In 2012, India led the world in terms of the number of quality certifications achieved by centres in any single country (NASSCOM, 2012). The US and the UK remain the key markets for Indian IT/BPO exports (excluding hardware), accounting for nearly 80% of total exports and the largest share of worldwide technology spends. In terms of global standing and competition, in the financial year 2013–2014 Indian IT/BPO providers have proved to be stiff competition for Western IT/BPO providers, as the Indian industry comprising over 16,000 firms, including over 3,000 software product firms, accounted for over 90% of the global incremental growth of US$11–12 billion (NASSCOM, 2014b).

HRM in Indian IT/BPO industry

This section will briefly introduce relevant strands of the literature on HRM in the Indian IT/BPO industry. Given the importance of India in the global economy (Budhwar and Varma, 2010; Kumar *et al.*, 2009; Nilekani, 2009), scholarly literature available on HRM in India is surprisingly scarce; and hence a comprehensive picture of HRM in the Indian context is lacking (Budhwar and Bhatnagar, 2009; Pio, 2007). This chapter identifies relevant gaps in this foundation literature in a context where patterns of HR practices relating to recruitment and retention, training and development, reward, and the management of the employment relationship in organisations in India have been subject to rapid change. International HRM practices have been 'imported' through the establishment of new business sectors supported by foreign direct investment (FDI) strategies and foreign firms operating in India (Budhwar and Baruch, 2003; Budhwar and Varma, 2010). At the same time, HRM and other features of management in India seem to be distinct from practices in Western developed countries (Cappelli *et al.*, 2010; Chatterjee, 2007; Sparrow and Budhwar, 1997), thus suggesting that HR practices in India are culturally specific, particularly in the areas of pay, recruitment, employee communication, and training and development (Budhwar and Khatri, 2001). The social and economic context of India comprising numerous cultural norms, beliefs and values including respect for seniority, status and group affiliation (Biswas and Varma, 2007) mandates this approach.

However, the experience of HRM in IT/BPO organisations in India may not reflect Indian HR traditions (Budhwar, Varma, Malhotra and Mukherjee, 2009; Khandekar and Sharma, 2005, 2006) and research by Budhwar *et al.* (2006) has suggested that in this sector, which is a fast-growing and significant part of the economic infrastructure in major cities in India, formal, structured and rationalised HRM systems comparable with the call centre industry in other countries have been developed. This may have significant effects on the labour market beyond the IT/BPO sector: attrition rates, for example which traditionally have been low in India (Singh, 2005; Taylor and Bain, 2005; Chatterjee, 2007) are found to be higher in its emergent business sectors such as IT, IT/BPO and financial services. BPO organisations, where they offer transactional services, are more likely to adopt HR practices in line with the call centre industry. However, should they be successful in developing their services to embrace business transformation services or 'Knowledge Process Outsourcing' (KPO), a range of different HR priorities may emerge (Raman *et al.*, 2007).

Som (2007) presented several propositions regarding the adoption of strategic HRM (SHRM) in India. He proposed that national environment (extent of unionisation and sector characteristics, technological sophistication), organisational restructuring and ownership structure, legitimising driver (use of international consultants), organisational culture and the role of HR department, have all influenced the adoption of SHRM in India. This in a way builds on Budhwar and Sparrow's (2002) work, which provides a comprehensive framework of factors and variables determining HRM in a given national context. Strategic international HRM (SIHRM) researchers attempt to overcome the intricacies of interpreting the conceptual and functional similarities of measures such as survey instruments (McGaughey, Iverson and Cieri, 1997) and need to address the many methodological problems innate in much of the existing international business literature (Cavusgil and Das, 1997; Nasif, Al-Daeaj, Ebrahimi and Thibodeaux, 1991). Furthermore, Cavusgil and Das note the need to address cross-cultural differences within India, noting, for example, that India has several official languages and numerous dialects.

Comparing HRM systems and practices between Western economies and India, Budhwar and Varma (2010, p. 347) point out, 'the Indian HRM system(s) is somewhat unstructured, and less formal, when compared to Western countries, though the gap is reducing rapidly'. Pio's (2007, p. 324) study also claims that in India the 'HRM function is increasingly gaining importance with a cross fertilisation of ideas between East and West'. Rapid liberalisation of markets and global linkages has created the context for a changed outlook towards HR policies and practices in India (Budhwar and Bhatnagar, 2009; Budhwar and Singh, 2007), but transposition of Western ideas is not straightforward. As a large country with numerous cultural norms and beliefs it is a challenge to examine the rationale of Western ideas of organisation in the changing social and economic scenario of Indian organisations (Biswas and Varma, 2007). So much so that 'many of the modern western concepts and theories do not always work in practice because there is a mismatch between western management theories and the Indian culture and value system to which they are applied' (Jain, 1991, p. 19). As a result HR practitioners are increasingly required to take a broader and more reflective view of HRM in India (Chatterjee, 2007) whereby many of the traditional Indian values (respect for seniority, status and group affiliation) are complemented by newer areas of attention that are more usually linked to globalisation, such as work quality, customer service and innovation (Chatterjee and Pearson, 2000).

Some work has already been done in certain areas, such as studies into managerial implications, HR strategies and practices. Studies have also critically discussed and argued the advantages and disadvantages for various actors within the employment relationships. For example, Ramesh (2004) describes IT/BPO employees as 'cyber coolies', D'Cruz and Noronha (2008, 2009) talk about their 'emotional labour', 'professionalism' and attempts to unionise. Still others focus on thematic areas such as conditions of work, employee rights and transnational cultural issues (e.g. Mirchandani, 2004). Other studies, from a managerial perspective examine 'best practices', 'indigenous practices' (e.g. Budhwar and Varma, 2010) and 'strategic practices' (Som, 2008), alongside 'internal marketing' strategies employed by some organisations (Budhwar *et al.*, 2009). A few have tried to compare Indian and Western practices (e.g. Russell and Thite, 2009; Taylor and Bain, 2004). Challenging and pressing issues such as attrition and retention have often been highlighted and featured (Budhwar and Varma, 2011a; Das, Nadialath and Mohan, 2012; Russell and Thite, 2009), amongst the issues, changes and evolution of employment relations in this pivotal industry in India (Kuruvilla and Ranganathan, 2010; Bhattacherjee and Ackers, 2010).

As is evident above, some research on HRM in the Indian IT/BPO industry exists. However, much more is needed to unbundle the complexities of this vast and globally influential industry. The next section discusses the theoretical underpinning of HRM and HPWS in the context of the Indian IT/BPO industry.

Theoretical underpinning: HRM–firm performance

Theoretically, the point of departure in the context of this chapter is the need to explain the decision to both initiate and sustain offshored provision of business services. One explanation is provided by transaction cost economics (TCE) theory (Williamson, 1975, 1985), which argues that transaction costs are all those costs that are incurred by a firm in operating in an economic system. TCE has been used to explain the entry mode strategies, foreign expansion, diversification, performance and forward-backward integration of the firm (North, 1990). In the internationalisation process, the firm comes across many types of external transaction costs such as that of coordinating activities in geographically and culturally distant home and host countries. Both TCE (Williamson, 1975, 1985) and internalisation theory (Buckley and Casson, 1976) share the view that the existence of external transaction costs deters the internationalisation of the firm. Further, these costs are external, imposed by the environment where the firm operates and thus, out of its control. Therefore, according to Tate, Ellram, Bals and Hartmann (2009, p. 513) 'in the context of TCE, if firms that offshore outsource services perceive the offshore outsourced market to be more efficient, we would expect offshore outsourcing to grow'.

However, to maintain sustainability over time, offshored business providers in India need to demonstrate sustained high performance to meet and exceed customer expectations. Hence, the argument we make is that, whilst technology underpins the delivery of services and processes, the employees of IT/BPOs are central to service offering and quality, and represent a cornerstone for value creation.

As a result, a second theoretical lens applied in this chapter relates to high performing work systems. Little consensus about the definition of HPWS is evident in the literature (Heffernan, Elood and Lui, 2011, p. 295). HPWS are work systems that are variously promoted as 'using a variety of complementary new work practices (HPWP). Interest in HPWS has emerged in the last two decades worldwide' (Bae, Chuma, Kato, Kim and Ohashi, 2011, p. 2) as people management and employment practices have been accepted as a critical part of practices in high performing work organisations (HPWO) and have been identified as high performance work practices (HPWP) (e.g. Bohlander and Snell, 2007; Boxall and Macky, 2009; Boxall and Purcell, 2003; Guest, 2011; Tregaskis, Daniels, Glover, Butler and Meyer, 2012).

Most HPWS accounts are grounded in assumptions derived from human capital theory and/or the resource-based view of the firm (RBV) theory. Human capital theory suggests that within a firm, the knowledge, skills and attributes of employees make an important contribution to performance and add economic value. The resource-based view (RBV) suggests that a firm's HRM resources such as its infrastructure, processes, and HR and people management systems are the variables that generate value and contribute to its performance. An ongoing and so far unresolved debate is whether concentration on people as assets (human capital) or on people-related systemic practices, processes and systems (RBV) has the greater explanatory value. From a longitudinal view-point, this argument is taken further through Mueller's (1996) evolutionary RBV ((e) RBV), which posits that this form of strategic HRM can lead to a com-petitive advantage for the firm, on the condition that effective resource mobility barriers exist.

Human capital is defined as:

> the individual's capabilities, knowledge, skills and experience of the com-pany's employees and managers, as they are relevant to the task at hand, as well as the capacity to add to this reservoir of knowledge, skills, and experi-ence through individual learning.
>
> (Dess and Picken, 1999, p. 8)

Human capital theory relies on the assumption that 'there is no substitute for knowledge and learning, creativity and innovation, competencies and capabil-ities; and that they need to be relentlessly pursued and focused on the firm's environmental context and competitive logic' (Rastogi, 2000, p. 196). There is a large evolving body of research that shows a positive linkage between the devel-opment of human capital and overall firm performance (e.g. Dess and Picken, 2000; Itami, 1987; Lepak and Snell, 1999, 2002; Rastogi, 2000). The importance of human capital in firms hence reflects the view that market value is increas-ingly predicated on intangible areas, such as human resources, and less dependent on tangible resources, such as technology or finance. The firm thus has to leverage the skills and capabilities of its employees by encouraging indi-vidual and organisational learning and creating a supportive environment in which knowledge can be created, shared and applied. The RBV theory, on the other hand, assumes the importance of building a valuable set of people pro-cesses and bundling them together in unique and dynamic ways to develop a firm's success. With this approach, competitive advantage depends on the valu-able, rare and hard-to-imitate people resources that reside within an organisation, rather than developing technological or structural resources that are easier to imitate. Human capital in a real sense is thus an 'invisible asset' (Itami, 1987). The importance to the strategic aims of the organisation of the human capital pool (the collection of employee capabilities such as knowledge, skill and attributes), and how it is managed through HR processes (its organisational resources) then becomes apparent.

Lepak and Snell (1999) attempted a synthesis of TCE, HC and RBV theories, which is further developed in this chapter. They argue that not all employees possess knowledge and skills of equal strategic importance. Drawing on the three theories, they develop a 'human-resource architecture' model comprising four different employment modes: internal development, acquisition, contracting and alliance. Although grounded in HC theory, TCE and RBV assumptions also influence the 'make or buy' decisions (Miles and Snow, 1984), associated with business development. Lepak and Snell identify these decisions as either 'inter-nalisation' or 'externalisation' of a firm's human capital. However, they caution that these decisions would not be either/or but, rather, complex and multifaceted. Within the first, internal development, a firm develops, invests and builds upon existing employees' skills, knowledge and attributes. The second, acquisition, is when a firm requires certain skills, knowledge and attributes unavailable internally so it has to 'acquire' them. The third, contracting, is linked to outsourcing, where a firm outsources work to an external agency or organisation. The fourth, alliance, is similar to collaboration between two firms, where mutually beneficial synergies are exploited. In the context of this chapter, all four modes of Lepak and Snell's architecture are of significance. Thus, the RBV perspective considers 'whether certain resources or capabilities contribute to a firm's competitive advantage. It is argued that if enhanced capabilities are experienced in offshore outsourcing, we would expect offshore outsourcing to proliferate' (Tate *et al.*, 2009, p. 513).

Figure 4.1 depicts the theoretical strands discussed and the interlinkages. These theories are general explanations of high performance (of people and firms) in work organisations. These are generated from the perspective and evidence base of employing organisations in Western developed economies and scant attention has thus far been paid to the issues in developing, dynamic and changing economies such as India. In the following sections we set out to examine the extent to which these theories explain sustained high performance in the dynamic context of the Indian IT/BPO sector. We suggest that in future research in Indian IT/BPO industry tests and develops these theories so that they would add new perspectives by assessing HRM and high performance in organisations outside of the developed economies.

Human capital, RBV and HRM in Indian IT/BPO industry

In terms of 'human resources', employees and their capabilities are an important resource, and are often referred to in the literature as 'human capital'. *Human capital* thus refers to the skills, education, experience and knowledge of a firm's employees (Becker, 1964; Hatch and Dyer, 2004). In relation to linking human capital with firm performance, scholars suggest that human capital is essential for firms to achieve above-average performance and competitive advantage (Hatch and Dyer, 2004). Thus, 'skills, knowledge, abilities arising from education and experience, and embedded within human actors allow precise comprehension of various organizational functions and subsequent efficient execution of those functions within stipulated time-frames' (Lahiri et al., 2012, p. 147). There

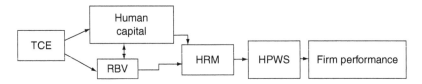

Figure 4.1 Theoretical strands and interlinkages.

is also an argument that being tacit and path dependent, human capital is not susceptible to easy imitation by industry rivals. Previous research (Hitt, Bierman, Shimizu and Kochhar, 2001; Lahiri and Kedia, 2009; Subramaniam and Youndt, 2005) including the offshoring industry has empirically tested for the positive association between human capital and firm performance.

'Organisational capital' according to Lahiri et al. (2012), represents codified knowledge and experience residing in databases, patents, manuals, structures and systems. Specifically looking at the offshoring industry in India, they claim such 'capital' is a resource which is more institutionalised and stable than human capital, which is susceptible to mobility. Authors such as Reed, Lubatkin and Srinivasan (2006) and Subramaniam and Youndt (2005) have argued that organisational capital favourably impacts firm performance, just as human capital does. Organisational capital is also asserted to be based on the dynamic capability view, an extension of RBV (e.g. Teece, 2007). Lahiri et al. (2012, p. 148) state, 'organizations require dynamic capabilities to effectively adapt to the changing market conditions and create value'. These capabilities, they go on, help organisations in creating and modifying existing operating routines, sensing and seizing entrepreneurial opportunities that, in turn, increase organisational effectiveness and competitive advantage. Agreeing with Lahiri et al. (2012), we argue that dynamic capabilities may include the capacity to integrate, learn and reconfigure internal and external organisational skills and resources. Thus management capability may allow Indian IT/BPO providers to integrate and support various intangible assets related to managing human resources, diverse project requirements, information systems and technology-related changes and also satisfy the expectations of their clients.

Lahiri et al. (2012) further contend that the positive effect of human capital on the performance of IT/BPO provider firms can be enhanced in the presence of strong management capability in at least three ways. First, a firm's superior management capability can enable top executives to recruit, place, train and develop, retain and replace employees with appropriate skill sets and industry experience. This, they argue, 'will ensure maintaining a steady pool of human capital that will lead to improved firm performance through learning over time' (p. 148). Second, high management capability allows more effective matching of employee talents to particular function or project requirements, contributing to greater individual and team-based performance. This ensures better utilisation of skills and experience in meeting clients' needs and subsequently to higher firm performance. Third, as a result of the above two, high management capability will be able to improve individual and team-based efforts through the creation of a better work environment for all, thereby culminating in higher firm performance (Budhwar et al., 2006). We could thus infer that this argument relates to the literature on HPWS (e.g. Bae et al., 2011; Heffernan et al., 2011). Lahiri et al. (2012) thus hypothesise that an offshore outsourcing service provider's human capital, organisational capital and partnership quality will be positively associated with firm performance. Future research needs to be undertaken to strengthen and also test this hypothesis in the context of the Indian IT/BPO industry.

Further evidence of HC's importance in the offshoring context is seen in Barthélemy and Quélin's 2006 analysis of 82 outsourcing contracts using three different dimensions (proximity to the core business, switching costs and adaptation costs) to assess the strategic importance of an outsourced activity. They argue that 'in the case of outsourcing, employees and equipment may be transferred to the vendor ... the transfer of tailor-made assets to a vendor is likely to make it quite costly to switch vendors or reintegrate an outsourced activity' (pp. 1777–1778). They refer to this as 'switching costs'. Additionally, they introduce a new characteristic of specificity, i.e. 'core-related specificity' which they refer to as 'the extent to which the resources that underlie an outsourced activity contribute to a firm's competitive advantage', which they believe is theoretically rooted in the RBV of the firm (see also, for example, Amit and Schoemaker, 1993; Barney, 1991; Dierickx and Cool, 1989).

RBV postulates that firms are repositories of resources and capabilities and although firms are viewed as bundles of resources, the interactions among resources are far more important than the resources themselves. They further introduce an additional concept of 'adapting human assets', wherein they argue that 'for an outsourcing client, *adapting human assets* refers to the extent to which specific assets have been developed to deal with a particular vendor as opposed to the activity's execution in-house' (Barthélemy and Quélin, 2006, p. 1778, emphasis added). They also contend (quoting Zaheer and Nilakant, 1995, p. 377) that 'in the context of service outsourcing, adapting human assets has both human and procedural dimensions'. Hence in the context of the Indian IT/BPO industry we argue that human specific assets are the skills and knowledge that employees working for the outsourcing client need to develop to deal with the supplier, whereas procedural-specific assets are the business processes of the outsourcing client that must be customised to meet the requirements of the vendor. Barthélemy and Quélin (2006, p. 1778), thus conclude that 'when outsourcing clients make specific investments to adjust to their vendor, the resulting routines have two characteristics. First, they are difficult to alter once they have been established. Second, it is hard to transfer them to another vendor'. In summary, adapting human assets increases switching costs and the extent of potential damage if the vendor delays a contract and at the same time, it also increases the value of the relationship for the partner, thus reducing the likelihood of a 'hold-up'. We suggest that research testing and developing their propositions/assertions in the Indian IT/BPO industry is needed in the future.

Another view is taken by Mueller (1996, p. 776), who came up with what he called an 'evolutionary resource-based approach' ((e) RBV), wherein, strategic HRM can lead to competitive advantage for the firm, on the condition that effective resource mobility barriers exists. These could be in the form of informal social architecture (other variants in the literature being social complexity and capital), tacit knowledge, cooperation, informal learning, etc., that '*emerge[s] over a long period of time and is largely emergent and unplanned*' (ibid., emphasis added). Herein, he stresses the role of HRM in harnessing these skills and competencies held within this informal system. This portrays the RBV of the firm in the context of HRM. Moreover, as it prescribes to be evolutionary in nature, it suggests an essential, integral longitudinal element. Thus, Mueller, in his conceptualisation of the (e) RBV suggests that there is an evolutionary approach to strategic HRM, whereby 'valuable strategic assets' would result not because of the management's *deliberate* strategy, but because of an organisation's *emergent* strategy. There are two further necessities and propositions for this postulation of the (e) RBV. First, the strategic assets grow slowly over time (are evolutionary in nature), and second, that codified policies are typically easy to imitate and hence unofficial, informal and tacit knowledge leads to inimitability. Principally Mueller (1996, p. 771) puts forward five propositions that would lead to an evolutionary approach to the development of strategic HR. First, it happens as a slow, incremental, evolutionary process. Second, it is facilitated by the existence of 'pertinent intent'. Third, it draws on underlying processes of skills formation. Fourth, it draws on established patterns of 'spontaneous cooperation'. And fifth, there needs to be 'HR interdependency' with other resources. We postulate that in the Indian IT/BPO industry, over time, the (e) RBV could be an approach that could lead to the development of strategic HR and HPWS. This hypothesis is worth testing.

High performance work systems (HPWS) in the context of Indian IT/BPO industry

The attempt to explain the relationship between HRM and firm performance is a central feature in the strategic HRM literature. Drawing on previous work on industrial relations, HRM, labour process theory and organisational sociology (e.g. Fox, 1974; Storey, 1989; Legge, 1995; Boxall and Purcell; 2003; Friedman, 1977; Crozier and Friedberg, 1977 respectively), Almond (2011, p. 260) reiterates the 'relational perspective' between the buyers and sellers of labour and argues that certain 'normative HRM theories such as the notion of "High Performance Work Systems" can be seen as an attempt to institutionalise a set of ideas about what is the "right" way to manage the effort–reward bargain within paid employment'. However, within individual MNCs such country of origin effects are mostly dependent on global dominance. The US, for example, Almond contends, has a global dominance and hence it could well be more likely that what are termed its best practices 'converge' at subsidiary level, in comparison to 'non-dominant' countries of origin MNCs where 'it is more likely to consist of an imitation, or interpretation, of dominant practice than to be strongly based on a country of origin model' (Almond, 2011, p. 263). The section below examines HPWS in detail.

The HPWS literature focuses attention on the HR practices required to increase performance (e.g. Huselid, 1995; Pfeffer, 1994, 1998). HPWS are composed of high performance working practices (HPWP) which, when placed together, form the HPWS. HPWS research provides important insights into studying the difficulties and complexities that can arise in what is known in the HRM literature as the 'black box' between HR management systems and firm performance (e.g. Purcell, Kinnie, Hutchinson, Swart and Rayton, 2003; Wright and Gardner, 2004). Importantly, a cluster of HRM practices forms the contents of the black box and impact on the profitability of the organisation (Boxall, Ang and Bartram, 2011). However, though these studies do not *establish* any relationship between HRM and performance, it is considered that they are likely to *show* if there is a tendency for such a relationship. HPWS studies also involve analysing the chain of links or mediators inside the black box of the firm's models of HRM (Boxall, 2012).

A key debate in the HPWS arena is grounded in the nature and degree of HR practice 'fit' (Wood, 1999; Boxall and Purcell, 2008), and bundling of HR practices (e.g. Pfeffer, 1998) perspectives. Wood (1999, p. 367) in his work on HRM and performance stated that 'synergy, fit and integration are key concepts in modern HRM theory', postulating four types of 'fit': internal, organisational, strategic and environmental. In terms of models of HPWS, internal fit involves the blending of HR practices to achieve synergy. Organisational fit entails aligning these identified HR practices or systems to other systems within the organisation. Strategic fit entails linking HPWS directly to organisational strategy and environmental fit aligns HPWS to the organisation's environment.

One development of the debate on 'fit' is the question of whether HPWS are universally or contingently relevant (e.g. Becker and Gerhart, 1996; Youndt, Snell, Dean and Lepak, 1996; Becker and Huselid, 1998). The 'universalist view' attempts to identify HR practices that will always result in superior performance whilst the 'contingent view' focuses on 'best fit' of practices to context (e.g. Boxall and Purcell, 2008). However, Youndt et al. (1996, p. 837) argue that 'although on the surface the universal and contingency perspectives may appear to be competing, we would argue that they can be complementary'.

HR 'bundling', which may be considered a development of the 'best-fit' approach, is also an important component of the RBV and more recent studies to do with High Performance Working (HPW) are a further development of this approach. Research has suggested that a combination of employee training and development, empowerment, participation, information sharing and compensation systems are commonly found in HPWS (Boselie and Dietz, 2003) although very little empirical certainty is possible. Moreover, research findings vary. For example, Batt (2002) found practices such as team working, high skills, discretion and commitment were critical. A Chartered Institute of Personnel and Development (CIPD, UK) study by Guest (2000) identified 28 key practices pertaining to high performance or commitment. Kling (1995) considered three main HPWP areas, namely training, compensation and employee involvement as having a major influence on performance. Pil and MacDuffie (1996) suggest six practices within the car manufacturing industry: line work teams; employee involvement; problem-solving groups; job rotation; suggestion programmes; and decentralisation. Thompson's (2002) work on the aerospace industry identifies 30 practices falling into three clusters: high involvement, human resource and employee relations. Ashton and Sung (2002) list four dimensions in their review: employee involvement and autonomy;

support for employee performance; rewards for performance; and sharing of information and knowledge.

Thus, a variety of approaches has been adopted to study HPWS. For example, Pfeffer initially (1994) advocated the adaptation of 16 HPWP including employment security, selectivity in recruitment, incentive compensation and work teams, which he later concentrated into just seven (Pfeffer, 1998). Similarly, Huselid (1995) described 13 HPWP that encourage employee involvement, including comprehensive employee selection, development procedures, incentive compensation, performance management and organisational work structures. Studies have shown HPWS can favourably affect turnover (Guthrie, 2001; Huselid, 1995) and labour productivity (Huselid, 1995). Organisations exhibiting HPWS have higher levels of training (Whitfield, 2000) and also make a significant investment in their pool of human capital so that employees are well trained, skilled and empowered to do their jobs (Becker and Huselid, 1998). The 'internal social structure' of the organisation mediates the relationship between the HPWS and organisational performance (Evans and Davis, 2005). It has also been found that the link between HPWS and firm performance relates to 'organisational culture' (Den Hartog and Verburg, 2004) and in becoming a HPWO organisation, the role of employment security, employee involvement and training (SET) is viewed as important (Brown, Reich and Stern, 1993). On pay as an important ingredient and key motivator for staff, there is growing empirical evidence that HPWP such as incentive compensation, employment security and good pay can have a significant impact on organisational performance, firm productivity (Guthrie, 2001), and firm financial performance (Guthrie, 2001; Huselid, 1995). With regard to MNCs operating in India, Björkman and Budhwar's (2007) study of 76 MNCs examined the implementation of HRM practices in their Indian subsidiaries and the linkage between these HRM practices and organisational performance. It showed that the introduction of HRM practices from the foreign parent organisation has a negative effect on performance, while local adaptation of HRM practices a positive one. Both studies illustrate the need for significant local responsiveness, mediated by the HR function within the Indian country specific headquarters (CSHQ).

Conclusion

As is evident from our critical discussion, HPWP within high performance work organisations (HPWO) are well documented in developed country economies (Bae *et al.*, 2011; Heffernan *et al.*, 2011). However, there is scant research available concerning the emerging Indian economy, including the Indian IT/BPO industry. Strategic HR awareness and practices may exist in nascent form (Budhwar and Varma, 2010; Som, 2008), but to date the relationship between HR practices and HPWS in the Indian IT/BPO industry remains unaddressed.

In conclusion we propose the following. *First*, we reiterate that the Indian IT/BPO sector is an ideal research area for HRM–firm performance (Lahiri *et al.*, 2012), with its challenges of servicing rapid growth, building long-term sustainability, advancing up the value-chain of provided services and coping with skills shortages and attrition. Hence we propose that with the Indian IT/BPO sector challenges and the considerable fluidity in the global business models being pursued by these firms, HRM–firm performance research will add value. *Second*, there are practically no studies to date that have enquired into what 'bundles' of high performance work systems (HPWS) strategies (e.g. Huselid and Becker, 2011) Indian IT/BPO organisations have used, and hence it is timely such research is conducted. Thus, Indian IT/BPO organisations adapt in order to be competitive and sustainable businesses. We propose that future research should aim to identify these HPWS bundles that are unique to the industry. *Third*, research in the area of international HRM from emerging markets such as India is largely missing (Brewster et al., 2008). Further, emerging market multinational enterprise (MNE) HRM policies and practices play crucial roles in helping facilitate reverse knowledge transfer to emerging market multinationals' other subsidiaries and in the success of the firm in diverse cultural environments. We propose that the Indian IT/BPO industry, with its multitude of MNEs is fertile ground where 'reverse' knowledge transfer, in the context of HPWS, can be studied. We further propose that HPWS research within the Indian IT/BPO industry would add to new knowledge in this area, as an emerging market, service and knowledge sector. *Fourth*, as was evident from the discussion in above sections, much of the literature about HPWS is based on normative characteristics. There is scant research to assess causal relationships between variables that are assumed to predict high performance and little is known about the relationship between the different factors. We propose that HPWS research within the Indian IT/BPO industry with its complexities and global influence could assess and unbundle causal relationships between 'unique' variables that would be identified, thus adding to knowledge. *Lastly*, theoretical underpinnings and synthesis in the context of HRM–firm performance or HPWS (such as Lepak and Snell's 1999 'HR architecture' or Mueller's 1996 (e) RBV) where well-established theories such as TCE, HC and RBV have been well researched in developed and mature economies and industries. We propose that future research in Indian IT/BPO industry tests and develops established theories so that they add new perspectives by assessing HRM and high performance in organisations outside of the developed economies.

References

Almond, P. (2011). Re-visiting 'country of origin' effects on HRM in multinational corporations. *Human Resource Management Journal*, *21*(3), 258–271.

Amit, R., and Schoemaker, P.J. (1993). Strategic assets and organizational rent. *Strategic Management Journal*, *14*(1), 33–46.

Aron, R., and Singh, J. (2005). Getting offshoring right. *Harvard Business Review*, *83*(12), 135–143.

Ashton, D., and Sung, J. (2002). *supporting workplace learning for high performance working*. Geneva: ILO.

Aubert, B., Patry, M., and Rivard, S. (1998). *Assessing the risk of IT outsourcing: Hawaii: Proceedings of the thirty-first Hawaii international conference on system sciences, Kohala Coast, HI, USA*. Los Alamitos, CA: IEEE Computer Society.

Bae, K.S., Chuma, H., Kato, T., Kim, D.B., and Ohashi, I. (2011). High performance work practices and employee voice: A comparison of Japanese and Korean workers. *Industrial Relations: A Journal of Economy and Society*, *50*(1), 1–29.

Barney, J. (1991). Firm resources and sustained competitive advantage. *Journal of Management*, *17*(1), 99–120.

Barthélemy, J., and Quélin, B. (2006). Complexity of outsourcing contracts and ex post transaction costs: An empirical investigation. *Journal of Management Studies*, *43*(8), 1775–1797.

Batt, R. (2002). Managing Customer Services: Human resource practices, quit rates, and sales growth. *The Academy of Management Journal*, *45*(3), 587–597.

Becker, B., and Gerhart, B. (1996). The impact of human resource management on organizational performance: Progress and prospects. *The Academy of Management Journal*, *39*(4), 779–801.

Becker, B., and Huselid, M. (1998). High performance work systems and firm performance: A synthesis of research and managerial implications. In K. Rowland and G. Ferris (Eds), *Research in personnel and human resource management* (pp. 53–101). Greenwich, CT: JAI.

Becker, G. (1964). *Human capital*. New York, NY: National Bureau of Economic Research.

Bhattacherjee, D., and Ackers, P. (2010). Introduction: Employment relations in India – old narratives and new perspectives. *Industrial Relations Journal*, *41*(2), 104–121.

Biswas, S., and Varma, A. (2007). Psychological climate and individual performance in India: Test of a mediated model. *Employee Relations*, *29*(6), 664–676.

Björkman, I., and Budhwar, P. (2007). When in Rome…? Human resource management and the performance of foreign firms operating in India. *Employee Relations*, *29*(6), 595–610.

Bohlander, G., and Snell, S. (2007). *Managing human resources*. Mason, OH: Thomson-Southwestern.

Boselie, P., and Dietz, G. (2003). *Commonalties and contradictions in research on human resource management and performance*. Seattle: The Academy of Management Conference.

Boxall, P. (2012). High-performance work systems: What, why, how and for whom? *Asia Pacific Journal of Human Resources*, *50*(2), 169–186.

Boxall, P., and Macky, K. (2009). Research and theory on high-performance work systems: Progressing the high-involvement stream. *Human Resource Management Journal*, *19*(1), 3–23.

Boxall, P., and Purcell, J. (2003). *Strategy and human resource management*. Basingstoke: Palgrave Macmillan.

Boxall, P., and Purcell, J. (2008). *Strategy and Human Resource Management* (2nd ed.). Basingstoke: Palgrave Macmillan.

Boxall, P., Ang, S., and Bartram, T. (2011). Analysing the 'black box' of HRM: Uncovering HR goals, mediators and outcomes in a standardised service environment. *Journal of Management Studies*, *48*(7), 1504–1532.

Brewster, C., Carey, L., Grobler, P., Warnisch, S., and Holland, P. (2008). *Contemporary issues in human resource management: Gaining a competitive advantage* (3rd ed.). Cape Town: Oxford University Press.

Brewster, C., Sparrow, P., and Harris, H. (2005). Towards a new model of globalizing HRM. *The International Journal of Human Resource Management*, *16*(6), 949–970.

Briscoe, D., Schuler, R., and Tarique, I. (2012). *International human resource management: Policies and practices for multinational enterprises* (4th ed.). New York, NY: Routledge.

Brown, C., Reich, M., and Stern, D. (1993). Becoming a high-performance work organization: The role of security, employee involvement and training. *The International Journal of Human Resource Management, 4*(2), 247–275.

Buckley, P.J., and Casson, M. (1976). *The Future of the Multinational Enterprise.* New York, NY: Holmes & Meier.

Buckley, P.J., Clegg, L.J., Cross, A.R., Liu, X., Voss, H., and Zheng, P. (2007). The determinants of Chinese outward foreign direct investment. *Journal of International Business Studies, 38*(4), 449–518.

Budhwar, P. (2012). Management of human resources in foreign firms operating in India: The role of HR in country-specific headquarters. *The International Journal of Human Resource Management, 23*(12), 2514–2531.

Budhwar, P. S., and Khatri, N. (2001). A comparative study of HR practices in Britain and India. *The International Journal of Human Resource Management, 12*(5), 800–826.

Budhwar, P., and Baruch, Y. (2003). Career management practices in India: An empirical study. *International Journal of Manpower, 24*(6), 699–719.

Budhwar, P., and Bhatnagar, J. (2009). *The changing face of people management in India.* Abingdon: Routledge.

Budhwar, P., and Singh, V. (2007). People management in the Indian subcontinent. *Employee Relations, 29*(6), 545–553.

Budhwar, P., and Sparrow, P. (2002). An integrative framework for determining cross-national human resource management practices. *Human Resource Management Review, 12*(3), 377–403.

Budhwar, P., and Varma, A. (2010). Guest editors' introduction: Emerging patterns of HRM in the new Indian economic environment. *Human Resource Management, 49*(3), 345–351.

Budhwar, P., and Varma, A. (2011a). Emerging HR management trends in India and the way forward. *Organizational Dynamics, 40*(4), 317–325.

Budhwar, P., and Varma, A. (Eds.) (2011b). *Doing business in India.* Abingdon: Routledge.

Budhwar, P., Luthar, H. K., and Bhatnagar, J. (2006). The dynamics of HRM systems in Indian BPO firms. *Journal of Labor Research, 27*(3), 339–360.

Budhwar, P., Varma, A., Malhotra, N., and Mukherjee, A. (2009). Insights into the Indian call centre industry: Can internal marketing help tackle high employee turnover? *Journal of Services Marketing, 23*(5), 351–362.

Budhwar, P., Varma, A., Singh, V., and Dhar, R. (2006). HRM Systems of Indian call centres: An exploratory study. *The International Journal of Human Resource Management, 17*(5), 881–897.

Cappelli, P., Singh, H., Singh, J., and Useem, M. (2010). The India way: Lessons for the U.S. *Academy of Management Perspectives, 24*(2), 6–25.

Cavusgil, S.T., and Das, A. (1997). Methodology issues in cross-cultural sourcing research: A primer. *Marketing Intelligence & Planning, 15*(5), 213–220.

Chatterjee, S. R. (2007). Human resource management in India: 'Where from' and 'where to?' *Research and Practice in Human Resource Management, 15*(2), 92–103.

Chatterjee, S.R., and Pearson, C.A. (2000). Work goals and societal value orientations of senior Indian managers: An empirical analysis. *Journal of Management Development, 19*(7), 643–653.

Crozier, M., and Friedberg, E. (1977). L'Acteur et le systeme: Les contraintes de l'action collective. In C. Geertz (Ed.), *The interpretation of cultures: Selected essays.* New York, NY: Basic Books.

D'Cruz, P., and Noronha, E. (2008). Doing emotional labour: The experiences of Indian call centre agents. *Global Business Review, 9*(1), 131–147.

D'Cruz, P., and Noronha, E. (2009). Experiencing depersonalised bullying: A study of Indian call-centre agents. *Work Organisation, Labour and Globalisation, 3*(1), 26–46.

Das, D., Nandialath, A., and Mohan, R. (2012). Feeling unsure: Quit or stay? Uncovering heterogeneity in employees' intention to leave in Indian call centers, *International Journal of Human Resource Management, 24*(1), 15–34.

Delbridge, R., Hauptmeier, M., and Sengupta, S. (2011). Beyond the enterprise: Broadening the horizons of international HRM. *Human Relations, 64*(4), 483–505.

Demirbag, M., Tatoglub, E., and Glaistera, K.W. (2009). Equity-based entry modes of emerging country multinationals: Lessons from Turkey. *Journal of World Business, 44*(4), 445–462.

Den Hartog, D., and Verburg, R. (2004). High performance work systems, organisational culture and firm effectiveness. *Human Resource Management Journal, 14*(1), 55–78.

Dess, G.D., and Picken, J.C. (1999). *Beyond productivity: How leading companies achieve superior performance by leveraging their human capital.* New York, NY: American Management Association.

Dess, G.G., and Picken, J.C. (2000). Changing roles: Leadership in the 21st century. *Organizational Dynamics, 28*(3), 18–34.

Dickmann, M., Bewster, C., and Sparrow, P. (2008). *International human resource management: A European perspective* (2nd ed.). Hoboken, NJ: Taylor & Francis.

Dierickx, I., and Cool, K. (1989). Asset stock accumulation and sustainability of competitive advantage. *Management Science, 35*(12), 1504–1511.

Dowling, P., Festing, M., and Engle, A. (2013). *International human resource management* (6th ed.), Melbourne: Cengage Learning.

Earl, M. (1996). The risks of IT outsourcing. *Sloan Management Review, 37*(3), 26–32.

Evans, W.R., and Davis, W.D. (2005). High-performance work systems and organizational performance: The mediating role of internal social structure. *Journal of Management, 31*(5), 758–775.

Fox, A. (1974). *Beyond contract: Work, power and trust relations.* London: Faber.

Friedman, A. (1977). *Industry and labour: Class struggle at work and monopoly capitalism.* London: Macmillan.

Glover, L., and Butler, P. (2011). High-performance work systems, partnership and the working lives of HR professionals. *Human Resource Management Journal, 22*(2), 199–215.

Guest, D. (2000, July 20). HR and the bottom line: 'Has the penny dropped?' *People Management,* pp. 26–31.

Guest, D. (2011). Human resource management and performance: Still searching for some answers. *Human Resource Management Journal, 21*(1), 3–13.

Guthrie, J. (2001). High-involvement work practices, turnover, and productivity: Evidence from New Zealand. *The Academy of Management Journal, 44*(1), 180–190.

Hatch, N.W., and Dyer, J.H. (2004). Human capital and learning as a source of sustainable competitive advantage. *Strategic Management Journal, 25*(12), 1155–1178.

Heffernan, M., Elood, P.G., and Lui, W. (2011). High performance work systems: International evidence of the impact on firms and employees. In A. Harzing and A.H. Pinnington (Eds.), *International human resource management* (pp. 291–342). London: Sage.

Hitt, M., Bierman, L., Shimizu, K., and Kochhar, R. (2001). Direct and moderating effects of human capital on strategy and performance in professional service firms: A resource-based perspective. *Academy of Management Journal, 44*(1), 13–28.

Hoecht, A., and Trott, P. (2006). Innovation risks of strategic outsourcing. *Technovation, 26*(5/6), 672–681.

Huselid, M.A. (1995). The impact of human resource management practices on turnover, productivity, and corporate financial performance. *Academy of Management, 38*(3), 635–672.

Huselid, M.A., and Becker, B.E. (2011). Bridging micro and macro domains: Workforce differentiation and strategic human resource management. *Journal of Management, 37*(2), 421–428.

Itami, H. (1987). *Mobilizing invisible assets*. Cambridge, MA: Harvard University Press.

Jain, H. (1991). Is there a coherent human resource management system in India? *International Journal of Public Sector Management, 4*(3), 18–30.

Khandekar, A., and Sharma, A. (2005). Organizational learning in Indian organizations: A strategic HRM perspective. *Journal of Small Business and Enterprise Development, 12*(2), 211–226.

Khandekar, A., and Sharma, A. (2006). Organizational learning and performance: Understanding Indian scenario in present global context. *Education + Training, 48*(8/9), 682–692.

Kling, J. (1995). High performance work systems and firm performance. *Monthly Labor Review, 118*(May), 29–36.

Kumar, N., Mohapatra, P., and Chandrasekhar, S. (2009). India's global powerhouses: How they are taking on the world. Boston, MA: Harvard Business School Press.

Kuruvilla, S., and Ranganathan, A. (2010). Globalisation and outsourcing: Confronting new human resource challenges in India's business process outsourcing industry. *Industrial Relations Journal, 41*(2), 136–153.

Lahiri, S., and Kedia, B.L. (2009). The effects of internal resources and partnership quality on firm performance: An examination of Indian BPO providers. *Journal of International Management, 15*(2), 209–224.

Lahiri, S., Kedia, B., and Mukherjee, D. (2012). The impact of management capability on the resource-performance linkage: Examining Indian outsourcing providers. *Journal of World Business, 47*(1), 145–155.

Legge, K. (1995). *Human resource management: Rhetorics and realities*. London: Macmillan.

Lepak, D. P., and Snell, S. A. (1999). The human resource architecture: Toward a theory of human capital allocation and development. *The Academy of Management Review, 24*(1), 31–48.

Lepak, D.P., and Snell, S.A. (2002). Examining the human resource architecture: The relationship among human capital, employment, and human resource configurations. *Journal of Management, 28*(4), 517–543.

Luo, Y., and Tung, R.L. (2007). International expansion of emerging market enterprises: A springboard perspective. *Journal of International Business Studies, 38*(4), 481–498.

Luo, Y., Zheng, Q., and Jayaraman, V. (2010). Managing business process outsourcing. *Organizational Dynamics, 39*(3), 205–217.

Luthans, F., and Slocum, J. (2011). Letters from the Editors. *Journal of World Business, 46*(4), 404–405.

Mathews, J. (2006). Dragon multinationals: New players in 21st century globalization. *Asia Pacific Journal of Management, 23*(1), 5–27.

McGaughey, S.L., Iverson, R.D., and Cieri, H.D. (1997). A multi-method analysis of work-related preferences in three nations: Implications for inter-and intra-national human resource management. *The International Journal of Human Resource Management, 8*(1), 1–17.

Miles, R., and Snow, C. (1984). Designing strategic human resource systems. *Organizational Dynamics, 13*(1), 36–52.

Mirchandani, K. (2004). Practices of global capital: Gaps, cracks and ironies in transnational call centres in India. *Global Networks, 4*(4), 355–373.

Mueller, F. (1996). Human Resources as Strategic Assets: An evolutionary resource-based theory. *Journal of Management Studies, 33*(6), 757–785.

Nasif, E.G., Al-Daeaj, H., Ebrahimi, B., and Thibodeaux, M.S. (1991). Methodological problems in cross-cultural research: An updated review. *MIR: Management International Review, 21*(1), 79–91.

NASSCOM. (2012). *NASSCOM strategic review*. Retrieved from www.nasscom.in/itbpo-sector-india-strategic-review-2012

NASSCOM. (2014a). *Positive outlook for IT-BPM industry in FY 2014*. Retrieved from www.nasscom.in/positive-outlook-itbpm-industry-fy-2014

NASSCOM. (2014b). *Strategic review report*. Retrieved from www.nasscom.in/itbpm-sector-india-strategic-review-2014

Nilekani, N. (2009). *Imagining India: The idea of a renewed nation*. New York, NY: Penguin Press HC.

North, D.C. (1990). *Institutions, institutional change and economic performance*. Cambridge: Cambridge University Press.

Pfeffer, J. (1994). *Competitive advantage through people*. Boston, MA: Harvard Business School Press.

Pfeffer, J. (1998). Seven practices of successful organisations. *California Management Review, 40*(2), 96–124.

Pil, F., and MacDuffie, J. (1996). The adoption of high-involvement work practices. *Industrial Relations: A Journal of Economy and Society, 35*(3), 423–455.

Pio, E. (2007). HRM and Indian epistemologies: A review and avenues for future research. *Human Resource Management Review, 17*(3), 319–335.

Purcell, J., Kinnie, N., Hutchinson, S., Swart, J., and Rayton, B. (2003). *Understanding the people and performance link: Unlocking the black box*. London: CIPD.

Raman, S.R., Budhwar, P., and Balasubramanian, G. (2007). People management issues in Indian KPOs. *Employee Relations, 29*(6), 696–710.

Ramesh, B.P. (2004). 'Cyber Coolies' in BPO: Insecurities and vulnerabilities of non-standard work. *Economic and Political Weekly, 35*(5), 492–497.

Rastogi, P.N. (2000). Sustaining enterprise competitiveness: Is human capital the answer? *Human Systems Management, 19*(3), 193–203.

Reed, K.K., Lubatkin, M., and Srinivasan, N. (2006). Proposing and testing an intellectual capital-based view of the firm. *Journal of Management Studies, 43*(4), 867–893.

Russell, B., and Thite, M (2009). 'Human resource management in Indian call centres/business process outsourcing', in B. Russell and M. Thite (Eds), *The Next Available Operator: Managing Human Resources in Indian Business Process Outsourcing Industry* (pp. 33–58). New Delhi: Sage.

Singh, H. (2005, February 10). Is the BPO iceberg melting under attrition heat? *The Economic Times*. Retrieved from http://articles.economictimes.indiatimes.com/ 2005-02-10/news/27490856_1_attrition-heat-bpo-hr-managers

Som, A. (2007). What drives adoption of innovative SHRM practices in Indian organizations? *International Journal of Human Resource Management, 18*(5), 808–828.

Som, A. (2008). Innovative human resource management and corporate performance in the context of economic liberalization in India. *The International Journal of Human Resource Management, 19*(7), 1278–1297.

Sparrow, P., and Budhwar, P. (1997). Competition and change: Mapping the Indian HRM recipe against world-wide patterns. *Journal of World Business, 32*(3), 224–242.

Storey, J. (1989). Introduction: from personnel management to human resource management. In J. Storey (Ed.), *New Perspectives on Human Resource Management*. London: Routledge.

Subramaniam, M., and Youndt, M.A. (2005). The influence of intellectual capital on the types of innovative capabilities. *The Academy of Management Journal*, *48*(3), 450–463.

Tate, W.L., and Ellram, L.M. (2009). Offshore outsourcing: A managerial framework. *Journal of Business & Industrial Marketing*, *24*(3/4), 256–268.

Tate, W.L., Ellram, L.M., Bals, L., and Hartmann, E. (2009). Offshore outsourcing of services: An evolutionary perspective. *International Journal of Production Economics*, *120*(2), 512–524.

Taylor, P., and Bain, P. (2004). Call centre offshoring to India: the revenge of history? *Labour and Industry*, *14*(3), 15–38.

Taylor, P., and Bain, P. (2005). 'India calling to the far away towns': The call centre labour process and globalization. *Work, Employment and Society*, *19*(2), 261–282.

Teece, D.J. (2007). Explicating dynamic capabilities: The nature and microfoundations of (sustainable) enterprise performance. *Strategic Management Journal*, *28*(13), 1319–1350.

Thite, M., Budhwar, P., and Wilkinson, A. (2014). Global HR roles and factors influencing their development: Evidence from emerging Indian IT services multinationals. *Human Resource Management*, *53*(6), 921–946.

Thompson, M. (2002). *High Performance Work Organisation in UK Aerospace – The SBAC Human Capital Audit*. London: The Society of British Aerospace Companies.

Tregaskis, O., Daniels, K., Glover, L., Butler, P., and Meyer, M. (2012). High performance work practices and firm performance: A longitudinal case study. *British Journal of Management*, *24*(2), 225–244.

Whitfield, K. (2000). High-performance workplaces, training, and the distribution of skills. *Industrial Relations: A Journal of Economy and Society*, *39*(1), 1–25.

Williamson, O.E. (1975). *Markets and hierarchies: Analysis and antitrust implications*. New York: Free Press.

Williamson, O.E. (1985). *The economic institutions of capitalism: Firms, markets, relational contracting*. New York: Free Press.

Wood, S. (1999). Getting the measure of the transformed high-performance organization. *British Journal of Industrial Relations*, *37*(3), 391–417.

Wright, P.M., and Gardner, T. (2004). The human resource-firm performance relationship: Methodological and theoretical challenges. In D. Holman, T. Wall, C. Clegg, P. Sparrow, and A. Howard (Eds), *The new workplace: A guide to the human* (pp. 311–330). London: Wiley.

Wright, P.M., Gardner, T.M., Moynihan, L.M., and Allen, M.R. (2005). Relationship between HR practices and firm performance: Examining casual order. *Personnel Psychology*, *58*(2), 409–446.

Youndt, M.A., Snell, S.A., Dean Jr., J.W., and Lepak, D.P. (1996). Human resource management, manufacturing strategy, and firm performance. *The Academy of Management Journal*, *39*(4), 836–866.

Zaheer, A., and Nilakant, V. (1995). Relational governance as an interorganizational strategy: An empirical test of the role of trust in economic exchange. *Strategic Management Journal*, *16*(5), 373–392.

Zaheer, S., Lamin, A., and Subramani, M. (2009). Cluster capabilities or ethnic ties? Location choice by foreign entrants in the services offshoring industry in India. *Journal of International Business Studies*, *40*(6), 944–968.

5 Orchestrating human capital in the Indian IT service market

From entrepreneurial management to professional management

Jagdish Sheth and Arun Sharma

Introduction

The rapid evolution of the Indian information technology (IT) services industry in the last 30 years has given us a front row seat to see how an industry evolves and has an the impact on its human capital. The Indian IT services industry employs more than two million people in India. What is unique about this industry is that the vast majority of employees are knowledge workers with a large number of firms employing more than 100,000 employees. Most of these workers have a bachelor's degree in engineering and a large proportion have a master's degree. The Indian IT services industry is also unique for the following reasons:

- Firms have human capital in terms of both quality and quantity that is unparalleled in the world. This scale has only been observed in a few industries. Recall that TCS had 290,000 employees in 2014. IBM, a global IT firm had 400,000 employees worldwide in early 2014 with about half of them in India. As parallels, Google had 46,000 employees in 2014 and Microsoft had 100,000 employees in 2013.
- In the initial stages of growth, the employees were recruited from best-of-class engineering and management schools that became the backbone of the managerial and senior executive talent in these firms. The industry has an executive team depth that is unique to the Indian IT services industry and has not been observed in any other industry.
- The rapid growth of the IT services industry has created unique and progressive career paths for employees.

Some may seek to derive parallels between the Indian IT services industry and Silicon Valley, but the IT services industry in India has scale that is not accessible in Silicon Valley. A report from American Electronics Association (2010) found that Silicon Valley, San Francisco, and Oakland (the wider Bay Area), long known as the world's "tech mecca" had less than 400,000 knowledge workers in 2009. This number is easily surpassed by the number of employees of the top two Indian IT services firms: TCS and Cognizant (460,000 employees in first quarter of 2014).

Table 5.1 The journey of IT services providers – the four stages of growth

Years	Conditions in India	Conditions in US/Europe	Offerings	Market behaviors	HR processes
1981–1990	• Small set of excellent engineers (IITs) • Lack of employment prospects	• Lack of skilled IT employees	• Labor arbitrage (hire engineers from IITs in India, place in US)	Four types of entrants: • Existing IT firms (e.g., HCL) • IT entrepreneurs (e.g., Infosys) • Multinational family firms (e.g., TCS) • Promoters (e.g., Wipro) • Tremendous growth for all firms • Emergence of small firms	• Selective hiring • Entrepreneurial HR and business processes • Emphasis on margins • India-based hiring
1991–2000	• Smaller set of excellent engineers (IITs) • Large set of good engineers • Better employment prospects	• Tremendous shortage of skilled IT employees – specifically for COBOL and SAP	• Labor arbitrage (hire engineers from India, place in US) • BPO • First stage of IT outsourcing		• Mass hiring • Mass HR processes (hiring, training, placement) • Entrepreneurial business processes • Emphasis on growth • India-based hiring
2001–2010	• Large set of good/marginal engineers • Good employment prospects	• Budget pressures increased the need for IT outsourcing	• Integrated IT outsourcing offerings • Focus on efficiency	• Size becomes a constraint (entrepreneurial processes do not match size needs) • Emergence of Cognizant with different model (lower margins, higher customer centricity) • Differential growth rates of TCS/Cognizant versus Infosys/Wipro • Decline of smaller firms.	• Segmented hiring (hiring to demand) • Emergence of standardized HR processes (versus entrepreneurial) • Emphasis on growth management (demand versus supply) • India- and advanced country-based hiring
2011 onwards	• Large set of good/marginal engineers • Mediocre employment prospects	• Increased emphasis on effectiveness (how does it help the business versus cost saving)	• Emerging domain-specific value-added offerings	• Emphasis on growth and profitability • Increased adoption of new technologies such as agile, mobility and cloud • Better domain knowledge	• Selective hiring (hiring to skills versus mass hiring) • Professional global HR processes • Emphasis on enabling growth and enhancing profitability • India- and advanced country-based hiring • Top management change

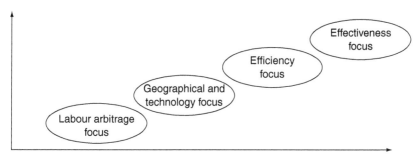

	1981–1990	1991–2000	2001–2010	2011 onwards
Stage	Introduction	Growth stage I	Growth stage II	Shakeout and maturity
Focus	Labor arbitrage	Supply of engineers	Cost savings, higher SLA	Enhancing client business
HR process	Indian-based individual hiring	Indian-based mass hiring	Indian-based mass hiring and global individual hiring	Global individual hiring; global management change

Figure 5.1 The four stages model.

How firms were able to develop and utilize the human capital is the focus of this chapter. We focus on external (non-Indian) markets although in the initial stages, a number of firms focused on domestic markets. In the following sections, we detail the four stages of growth that was observed. We present our analysis based on our own ethnographic accounts of engagements with the Indian IT industry as well as through secondary data of organizations operating in the Indian IT industry (Van Maanen, 1988, 1998, 2006) to develop new understandings of the phenomenon (Geertz, 1973). The role of senior management in reinventing the business model of the Indian IT industry is also highlighted here (Govindarajan and Trimble, 2011). The industry pattern of Introduction, Slow Initial Growth, Rapid Growth, and Shakeout and Maturity, was followed. This classification is based on each decade in the industry and the titles are based on product life-cycle labels. This chapter defines the drivers of growth and the human capital implications. The findings are summarized in Table 5.1 and the conclusions provided in Figure 5.1.

The introduction stage: 1981–1990

In the introduction stage, India was not seen as a country that would create an IT services industry. The communications infrastructure was poor and personal/ business communication systems were almost nonexistent. In 1980, firms had to wait almost 5 years to obtain a telephone line, and long-distance calls had to be booked through operators. Previous governments had forced IBM to leave the country and very few firms and students had access to computers. There was very little computer training provided in schools and colleges. Foreign exchange was restricted and business travelers had difficulty travelling abroad to conduct business. Combined with an overbearing bureaucracy that made doing business very difficult, the overall infrastructure was poor with an inadequate electricity supply and with inadequate transportation systems.

Demand and supply side trends led to the initial stages of the industry. On the demand side, with the introduction of minicomputers by Digital Equipment Corporation, computer systems were widely adopted by U.S.-based firms. As the adoption of computers increased, there was a skills shortage – a lack of qualified computer programmers. On the supply side, India did not have the capacity to absorb the large number of highly qualified engineers and managers that the top institutions were producing. Although not proficient in computer programming, these engineers and managers could be quickly trained to be computer programmers. Indian engineers and managers had three other characteristics that were important. First, admissions to the best engineering and management schools were based on meritocracy and these schools selected the best students in the country. Less than 0.01% of the students made it to the top schools in a country that emphasized education. Second, the starting salaries of engineers were about 10% of U.S. wages. Even after paying higher wages and allowances, firms could arbitrage the salary difference between US and India. Finally, most of the engineers and managers spoke English, which allowed them to communicate with U.S.-based firms. Therefore, India could supply the demand for software engineers in the U.S.

The earliest business models were pure labor arbitrage. Firms would hire engineers and management graduates from India (pay them Indian wages) and place them in the U.S. This was the dominant business model for the first 10 to 15 years of the industry. Because of the low barriers to entry and high service demand, a large number of firms entered the market during this period.

Two of the earliest firms to recognize this potential were HCL and Tata Burroughs. HCL was established in 1976 to manufacture computers. In 1979, HCL set up a venture in Singapore named Far East computers. The firm provided hardware and software solutions and HCL set up a software facility in Chennai. Tata Burroughs was established in 1977 by Tata Sons and Burroughs Corporation, U.S.A. to manufacture of computer peripherals in Mumbai. It soon started providing computer consultancy and development services for the overseas market. The name was changed to Tata Unisys in 1987 and then to Tata Infotech in 1997 before the firm merged with TCS in 2006.

Based on the initial success of the firms and the rising demand from developed markets, more firms entered the market. We classify these firms into four categories:

1   *Incumbent computer manufacturing/marketing firms.* In 1984, India opened its market to foreign computer manufacturers. This led to an expansion of

the computer market and a large number of entrants, both domestic and global, simultaneously entering into the IT services market. The computer firms that operated in the Indian market (e.g., HCL) recognized the opportunity and entered the IT services market. These firms had strong technological skills and understood the potential markets. The negative aspects of this decision were the loss of intellectual property and knowledge management that product firms created and had access to (with subsequent higher margins). However, the IT services market was larger than the products markets moving firms into the IT services markets.

2   *IT entrepreneurs.* The second group of firms were IT entrepreneurs who were able to recognize the impending shift in the industry. An example is Infosys, which was established in 1981. These firms typically obtained outsourcing contracts from Western countries and set up an Indian organization to provide software programming.

3   *Multinational family firms.* The third types of firms that entered the industry were multinational family firms (e.g., TCS). These firms were in multiple industries and constantly sought new industries to enter. For example, Tata Sons entered the IT services market and later spun off TCS in 1995.

4   *Promoters.* The last group of firms that entered the market were promoters (e.g., Wipro). Like multinational family firms, these firms were attracted to the industry because of market size and potential. Wipro was established in 1945 as a vegetable-product company, but moved to the computer industry in 1981 and later moved to the IT services industry.

Orchestrating the human capital

Hiring

The hiring in the initial stages of this era was predominantly from the best engineering and management schools. Because of the higher than local wages provided by Indian IT services firms, the only competition for hiring these graduates were Western universities (students who had obtained scholarships to study in the West, predominantly in the U.S.). However, as the Indian market started expanding due to deregulation, firms started recruiting from the top tier, but not the best, engineering and management schools (e.g., regional engineering colleges).

HR processes

The human resource processes at this stage were predominantly entrepreneurial (the only exception were the Tata firms). Led by strong leaders such as N. R. Narayana Murthy (Infosys), Aziz Premji (Wipro), and Shiv Nadar (HCL), the firms reflected the vision of the leaders and the HR processes were entrepreneurial. Most of the firms were self-governing with key decisions being made by the leaders. However, the opportunities of intellectual property creation and knowledge management were not the focus at this stage as managing growth and enhancing the HR engines were key priorities and limited managerial resources reduced leaders' attention to the creation of intellectual property. Professional management at this stage may have led to higher attention to intellectual property.

Emphasis on margins

The emphasis at this stage was on margins and costs were tightly controlled. Focus on costs was regarded as the standard operating procedure.

The slow growth period: 1991–2000

The second decade was the era of slow growth. Although, it may have been seen as rapid growth by participants at this stage, more rapid growth came in the next decade. As an example, the 2000 revenues for TCS were about $600 million, which increased to $8 billion by 2010.

By the end of the decade, India had been recognized as a country for outsourcing services. The focus of Indian IT services firms in this decade was on technology (e.g., SAP) and geography (U.S. and Western Europe). In IT services, with a large number of firms providing services to U.S.- and Western European-based firms, India had developed a reputation for low-cost IT services by the middle of the decade. There were supply and demand side reasons for the recognition. On the demand side, Western economies boomed during the 1990s. For the U.S. market, the Clinton administration increased the number of H1B visas that could be issued. However, the biggest demand side contributor was Y2K. Computers had been programmed with two-digit numbers for years, and with the year 2000 approaching, the computer systems were not expected to work in the new millennium. In this context, firms needed to go through their computer programs, identify the two-digit year code and convert them to four-digit codes. There was a labor shortage that was exacerbated by two factors. First, most of the mainframe programs were written in COBOL, an old language that did not have enough programmers. Second, a substantial number of firms decided to scrap their old systems and move to new enterprise systems, specifically SAP. This created an extreme shortage of SAP programmers.

On the supply side, there were multiple reasons for growth. First, after the opening up the economy in the early 1990s, the Indian government also started supporting the IT and call center services industries through special zones that reduced regulation and taxes and gave special access to power and better telecommunications links. NASSCOM, an industry lobby established in 1988, also started advocating for IT service providers. Second, seeing the need for engineers, a number of engineering schools were opened that provided a steady supply of engineering talent to Indian IT services firms. Finally, due to the establishment of a special economic zone, the growth of Infosys, a good location, and a number of engineering schools, Bangalore became the growth engine for this industry.

This was also the era of the voice business (or the call center business). India's having a core group of people who could speak English, employees that were motivated, and wages that were a tenth of those in the U.S. created a demand for voice services. This was also when the first generation of captives (Western firms located in India) emerged. A prominent example is Genpact, which started in 1997 as a business unit within GE, focusing on outsourcing business processes including voice. However, with the growth of voice came the issues that later made India a less attractive destination for call centers. The lack of cultural sensitivity combined with strong accents, made up Western names, and a lack of knowledge of how the U.S. economy functioned, reduced the importance of this industry. Since higher education was not central to the call center business, the natural advantages of the IT services industry did not translate into the call center business, which eventually gravitated to the Philippines due to its cultural proximity to the United States.

In this era of extremely short supply of professionals in the U.S. and Europe, large and small Indian firms stepped in to fill a void and delivered IT professional services that Western firms could not provide. The larger firms with expertise and experience understood the benefits of long-term contracts and started signing service contracts rather than just providing inexpensive software engineers. In the process, they developed processes to ensure high quality service outcomes. The smaller firms operated on labor arbitrage. Similar to the initial period, firms would hire engineers and management graduates from India, pay them Indian wages, and place them in the U.S. Again, because of the low barriers to entry and high demand, a large number of firms entered the market during this period.

As in the earlier phase, most leaders concentrated on the twin engines of growth – sales and delivery. In addition, firms had to concentrate on their operations in India, a difficult business environment. This phase was also characterized by firms learning and understanding the intricacies of customer IT services organizations and training their employees. The slow growth was a result of the tremendous amount of learning that was required by IT services firms. Again, due to limited attention by leaders, intellectual property and knowledge management were not paid the attention that they needed.

An interesting facet of human capital is that most firms used their current India-recruited employees as salespeople. This was a different strategy from most industries that tended to recruit locals to be salespeople. There were two reasons for recruiting Indians as salespeople. The first advantage was the cost (Indian salespeople could cost as little as 30% of U.S.-based salespeople). The second was cultural understanding. Indian salespeople understood their firms and could navigate their internal ad hoc systems.

Based on the initial success of the firms and the rising demand from developed markets, more firms entered the market. We classify these firms into three categories:

1   *Incumbent large IT services firms.* The five firms that started growing rapidly were the early entrants. These included the Tata firms, Infosys,

Wipro, Satyam, and HCL. At this stage, Infosys, which modeled itself as the Indian equivalent of IBM and Accenture, had the highest quality perceptions in the industry.

2   *Small firms.* The second group of firms were IT entrepreneurs who were able to observe the high demand for IT professionals. These were predominately small firms and an exception was Cognizant. Cognizant started as an in-house technology unit for Dunn and Bradstreet in 1994, started taking clients in 1996, and had an IPO in 1998. Cognizant was small at this stage with revenue of $137 million in 2000.

3   *Promoters and very small entrepreneurs.* The last group of firms that entered the market were promoters (e.g., Mahindra Infotech) and very small entrepreneurs that saw the potential profits.

Orchestrating the human capital

Hiring

The hiring in this stage was predominantly from the top tier, but not the best engineering and management schools. The competition from global and local firms for hiring the graduates from the best engineering and management schools reduced the number of students that could be hired by each firm from the best schools. After deregulation and as the Indian economy expanded, non-IT services firms started recruiting from the best schools, reducing supply. In response, IT services firms started recruiting from the second and third tier engineering and management schools. At this stage, the larger firms recognized that recruitment would be a strategic differentiator. Therefore, most large firms started developing a robust and scalable recruiting engine.

HR processes

The human resource processes at this stage remained entrepreneurial (the only exceptions were the Tata firms and Cognizant). Again, led by strong leaders such as N. R. Narayana Murthy (Infosys), Aziz Premji (Wipro), Ramalingam Raju (Satyam), and Shiv Nadar (HCL), the firms reflected the vision of the leaders and the HR processes were entrepreneurial. Most of the firms were self-governing with key decisions being made by the leaders.

Emphasis on growth and margins

The emphasis at this stage was on both growth and margins and costs were tightly controlled. Focus on costs was regarded as the standard operating procedure.

The period of high growth: 2001–2010

Starting in 2001, the overall market changed. The Y2K projects had been completed, the dotcom bust had taken place, and the U.S. entered a recession in late 2001. The impetus for the previous growth had come to a halt. However, it is at this stage that India-based IT services firms matured and created their current business focus. They started providing IT services such as application management, software implementation, infrastructure management, and business process outsourcing. The Indian IT services firms applied their learning from the previous decade and found immediate success in these areas. In this decade, the focus was on enhancing the efficiency of IT operations. Firms started verticalizing their business. Because of their high expenditure on IT services (10%+ of revenues), the biggest vertical for most firms was banking and financial services.

In India, the government continued to open new export zones with lower taxes in smaller cities and supported the IT services industry. Due to the importance of telecommunications links, Tata Communications started investing in global fiber networks and installed the first "round the world" fiber-optic cable in 2012. The country increased the size of the engineering colleges ensuring a supply of engineering graduates that is unparalleled in the world. Finally, with the trend starting in late 1990s, the voice business moved to the Philippines.

There were other major trends. First, scale arrived in the industry. TCS was the first firm to cross the $8 billion mark in revenues and Cognizant followed soon afterwards. Second, Satyam was indicted for financial fraud in 2009. It was critical moment for the Indian IT services industry and there were concerns that the entire industry would be tainted with the misdeeds of Satyam. However, this incident was regarded by IT service customers as isolated. Finally, although other countries attempted to enter the outsourcing market, the scale in India overwhelmed other countries. India graduates about 500,000 engineering graduates annually that Indian IT service firms have learned to train and utilize. In comparison the number of engineering graduates for other countries was less than 50,000 per year. India won the outsourcing battle.

The focus of the industry was initially (in this stage) on cost reductions or efficiency. Outsourcing activities to Indian IT services providers would reduce costs by 30%–50%. Since most of the larger Indian IT services firms were seen as having similar capabilities, this strategy led to undifferentiated services. Indian IT services firms realized that they needed to provide more brand differentiation. The larger firms developed domain knowledge and created products and solutions for their customers. This created a gap between the larger firms and smaller firms.

The second interesting aspect of the industry during this period was the interaction of scale and management methods. It was initially seen at this stage, but the trends became more evident in the next decade. Firms started to realize that they could not rely on India-based talent and began recruiting salespeople and domain experts from the West. The conflict between India-based HR management (predominantly ad hoc) and the Western system (predominantly professional) became more apparent. It is important to note that the firms that had traditional professional management (e.g., TCS and Cognizant) or developed professional management through acquisition (e.g., HCL) had started having higher growth rates compared to firms that had a slower transition from entrepreneurial to professional management. The phase was very challenging for entrepreneurial firms and their practices had a mismatch with the market. This trend became stronger in the next decade. In Cognizant's case, it became the second-largest India-based IT services supplier.

The final area of growth were the captives. Captives are firms set up in India by global firms to provide low-cost IT services and process outsourcing to the parent firms. The number of captives grew as firms wanted to retain their imbedded knowledge and at the same time take advantage of India-based talent and costs.

We classify firms into four categories:

1   *Large IT services firms.* Three firms in this category started having higher growth rates: TCS, Cognizant, and HCL. TCS was one of the first Indian firms to develop a professional management core and it created an academy called Tata Administrative Services to train their mangers. Due to its Dunn and Bradstreet heritage, Cognizant always had a professional management core. HCL had changed its management focus toward a more professional style. There were two major firms that started having lower than industry growth rates: Infosys and Wipro, which had problems moving from an entrepreneurial management culture to a professional management culture. These firms combined were also known as WITCH.
2   *Medium-sized firms.* There were a number of medium-sized firms (annual revenues from $200 million to $2 billion): iGate, Tech Mahindra, Mphasis, L&T Infotech, Hexaware, Syntel, and UST Global. With the exception of a few firms, most firms in this category started having slower growth rates and the growth rates of firms with more than $1 billion annual revenue started being severely curtailed. Scale and the ability to create value for customers were emerging issues in this group.
3   *Small firms.* As in most contexts, small firms continued to emerge providing IT services to the industry. As an example, a number of firms supplied software engineers to large IT services firms such as IBM and Accenture.
4   *Captives.* The final category of firms were captives. Firms such as American Express, JP Morgan Chase, Target, and Tesco set up captives in India to aid them in process improvement and cost reduction.

Orchestrating the human capital

Hiring

The hiring in this stage was predominantly volume based. The large growth in demand of engineers created large-scale processes of recruitment, training, and even retrenchment. These processes later spilled into other HR processes.

The traditional hiring of the "best athlete" and providing them with required skills also became less efficient as new software emerged and customers sought experienced engineers that the traditional model could not provide. At this stage two models appeared. The first model was hiring to demand. Firms did not hire engineers unless there was demand. The second model was hiring experienced employees in both India and the West. The experience could either be in the domain (e.g., banking) or in a specific technology (e.g., SAP). Most large firms were able to excel with both models.

HR processes

The human resource processes at this stage became bimodal. Firms such as TCS, Cognizant, HCL, and the captives were employing professional management practices. These firms were able to recruit and retain global talent. Most other firms were attempting to transition from entrepreneurial process to professional management processes. Professional firms managed this transition very well.

Emphasis on skills

The emphasis on growth and margins continued. Additionally, skill management became the key component for success. Firms sought skills in domain and practice areas.

The shakeout and maturity stage: 2011–2020

As we are in the middle of the shakeout and maturity stage, some trends are becoming more apparent. First, the heady growth of 30% plus annually is slowing down to the teens. Second, there are clear winners and losers in the industry. The India-based firms are growing, whereas, the growth of U.S.-based firms such as IBM and Accenture is slowing down. Even among India-based firms, some firms are growing at rapid rates and the growth of some firms has slowed. TCS and Cognizant, and lately HCL, have growth rates that are higher than their peers. The growth of Cognizant may be derived from their model that emphasizes lower margins to investors so that Cognizant can invest in the firm and clients. Third, customers are increasingly asking for Indian IT service firms to enhance their effectiveness rather than just enhancing efficiency. This is leading to a talent war where India-based firms are recruiting global industry and technology experts to help them better understand customer issues. Indian IT services firms need to address effectiveness issues rather than just focusing on efficiency issues.

Based on the industry structures, we expect the following trends regarding firms that will exists in the industry.

Industry structure

In the emerging era, we suggest that there will be four types of firms operating in this industry:

1   *High-growth large IT services firms.* Firms that are able to combine customer-centricity, domain expertise, professional management, and industry and technology expertise in their offerings will continue to grow at faster than market growth rates. Early successes in this segment have been achieved by TCS, Cognizant, and HCL.
2   *Low-growth IT services firms.* Firms that will not be able to incorporate customer-centricity, professional management, and industry and technology expertise in their offerings will see slower that market growth rates. Size or scale will itself not be critical for this group, but smaller firms will have the additional burden of lack of scale. We expect mergers and acquisition activity to take place in the group. Firms with sizes between $400 million and $2 billion will have an exceptionally hard time growing. They are too small to be generalists and too big to be specialists. These firms will be targets for acquisitions.
3   *Niche specialists.* Firms with niche specialties will continue to grow. These firms will provide targeted solutions to specific customers. Also, there is still a demand for basic outsourcing of talent from low-wage countries to high-wage countries. As most firms migrate to higher level services, a market-space will be created for basic outsourcing firms.
4   *Captives.* With increases emphasis on "insourcing," captives will continue to grow. Captive retain key industry knowledge and CIOs are supporting enhanced use of captives.

Orchestrating the human capital

We expect the following four trends in HR management.

Shift from Indian HR mindset to global HR mindset

The hiring in this stage will be predominantly talent-based. Rather than just scale, firms will seek employees with specific skills or traits. Recruiting will also shift away from exclusively recruiting from colleges in India to a large amount of recruiting taking place off-campus outside India. Firms will have to develop engines to recruit experienced employees from across the globe. The India-based ethnocentric mindset will no longer suffice. As global recruitment will be a priority, HR practices will also have to be global. Recruiting and retaining talent from global organizations will require HR policies that are global.

Shift in top management

The traditional top management of Indian IT services firms is typically Indian, seniority based, and too set in its ways. The next generation firms will have senior leaders from across the globe that are younger and have a more open and global perspective. This shift will be very challenging for firms, but will be required to ensure success. Also, firms will have to create outplacement services for their older managers.

The service factory

Indian IT services firms regarded revenues and number of employees to be highly correlated. This is the reason that Indian IT services firms recruited to future revenue expectations. As in manufacturing, automation is coming and it will bring increased productivity and efficiency to the IT services industry. Firms have already developed some IT services tools to enhance automation, and this trend is expected to grow faster. The consequence will be that the recruitment of fresh graduates will no longer be a source of competitive advantage. Rather, automation and higher level skills will define competitive advantage.

Increased focus on domain

To enhance the effectiveness of clients, domain expertise will become important for firms. As firms cannot create domain expertise, recruiting training and managing domain experts will become critical. The ability to hire experienced domain experts will create a competitive advantage for firms.

Conclusion

This chapter has outlined the four stages of IT industry development with implications for human capital. We suggested that the industry evolved from an Indian entrepreneurship-based human capital to a more global managerial-based human capital with implications for the industry, people, and profits. We suggest, like other industries, the IT industry has moved away from seeking the "best athlete" in India to seeking individuals with global industry and technology skills. We also suggest that a delay from moving from an entrepreneurial to a professional global management culture may have hindered the growth rate of some firms. We also looked at the future and predicted human capital trends.

References

American Electronics Association (2010). High-tech jobs evaporate by the thousands in Detroit and San Francisco Bay Area; Boston, San Diego, Seattle hold their own. Retrieved from www.xconomy.com/national/2010/12/09/high-tech-jobs-evaporate-by-the-thousands-in-detroit-and-san-francisco-bay-area-boston-san-diego-seattle-hold-their-own.

Geertz, C. (1973). Thick description: Toward an interpretive theory of culture. In C. Geertz (Ed.), *The interpretation of cultures: Selected essays* (pp. 3–30). New York, NY: Basic Books.

Govindarajan, V., and Trimble, C. (2011). The CEO's role in business model reinvention. *Harvard Business Review, 89*(1/2), 3–8.

Van Maanen, J. (1988). *Tales from the field.* Chicago, IL: University of Chicago Press.

Van Maanen, J. (1998). *Qualitative studies of organizations.* London: Sage.

Van Maanen, J. (2006). Ethnography then and now. *Qualitative Research in Organizations and Management, 1*(1), 13–21.

Websites

Miscellaneous company data accessed through financial data via organizational websites.

NASSCOM (various dates). Employment data accessed at NASSCOM website at www. nasscom.in.

6 Innovative HR practices

Evidence from three IT software services organisations

Ashish Malik

Introduction

The increasing pace of globalisation and, in particular, the offshoring of goods and services has contributed to widespread geographical dispersion and the disaggregation of a firm's production function. These changes have led to the reallocation of work activities and the development of new forms of work organisation, such as networked firm designs, offshore strategic alliances and business-to-business service relationships (Bruche, 2009; Immelt, Govindarajan and Trimble, 2009; Mudambi, 2008). It is not surprising then to see renewed calls for reconceptualising theories of work and working, especially as the manufacturing mindset of producing tangible goods and products in local proximity is no longer fully applicable to such newer forms of work, which often involves technology-mediated co-creation of intangible services across borders (Ashcraft et al., 2011). The literature on strategic human resources (HR), HR management (HRM) and work organisation highlights the importance of the integration and alignment of multiple types of internal and external fits namely, vertical (strategic), horizontal (HR practices), organisational (for example, history, culture, ownership and technology) and institutional (for example, legislation, norms, values and firm population) for achieving high firm performance (Boon, 2008; Boselie, 2010; Deephouse, 1999; Paauwe, 2004). The general argument is that the closer the fit and alignment the better will be the performance outcomes (Boon, 2008).

Successful offshore information technology (IT) outsourcing firms depend significantly on the quality of HR employed. A firm that lacks any strategic initiative for developing its workforce and relies exclusively on factor markets will find it difficult to become strategically distinctive and efficient in the longer term to sustain the pervasive influence of its clients. Further, to the best of the author's knowledge, earlier research has neither dwelt upon investigating a set of innovative HRM practices in IT software services nor considered the impact of a firm's external stakeholders, including its clients, in shaping its HRM practices. This chapter, therefore, is aimed at, first, broadening our understanding of what are the key innovative HRM practices, by incorporating the influence of external stakeholders. Second, by studying the key HR practices employed by IT software services firms, one can understand why some firms invest in certain types of human capital and organisational capabilities and, thus, uncover what skills and capabilities are critical in developing better a *strategic fit*. This is done in the context of software services firms operating in the Indian IT industry.

This chapter makes the following contributions. In terms of *originality* this chapter focuses on an organisational-level understanding of internal and external factors and how they interact in shaping HR practices in an unique contextual setting – India's offshore outsourcing IT services industry. In terms of its *utility*, the development of a novel theoretical framework for business-to-business IT outsourcing service firms is highly relevant here, to understand the influence of external factors. Finally, by uncovering IT firms' strategic choices in relation to training and HRM practices, we can unbundle the strategic dimensions of training and capability development critical in achieving a strong *strategic fit*. The rest of the chapter is organised as follows. First, a brief review of India's IT sector is offered. Second, a short review of the extant literature on innovative HR practices is presented. Third, a case is made for incorporating *relevant* theories to construct a novel theoretical framework. This is followed by the methodological and analytical strategies and discussion.

The Indian IT sector

Indian IT sector: institutional environment, growth explanations and structure

During the 1990s and 2000s, the revenues derived from India's IT sector increased 15-fold, from an estimate of US$150 million in 1989 to US$71.7 billion in 2010 to its current level of more than $118 billion (NASSCOM, 2014). In that same period, the sector's contribution to India's GDP grew five-fold to an estimated 8% of the GDP in 2013, generating direct employment of 3.1 million (NASSCOM, 2014). Explanations for this phenomenal growth have focused mainly on the role of human capital agglomeration, comparative advantage of human resources, and the impact of knowledge diffusion from transnational corporations (TNCs) (Athreye, 2004, 2005; Patibandla and Petersen, 2002). Others, though, have pointed to the role of public policy, institutional dynamics and the evolving service capability of Indian firms in supporting sustained growth (Arora, Arunachalam, Asundi and Fernandes, 2001; Athreye, 2005; Dossani, 2005; Nilakant, 2005). The above studies point to the favourable changes in the wider institutional environment, thus improving the degree of strategic choice and leeway available to supplier firms. Nevertheless, strategic management scholars have highlighted the role of dynamic coordination between clients and service providers (Banerjee, 2004) and the development of strong client-specific, people management capabilities (Athreye, 2004; Ethiraj, Kale, Krishnan and Singh, 2005) as important factors in explaining its growth and the strategic choices firms exercise.

The Indian IT industry can be grouped into three sub-sectors: IT hardware manufacturing (ITHM); IT software and business services (ITSS); and business processes outsourcing (BPO) services. This study focuses mainly on the ITSS sub-sector. Typical ITSS activities include IT consulting, infrastructure management, networking services, product development and embedded software design, and development of customised software. As identified in Chapter 2, firms may undertake services for the entire software development cycle, typical of firms in a 'product development' environment, or provide services for various stages of the software development cycle. Broadly, the nature of client-supplier relationships in the sector includes third-party service provision undertaken mostly by large domestic organisations, wholly-owned subsidiaries of multinational corporations (MNCs), and joint venture business partnerships. The nature of contracts for third-party service providers are mainly 'time and materials' (T&M) contracts, wherein projects are undertaken on the basis of billable time and materials (labour and infrastructure) supplied for clients' projects. While such contracts are still prevalent, improving organisational capabilities, changing environmental conditions and the competencies of established domestic firms have led them undertaking an increasing number of fixed-price (FP) contracts (Athreye, 2005). Organisations in this sector vary greatly in the size and range of services offered; hence, there are also likely many explanations for why and how these organisations invest in their people management practices and innovation is often regarded as a key differentiator in explaining organisational growth (Coad and Rao, 2008). To this end, the following section offers a brief review of innovative HRM practices.

Innovations in human resource management practices

Developing human resource management practices that can provide innovation stimulus for building of innovation capacity is critical in realising high innovative performance (Prajogo and Ahmed, 2006). By focusing on both human and technological elements in a firm's production function (Prajogo and Ahmed, 2006), firms can, for example, achieve high innovation outcomes, a view that is well acknowledged in the innovation management literature (Kanter, 1985; Lado and Wilson, 1994; Mumford, 2000) and studies of strategic HRM (Schuler and Jackson, 1987). Where the focus is on innovation outcomes, among other practices, Schuler and Jackson (1987) suggest empowerment- and trust-based *job designs*, incorporating ideas such as flexible work hours. Similarly, broad-based position descriptions and allowing discretion to schedule and manage one's work tasks is critical in an innovation strategy. Others studies have highlighted the importance of training and developing a culture of learning (Mark and Akhtar, 2003; Laursen and Foss, 2003), skills development (Gupta and Singhal, 1993), focused approach to staffing (Gupta and Singhal, 1993; Schuler and Jackson, 1987; Storey, Quintas, Taylor and Fowle, 2002), as necessary stimuli for developing innovative capacity.

Studies of high performance work systems have advocated the bundling of HR practices and key organisational capabilities to realise innovation outcomes. In a study of 173 Spanish firms, support was found for the relationship between a bundle of HRM practices and innovation outcomes (Jiménez-Jiménez and Sanz-Valle, 2008). Laursen and Foss (2003), for example, found interdependencies between the implementation of new HRM practices and innovation performance. In the main, the authors identified two HRM systems conducive to innovation performance: one each for manufacturing and services. They found strong support for two sets of training practices – provision of internal and external training – as most important in improving firms' ability to innovate. Overall, there seem to be high levels of support for the two key HRM practices that are commonly found in developing human capital and innovative capacity: a learning orientation and flexible work design (Beugelsdijk, 2008; Ceylan, 2012; Jain, Mathew and Bedi, 2012; Shipton, West, Dawson, Birdi and Patterson, 2006). To this end this chapter focuses on the role played by these two practices in relation to other HRM practices in developing innovative capacity of firms. Thus, a review of training and development literature is followed by work design.

Training and development research in India

Much of the training and development research in India has focused on human resource development (HRD) at national and sectoral levels (e.g. Rao and Abraham, 1986; Yadapadithaya, 2001). Research on the Indian IT sector that has focused on human resource development issues, nevertheless, is mostly in the form of teaching cases (e.g. Hoyt and Rao, 2007; Purkayastha and Fernando, 2007). Where empirical HRD studies exist (Paul and Anantharaman, 2004; Wadhwa, de Vitton, and Gereffi, 2008), those studies have a broader industry focus and adopt an inward-looking HRM focus. Despite its broad cross-sectoral focus, Yadapadithaya's (2001) work surveying and evaluating the training and development practices of Indian organisations, offers a valuable contribution. In this study, Yadapadithaya found that competition – global and local – caused firms to make changes to their training and development infrastructures to enhance productivity, innovation and the quality of services. India's IT services sector invests between US$1.5 billion and $2.0 billion per year on training and the sector's four largest players account for close to a quarter or US$500 million of the total amount spent, or an annual average of about US$5,000 per person (*Economic Times*, 2007). Supporting this conclusion, Wadhwa et al.'s (2008) survey of fast-growing Indian companies revealed significant levels of investment in training by both IT companies and MNCs operating in India. Nevertheless, the inward-looking focus adopted by most studies has tended to neglect the needs of multiple stakeholders, including a firm's clients, thus limiting our understanding of training and capability development approaches in IT software services firms in India.

Work design and other practices

IT firms in India rely extensively on the adoption and implementation of numerous quality management frameworks, which would suggest that there exists high managerial control over work activities and limited leeway and choice in workflow decisions (Athreye, 2004, 2005; Malik, 2009; Malik, Sinha and Blumenfeld, 2012). Investment in learning and development is often associated with the nature of work design (Ashton and Sung, 2006). A review of the literature examining training and work design further reveals that researchers have tended to employ a range of theoretical lenses to consider the impact of, for example, business strategy, technological change, work organisation, adoption of new management practices (NMPs) and high performance work systems (HPWPs) on training provision (Ashton and Sung, 2006; Dawe, 2003; Dostie and Montmarquette, 2007; Green, Mayhew and Molloy, 2003; Mason, 2004; Ridoutt, Dutneall, Hummel and Smith, 2002; Smith and Dowling, 2001; Smith and Hayton, 1999). In general, the above studies found a range of organisational factors – including technology, workplace change, competitive strategies, the introduction of quality management and other NMPs, and trade unions – to be the primary influences on training decisions in organisations. The findings from these studies, however, yield equivocal results. To this end, this study incorporates multiple theoretical perspectives in analysing the following key questions this study seeks to answer:

1 What are the main innovative HRM practices employed by ITSS firms in India?
2 What are the main factors that influence a firm's decision to invest in training in Indian IT sector?
3 How do various factors – internal and external to the firm – interact with one another in the provision of training and designing work in India's IT sector?
4 Why do some firms invest more than others in training in the Indian IT industry sector?

Building a theoretical framework for understanding innovative HRM

In line with the philosophical assumptions of HRD, organisations in India's ITSS sector are considered in this chapter as purposive economic entities, operating for a surplus. This assumption underpins a number of theoretical perspectives such as human capital theory (Becker, 1962), neo-human capital theories (Acemoglu and Pischke, 1998a, b; Bartel and Lichtenberg, 1987; Wozniak, 1984, 1987), strategic human resource management in service sector firms (Boxall, 2003), and studies of high performance work practices (HPWPs) (Becker and Huselid, 1998; MacDuffie, 1995; Pfeffer, 1998). Further, given the presence of quality management practices in most studies of HPWPs and their widely acknowledged role in achieving sustained competitive advantage, the role of quality management capabilities is also included in the theoretical framework (Reed, Lemak and Mero, 2000; Ridoutt et al., 2002; Smith, Oczkowski, Noble and Macklin, 2004).

Finally, the study incorporates the concept of market and learning orientations (Argyris and Schön, 1978; Kohli, Jaworski and Kumar, 1993; Narver and Slater,

1990), as the key elements of a market-based organisational learning framework (Sinkula, Baker and Noordeweir, 1997), in explaining why certain organisational values drive managerial behaviours and actions. The following section provides a brief overview of the underpinning theories that individually and collectively shape our understanding of the design and implementation of innovative HRM practices.

Human capital theory (HCT)

The human capital theory has highlighted that education and training are key inputs for better learning and improved organisational productivity (Becker, 1962). Becker was the first to differentiate between firm-specific and generic training. He suggested that firms are more likely to invest in firm-specific human capital than generic human capital, as the former is concerned with the individual's immediate job requirements and in most cases is not transferable to other organisations, whereas the latter is transferable to other employers because it is of the same value to other employers. Hence, organisations are likely to invest in training and development of its human resources.

Neo-human capital theories

Proponents of neo-human capital theory argue that highly trained and educated employees are more likely to adopt technological change than less-educated and less-skilled employees (Wozniak, 1984, 1987) and that new technology is a means of improving productivity. Further, neo-human capital theory suggests that the demand for highly educated workers would decline with increases in experience on a particular technology (Bartel and Lichtenberg, 1987). This would suggest that for managing technological, managerial and workplace changes, training is a critical HRM practice.

Strategic Human Resource Management (SHRM) and HPWPs

The role of training and HRM in implementing strategic change was noted by Warwick scholars in the UK (Pettigrew, Sparrow and Hendry, 1988). Their model proposed that changes to a firm's strategy had a profound impact on its skills requirements and as a consequence, on its training provision. As noted earlier in Chapter 3, Boxall (2003) identified the variations in the nature of knowledge content, typical work design, competitive dynamics and the predications for appropriate HR strategy. Researchers from the UK (Green et al., 2003; Mason, 2004) who found the influence of product/service specification (complexity) also found higher demand for skills in high-value added product and service specifications relative to low and medium value added services. Thus, the nature of service markets, product or service specification and strategic orientation had a profound impact on the choice of a range of HRM practices. Studies of SHRM suggest that firms successfully implement changes to their production practices by introducing a bundle of HPWPs (Becker and Huselid, 1998; MacDuffie, 1995; Pfeffer, 1998). The provision of training and the inclusion of some form of quality management practices are often part of such bundles (de Menezes and Wood, 2006) of new management practices (Smith et al., 2004). HPWPs or new management practices that focus on a control-oriented or commitment-based work design are likely to have lower or higher levels of investment in skills, respectively (Ridoutt et al., 2002).

Total quality management (TQM)

Following an extensive review of the key content areas that encapsulate a TQM approach (Parzinger, 1997; Prajogo, 2007; Prajogo and Brown, 2004; Reed et al., 2000; Sitkin, Sutcliffe and Schroeder, 1994) incorporating three commonly understood areas: (1) an organisation's *commitment* to investment in quality and *information sharing* (similar to leadership commitment, shared beliefs, and values regarding systemic information sharing); (2) its focus on *continuous improvement* (which comprises its internal and external customer focus and process management); and (3) *team working* (involving functional teams and cross-functional integration). Research suggests that higher levels of investment are required in quality processes and personnel training in the early stages of product, service, process and TQM implementation life cycles to realise productivity (Krishnan, Kriebel, Kekre and Mukhopadhyay, 2000; Parzinger, 1997). Further, a high level of process maturity assessed against the Capability Maturity Model (CMM) standard, a commonly used quality management standard for ITSS organisations, is associated with high training volume, product quality and reduced development effort (Harter, Krishnan and Slaughter, 2000). This suggests that for firms to implement an integrated approach to quality to increase customer retention and satisfaction, they must also invest in HRM practices of training, team working and information sharing, including sharing information critical to performance metrics within and across employee teams.

Market-based organisational learning

Sinkula et al.'s (1997) conceptualisation of a market-based organisational learning analytical framework provides us with an understanding of how firms can effectively transform market information and organisational values into appropriate behavioural responses. This process of market-based organisational learning is facilitated by three elements: *organisational values* that promote learning; an organisation's *market-information processing behaviours*; and *organisational actions*. The framework has two main constructs – an organisation's learning orientation (LO) and market information processing (MIP).

Learning orientation involves three sets of organisational values associated with an organisation's tendency to learn. These are: *commitment to learning*; *open-mindedness*; and developing a *shared vision* to influence a firm's ability to create and use knowledge (Argyris and Schön, 1978; Garvin, 1993). *Commitment to learning* is fostered through ongoing training and development of its employees and the resources a firm allocates for such development. *Open-mindedness* requires an organisation to challenge its current theory-in-use and any new information it processes from its internal and external sources. *Shared vision* encompasses the organisation's ability to communicate and disseminate its theory-in-use and any new knowledge and competencies that it has developed throughout the organisation. These values can be implemented partly by direct investment in training and partly by fostering a culture of supporting and sharing new learning and skills development at all levels.

In globally dispersed production functions, the influence of client needs on training and transfer of knowledge can be better understood through market information processing behaviours. Market information processing is the process by which external market (client and competitor) information is sensed and transformed into knowledge (Sinkula et al., 1997) and disseminated across the organisation. Market information processing is developed from a key marketing construct, market orientation, which consists of three behavioural components: *information sensing* or acquisition from an organisation's customers and competitors; horizontal and vertical *dissemination* of such information within the organisation; and framing appropriate organisational *responses* in relation to such information via inter-functional coordination (Kohli et al., 1993; Narver and Slater, 1990). Of more importance is information sensing or generation because it involves capturing precise and critical information about a customer's needs and the external competitive environment. Sinkula et al. (1997) found that a more positive learning orientation (a values-based construct) will lead to increased market information generation and dissemination (knowledge-based construct), which, in turn, affects the degree to which an organisation makes changes to its strategies (a behavioural construct). Organisations with high levels of learning orientation are more likely to question their current theory-in-use, challenge basic assumptions and be open to new ideas and knowledge. While new knowledge is procured through an organisation's market information processing behaviours, it can be refined, redefined and challenged through its learning orientation, depending on the extent to which its learning orientation and market information processing are developed. Thus, knowledge generated through this mechanism can both shape and inform training and work design practices.

Methodology

A qualitative case study methodology is appropriate when a novel and relatively less researched phenomenon is being investigated (Eisenhardt, 1989). The Indian ITSS is an appropriate research setting for undertaking a case study because the complex team-based co-development processes that need to be analysed require information to be collected from more than one informant. As such the multi-case study design chosen here is appropriate (Yin, 2003). Yin highlights the importance of a priori constructs and theoretical framing for guiding data collection and analysis as well as for improving construct validity (Eisenhardt, 1989; Miles and Huberman, 1994; Yin, 2003). Thus, the multi-case study design employed here aims at literal (likelihood of predicting similar findings) and/or theoretical (likelihood of predicting rival findings with understandable and predicted rationales) replications.

By including organisations from a single industry sub-sector (IT software services) better cross-case comparisons can be made as well as this helps in strengthening construct and external validity caused by minimal extraneous variation in the sample. The choice of a maximum variation purposive sampling (Eisenhardt, 1989; Miles and Huberman, 1994; Yin, 2003) was deliberate to observe any common patterns despite differences in certain organisational characteristics. The case selection criteria were developed using extant literature on enterprise training (Ashton and Sung, 2006; Boxall, 2003; Smith and Dowling, 2001), and the structure of the Indian IT industry (Banerjee, 2004; Ethiraj et al., 2005; Heeks, 1998) and by using available details from industry association's directory of ITSS providers.

The following selection criteria were employed:

- enterprise size, expressed in terms of employee headcount: small (less than 150), medium (151–1,000), large (1,001);
- ownership: MNC, Indian, and MNC joint venture;
- business model: wholly owned subsidiary of a MNC, third-party service provider, and a variant of the above two categories; and
- the nature of product-market strategy: slightly differentiated and highly differentiated and specialised services.

To maintain reliability, a case study protocol containing semi-structured questions was developed after feedback from Marketing and HRM colleagues. Additionally, separate databases were created for within- and cross-case analyses. These databases included field notes, transcripts, a coding manual, protocol, organisational documents, news clippings, operational data, quality management performance data, and tables, matrices, displays and figures for analysis. To maintain the confidentiality of the participating organisations, the exact numbers of employees have been rounded off and pseudonyms are used for case organisations. Firms are labelled as SOFTSERV 1, 2 and 3. To get a holistic understanding of the phenomenon and to reduce single respondent bias, semi-structured interviews of 90–120 minutes duration were undertaken with 19 informants: CEOs or country heads, HR managers, project or product managers, project or product employees, business development managers and quality managers (see Table 6.1 for details).

Case reports were developed and sent to participating organisations for validation, feedback and release. Pattern matching and explanation building analytic strategies were employed at within- and cross-case levels. The use of visual displays and matrices and feedback from case organisations helped in strengthening the validity of the data analysis.

Table 6.1 Key informants

Case organisations	CEO/ country manager	HR manager	Project manager	Quality manager	Employees	Business development manager	Total
SOFTSERV 1		2	2	1	1		6
SOFTSERV 2		2	2	1	1		6
SOFTSERV 3	1*	1	2		3	1*	7
Total	1*	5	6	2	5	1*	19

Note

* is only counted once as the CEO/country manager is also the business development manager of SOFTSERV 3.

Analysis

An analysis of the key factors that shaped the development of training, work design and HRM practices is presented in the form of key themes emerging from within- and cross-case analysis. Visual displays of the nature and extent of training undertaken, the case descriptions, strength of key factors and HRM practices are provided in Tables 6.2 and 6.3, respectively. Figures 6.1–6.5 will provide further comparative analysis between various practices and its impact on training volumes.

Table 6.2 Nature and extent of training

	SOFTSERV 1	SOFTSERV 2	SOFTSERV 3
Training characteristics			
Extent (volume)			
1 Induction (weeks)	2	2–6	1
2 Product/project specific (weeks)	6–8	2–3	3–8
3 MDP[1] (weeks)	2	0	0
4 Total (weeks)	10–12	4–9	4–9
5 Classification	H[2]	M–H	M–H
6 Expected annual training (for all staff, post-induction)	80 hours	40 hours	Needs based
Training characteristics			
Nature (diversity)			
1 Internal	H–Mix	L	M
2 External	M–H	H	M–L
3 Formalisation (assessment)	H	M–H	L
4 Training type:			
• Technical (%)	85–90	90	90–95
• Behavioural (%)	10–15	10	5–10

Notes

1 MDP = Management development programmes.

2 H = High, M = Medium, L = Low, M–H = Medium to High, M–L = Medium to Low.

Table 6.3 Case description and impact of key factors on training provision

Case organisations Case description and impact of key factors on training	SOFTSERV 1	SOFTSERV 2	SOFTSERV 3
Ownership	MNC	Indian/US joint venture	MNC
Business model	MNC subsidiary and third-party accounts	MNC subsidiary and third-party accounts	Mostly MNC subsidiary accounts
Nature of services and product-market strategy	Highly differentiated	Slightly differentiated	Slightly differentiated
Number of employees (rounded)	35,000+	800+	30+
Industries served[1]	Media, automobiles, telecom, petroleum, business and IT consulting	BFSI, health, energy, technology, manufacturing, and public service	SAP solutions for health, oil and gas, government, technology and BFSI sectors
Key business lines[2]	AMS, BPO, R&D, and consulting services	AMS, CRM, ERP, Web services	Business process outsourcing and SAP solutions provider
Workplace change *(structural, ownership and technology)*	H[3]	M, M, H	H, L, H
Market orientation *(information sensing, dissemination and organisational response)*	M–H	M	M-H
Learning orientation *(commitment to learning, open-mindedness and shared vision)*	H	M–L	M–L
Quality management systems *(commitment, sharing information, continuous improvement and teamwork)*	H	M	M
Employee turnover	H	M–L	M
Enterprise size	H	M	L
Strategic HRM approach • *rewards and performance management systems* • *career planning* • *recruitment skills level and operating role*	H H H	M M–L M–H	M–L M–L H

Notes

1 BFSI: Banking, Financial Services and Insurance; SAP: SAP is an integrated enterprise resource planning (ERP) software product developed by SAP-AG (Germany).

2 AMS: Application management and development Services; ERP: Enterprise resource planning software; CRM: Client/customer relationship management.

3 H = High, M = Medium, L = Low, M–H = Medium to High, M–L = Medium to Low.

Internal factors

Enterprise size and HRM orientation

SOFTSERV 1, the largest of the three firms and had a 'strategic' approach to its HRM infrastructure. SOFTSERV 1 invested in building a training infrastructure and leveraged their training and quality management infrastructure to offer training to an increasing number of recent college graduates. As part of the HR strategy, it focused on increasing the percentage of graduate engineers with less than four years of work experience to 60%–70% of the total workforce composition. Since it was also experiencing a high growth rate, the training infrastructure supported development of *learning pathways* for structured career development and talent retention. It had well-developed and formalised HRM practices to service to its large, complex and geographically diverse employee population and service offerings. Clearly, its labour orientation was leaning more towards 'make' or investing in people and skills (Stewart and Brown, 2009), however, the most important HRM practices for fuelling its growth trajectory were its recruitment and selection, and training and development. SOFTSERV 1 employed a strong differentiation strategy in managing its people and services (Boxall, 2003).

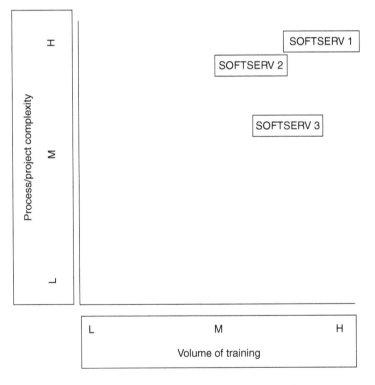

Figure 6.1 Process or project complexity and volume of training.

Being an extremely small start-up, SOFTSERV 3 relied extensively on informal and incidental learning (Watkins and Marsick, 1992). Such an approach to learning was logical given its firm size and an 'evolving' HRM infrastructure. As such it employed a 'buy' orientation towards HRM and training practices (Stewart and Brown, 2009). SOFTSERV 2 on the other hand, a mid-sized joint-venture between a diverse Indian multinational and a US-based IT MNC, had established a basic HRM 'operational' framework and relied on a combination of 'make' and 'buy' orientations towards its people management strategy (Stewart and Brown, 2009). This was primarily owing to its size, ownership structure and the narrow range of service offerings. SOFTSERV 2 and 3 thus hired experienced and relatively expensive employees and offered them with little or no structured career development.

In terms of training provision, all firms usually began with in-house internal induction training, followed by project- and process-specific training, and for various employee groups, as per need, invested in a range of leadership and management development programmes (MDPs). The latter was mostly evident in SOFTSERV 1 and 2. A differentiating emphasis in training was found in SOFTSERV 1. In addition to the above training content areas, it also focused on developing domain- and industry-specific human capital for its frontline and

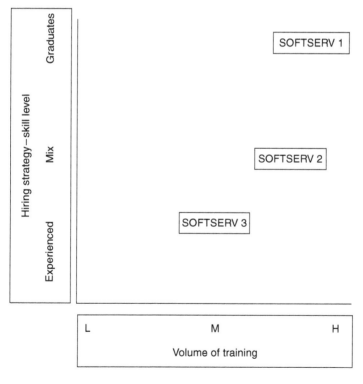

Figure 6.2 Hiring strategy and volume of training.

senior employees. SOFTSERV 1's learning and development approach was also different as it employed resources from its global learning campuses to offer training programmes from a range of about 4,000 courses covering technical, behavioural and personal needs training modules. SOFTSERV 1's decision to rely on global modules rather than developing local content was partly influenced by the worsening geopolitical climate of IT services offshoring.

In terms of the focus of all training activity as in generic versus firm-specific training, responses were often blurred and respondents noted that an element of each was present in the other. Further, the data suggests that bulk of the technical training in the technology domain is generic and transferable, locally and globally. Most general skills training such as people management, leadership and communication skills, and domain-specific skills, are transferable. The issue of firm-specific skills and transferability was not on the agenda of these case organisations. Choices between providing generic and firm-specific training was often linked to business needs more than the tenets of human capital theory (Becker, 1962). For example, contrary to extant research (Ridoutt et al., 2002; Smith et al., 2004), quality management training was an integral part of technical, rather than behavioural, training. The explanations lie at the heart of organisations' strategic milieus (both external and internal), the dynamic coordination that exists between a service provider and its clients (Banerjee, 2004) and the unique configurations of choices that firms exercise in investing in specific organisational capabilities and HRM practices that eventually shape the nature and extent of training.

Employee turnover and temporal dimension

Employee turnover was very high in all the software service firms and had an ongoing cost impact on the nature and extent of training. Although employee turnover explained variations in training volume, further variations in training demand can be explained by the temporal dimension training in a project's life cycle. Applying the classic organisational lifecycle 'S' curve to the training function, and following the neo-human capital assumptions of Bartel and Lichtenberg (1987), an organisation's need for learning should decline with experience on a given process or technology. While this theory may hold true for stable and simple process environments, it was not true in a dynamic outsourcing services environment witnessing high growth rates. The findings suggest that an organisation's training volume and diversity did not decline as firms developed maturity in a given process or technology; additional units of training were necessary because of two key factors – high and ongoing employee turnover and the ongoing process, product or project enhancements and changes requested by clients. Thus, additional training 'spikes' or new 'S' curves were formed.

Work design

To overcome competition and market positioning firms invested in a range of NMPs and HPWPs. These changes had a positive impact on skills demand. The relationship between the adoption of NMPs and HPWPs for a control- or commitment-based work design and training was not straightforward. The majority of firms adopted some mix of NMPs and commonly noted HPWPs such as TQM, team working, lean management, Six Sigma, organisational learning cultures, employee rewards and business process reengineering. The focus of these changes, for the majority of the workforce, was to increase control in order to ensure predictable service delivery in this globally distributed model of software co-development. Training was provided to deal with technological, managerial and structural changes associated with the introduction of these NMPs.

Quality management capabilities

The adoption of quality management accreditations by ITSS firms served multiples purposes: from market signalling for high quality services, through to cost reduction and improvement of services, to work process control and competitive positioning. SOFTSERV 1 had invested heavily in quality management capabilities and formal accreditations, whereas SOFTSERV 2 and 3 had medium levels of investment in its quality management infrastructure. Inbuilt in most quality management accreditations and approaches is a requirement to train people on

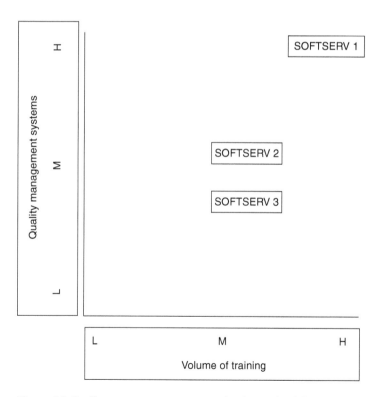

Figure 6.3 Quality management systems and volume of training.

quality management methodologies and process knowledge, and to address any gaps that arise from continuous improvement and monitoring projects. The strength of the quality management capabilities helped these firms to develop partnerships with HR, marketing, sales, operations and training. However, the extent to which these partnerships were successful was a function of the strength of firms' quality management capabilities. Hence, SOFTSERV 1 had strong influence from its quality management accreditations in shaping its recruitment and selection, performance management and training and development capabilities. The other two firms had more of an ad hoc approach in dealing with most people management issues.

External factors

Market-based organisational capabilities

SOFTSERV 1 had high levels of market and learning orientations as well as developed quality management capabilities. It is important to note here that even if firms have high levels of learning commitment and well-developed platforms for promoting a shared vision and key values, their overall learning orientation

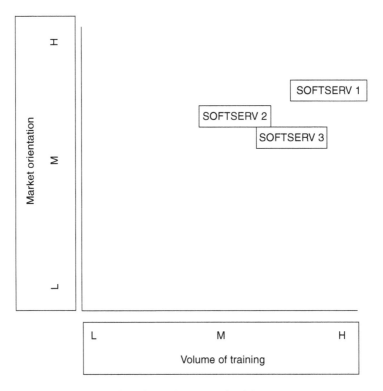

Figure 6.4 Market orientation and volume of training.

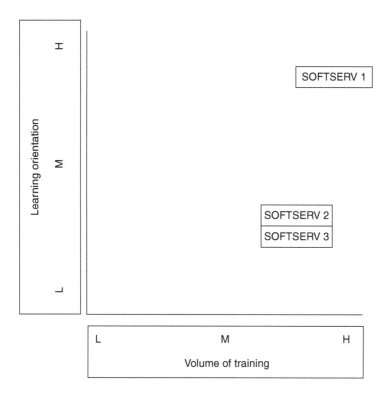

Figure 6.5 Learning orientation and volume of training.

can be adversely affected by its medium to low levels of *open-mindedness*: the ability to critically challenge clients' and business assumptions and a precursor for encouraging exploratory or innovative learning. The findings support that this was the case in SOFTSERV 2 and 3, where the focus was more on conformance to clients' expressed needs with little evidence of double-loop learning (Argyris and Schön, 1978) in its daily routines. These service providers lacked in their capability to engage in higher order learning. In the absence of high learning orientation, new knowledge is rarely produced and as such firms typically demonstrate single-loop learning and development programs to support their problem-solving.

Client specifications, project/product complexity and geographical location

The findings support a positive impact of client specifications on the nature and extent of HRM practices and training. The extent to which firms were influenced by external knowledge of their clients and their agreed specifications varied with the nature and extent of service/project complexity, its contract duration and the maturity (technology and domain experience) of the service provider. The total number of clients and the service provider's ability to integrate and offer cross-functional solutions to its clients depended on the provider's technology, consulting, BPO and quality capabilities. The high levels of skills needed for complex projects had a strong impact on training demand. In some cases, clients' proprietary tools, processes and software applications resulted in a greater level of training provision and influence being exercised by clients. Relative to SOFT-SERV 2 and 3, SOFTSERV 1 had highly developed training, quality and market-based organisational learning capabilities and, hence, was able to demonstrate higher order learning skills needed for delivering higher value-added services. Such an approach resulted in better performance outcomes for SOFTSERV 1 and as a result helped it achieve a better degree of *strategic fit.*

Gaps in the educational curriculum

Despite the strong analytical and problem-solving skills that most Indian engineers bring to the job, there is a significant level of mismatch between industry needs and the national engineering educational curriculum (Narayanan and Neethi, 2005), which meant that additional training for non-computer-science graduates was necessary. For example, the compounded annual growth rates of 40% and an annual attrition rate of more than 10% meant that SOFTSERV 1 had high levels of annual hiring (of about 20,000 engineers annually), for which they had to rely on all streams of engineering disciplines, not just computer science graduates. Thus, its huge training infrastructure was a highly relevant strategic lever to impart highly structured technology, domain, soft skills and quality management-related process training to large numbers of recent college graduates (nearly 75% of the annual intake of 20,000). Relative to this, SOFTSERV 2 and 3 continued to employ a combination of buy and make strategies for various job roles.

Discussion

From the above analysis, it follows that an organisation's strategic and contextual milieus have strong influence in shaping the nature and extent of HRM practices and its approaches towards training and work design. An organisation's strategy is best discerned by its behaviours and actions. Behaviours are driven by what a firm values most, which manifests in the capabilities and HRM practices it wants to develop to suit its competitive position in the marketplace. Such a view is common in strategic management literature and also forms a key basis for Sinkula et al.'s (1997) market-based organisational learning framework. From a training and, more broadly, from an HRM perspective, once an organisation has decided in which market it wants to operate, it has to exercise a choice whether to 'make' (develop) and/or 'buy' (acquire) resources from the external labour market (Stewart and Brown, 2009). The largest firm in this sample (SOFT-SERV 1) followed the practice of hiring young, less experienced and inexpensive resources from engineering backgrounds. While such a strategic choice sets the tone for investment in hiring and training, the exact nature and extent of training was also shaped by a number of changes in its internal and external environment. Large-scale investments in learning and development were also logical for large players, as the Indian IT engineering curriculum did not fully cater to the IT industry's skills needs. For example, the need to have a global expertise in new technology domains and the ability to manage changes to and from client accounts necessitated such investments. SOFTSERV 1, being a subsidiary of a large US-based IT MNC, also had the challenge of managing its investments due to the uncertain global geopolitical climate for offshoring.

From the above analysis and discussion, it follows that the most innovative HRM practices employed by SOFTSERV 1 were its ability to have a scalable attraction and selection workgroup and efficient supporting human capital development infrastructure to make these relatively young and inexperienced engineers employable and productive. However, these HRM practices also relied on the strength of other complementary organisational capabilities such as quality management and market-based organisational learning capabilities and how these concurrently supported the organisation's entry into the higher order and complex products and services. For small and medium enterprises such as SOFTSERV 2 and 3, the focus was less on having a strong training system and more on their ability to attract highly experienced and skilled resources and have medium levels of investment in quality management, learning and market orientations. Interestingly, all three firms had a relatively strong control-oriented mindset with regard to workflow and scheduling of their employees' activities. As such, the presence of a cost-focused and control-oriented work design prevailed across all firms.

A distinctive theoretical contribution from this study to the literature on strategic HRM in IT software services firms is the need for firms to simultaneously manage the tensions between a strong 'client fit' and *strategic, vertical,* and *horizontal fits. Client fit* is a highly dynamic construct, which, although temporally and contractually bound by service level agreements, changes through a dynamic coordination and information exchange between the contracting parties as each party gradually reduces their information asymmetries (Banerjee, 2004). Organisations serving multiple clients in different technology and industry domains have to invest selectively in capabilities such as market-based organisational learning, training and quality management to achieve a better overall fit for different competitive positions.

Conclusion

In answering the first research question, this study found three innovative HRM practices: scalable recruitment and selection practices; strategic approach to learning and development; and a control-oriented work design. The ability to exercise control over the youthful employee population was in part assisted by the strength of the firms' quality management systems and partly through work design. In answering the second research question, this study found that training and development practices are shaped by a combination of internal (competitive strategy, workplace change, employee turnover, quality and market-based organisational capabilities, temporal dimension of project/product lifecycle, and enterprise size) and external (client specifications, product/project complexity, and gaps in educational curriculum) factors. In answering the third question we found that the interaction between various factors varied with firms' strategic choices in regard to investment in key organisational capabilities and the dynamic coordination that occurred between the client and service provider (Banerjee, 2004). Depending on the service markets in which a firm operates, it has to keep up with technological and domain changes. To maintain and/or improve its competitive positioning, firms have to decide and choose the organisational capabilities that are critical to sustained performance. Depending on the choices firms exercise in developing their training, quality management and market-based organisational learning capabilities, the impact on the nature and extent of training provision varied. Additionally, if there is low dynamism in project/product life cycle, low employee turnover, and improvements in the educational curriculum or availability of industry-ready talent, the need for higher levels of training will decline.

In answering the study's last question, it is important to understand the reasons why firms in the Indian IT sector invest in training. Employee performance, organisational productivity and reduction in costs and thus servicing a firm's strategic orientation and its client specifications were the key reasons for investment in training. Additionally, firms that were following a 'make' strategy also invested in training to retain employees by providing training that supported both the organisational needs and employee career aspirations. The dynamism in project/product life cycles also influenced the nature and extent of training.

From the above analysis a number of theory and practice implications arise. HRD practitioners need to understand the differences between key factors impacting small, medium-sized and large firms so that they can allocate resources accordingly. Further, developing an appreciation of a temporal dimension of training will help practitioners develop and dedicate training resources at different stages. Additionally, sustained investment in quality management and market-based organisational capabilities will help firms achieve better client-fit outcomes. To manage growth and contain high employee turnover, HR and HRD practitioners need to invest in focused career-development programmes. The theoretical and policy argument of 'high-skill and high-wage route' to national competitiveness and prosperity is questionable as it ignores the impact that the abundant supply of relatively highly skilled resources has on 'high wages'. There is sufficient evidence from China and India's labour market that challenges such policy assumptions. A changing economic climate offers a rich opportunity to undertake future research that compares these factors in less munificent macro environments and to look for any rival explanations should the wider economic parameters of performance and trade continue to worsen. Although this study is set in the Indian cultural context, however, owing to the 'born global' nature of this industry, findings from this research can be tested following ex post facto designs in similar high growth and knowledge-intensive firms from different emerging markets.

References

Acemoglu, D., and Pischke, J.-S. (1998a). Why do firms train? Theory and evidence. *Quarterly Journal of Economics*, *113*(1), 79–119.

Acemoglu, D., and Pischke, J.-S. (1998b). Beyond Becker: Training in imperfect markets. *The Economic Journal*, *109*(453), 112–142.

Argyris, C., and Schön, D.A. (1978). *Organizational learning: A theory of action perspective*. Reading, MA: Addison-Wesley.

Arora, A., Arunachalam, V.S., Asundi, J.V., and Fernandes, R. (2001). The Indian software services industry. *Research Policy*, *30*(8), 1267–1287.

Ashcraft, K., Labianca, G., Lepak, D., Okhuysen, G., Smith, V., and Steensma, K. (2011). Theories of work and working today: Special topic forum. *Academy of Management Review*, *36*(2), 432–435.

Ashton, D., and Sung, J. (2006). *How competitive strategy matters? Understanding the drivers of training, learning and performance at the firm level*. Research Paper No. 66. Oxford: Oxford and Warwick Universities, Centre for Skills, Knowledge and Organisational Performance.

Athreye, A. (2004). 'The role of transnational corporations in the evolution of a high-tech industry: The case of India's software industry' – A comment. *World Development*, *32*(3), 555–560.

Athreye, A. (2005). The Indian software industry and its evolving service capability. *Industrial and Corporate Change*, *14*(3), 393–418.

Banerjee, P. (2004). *The Indian software industry: Business strategy and dynamic co-ordination*. New Delhi: Palgrave Macmillan.

Bartel, A.P., and Lichtenberg, F.R. (1987). The comparative advantage of educated workers in implementing new technology. *The Review of Economics and Statistics*, *69*(1), 1–11.

Becker, B.E., and Huselid, M.A. (1998). High performance work systems and firm performance: A synthesis of research and managerial implications. *Research in Personnel and Human Resource Management*, *16*, 53–101.

Becker, G. (1962). Investment in human capital: A theoretical analysis Part 2 – Investment in human beings. *Journal of Political Economy*, *70*(5), 9–49.

Beugelsdijk, S. (2008). Strategic human resource practices and product innovation. *Organisation Studies*, *29*(6), 821–847.

Boon, C. (2008). HRM and Fit: Survival of the fittest!? Unpublished dissertation, Rotterdam: Erasmus Research Institute for Management (ERIM).

Boselie, P. (2010). *Strategic human resource management: A balanced approach*. Maidenhead: McGraw-Hill.

Boxall, P. (2003). HR strategy and competitive advantage in the service sector. *Human Resource Management Journal*, *13*(3), 5–20.

Bruche, G. (2009). The emergence of China and India as new competitors in MNCs' innovation networks. *Competition & Change*, *13*(3), 267–288.

Ceylan, C. (2012). Commitment-based HR practices, different types of innovation activities and firm innovation performance. *The International Journal of Human Resource Management*, *24*(1), 208–226.

Coad, A., and Rao, R. (2008). Innovation and growth in high-tech sectors. *Research Policy*, *37*(4), 633–648.

Dawe, S. (2003). *Determinants of successful training practices in large Australian firms.* Leabrook, SA: NCVER.

de Menezes, L.M., and Wood, S. (2006). The reality of flexible work systems in Britain. *International Journal of Human Resource Management, 17*(1), 106–138.

Deephouse, D.L. (1999). To be different, or to be the same? It's a question (and theory) of strategic balance. *Strategic Management Journal, 20*(2), 147–66.

Dossani, R. (2005). *Origins and growth of the software industry in India.* Working paper. Palo Alto, CA: Stanford University, Asia-Pacific Research Center.

Dostie, B., and Montmarquette, C. (2007). *Employer sponsored training in Canada: Synthesis of using data from the workplace and employee survey.* Quebec: Human Resources and Social Development Canada.

Economic Times. (2007, March). $2bn spent for IT/ITeS Co's on training in '07. Formerly available at www.economictimes.com

Eisenhardt, K.M. (1989). Building theories from case study research. *Academy of Management Review, 14*(4), 532–550.

Ethiraj, S.E., Kale, P., Krishnan, M.S., and Singh, J.V. (2005). Where do capabilities come from and how do they matter? A study in the software services industry. *Strategic Management Journal, 26*(1), 25–45.

Garvin, D.A. (1993). Building a learning organization. *Harvard Business Review, 71*(4), 53–58.

Green, F., Mayhew, K., and Molloy, E. (2003). *Employers' perspectives survey, 2000.* Sheffield: Department for Education and Skills.

Gupta, A.K., and Singhal, A. (1993). Managing human resources for innovation and creativity. *Research Technology Management, 36*(3), 41–48.

Harter, D.E., Krishnan, M.S., and Slaughter, S.A. (2000). Effects of process maturity on quality, cycle time and effort in software development. *Management Science, 46*(4), 451–467.

Heeks, R. (1998). *The uneven profile of Indian software exports.* Development Informatics Paper No. 3. Manchester, England: University of Manchester, IDPM. Retrieved from www.sed.manchester.ac.uk/idpm/research/publications/wp/di/ di_wp03.htm

Hoyt, D., and Rao, H. (2007). Infosys: Building a talent engine to sustain growth. Case no. HR-30, Stanford Graduate School of Business, Stanford, CA.

Immelt, J.R., Govindarajan, V., and Trimble, C. (2009). How GE is disrupting itself. *Harvard Business Review, 87*(10), 55–65.

Jain, H., Mathew, M., and Bedi, A. (2012). HRM innovations by Indian and Foreign MNCs operating in India: A survey of HR professionals. *The International Journal of Human Resource Management, 23*(5), 1006–1018.

Jiménez-Jiménez, A., and Sanz-Valle, R. (2008). Could HRM support organizational innovation? *The International Journal of Human Resource Management, 19*(7), 1208–1221.

Kanter, R. (1985). Supporting innovation and venture development in established companies, *Journal of Business Venturing, 1*(1), 47–60.

Kohli, A.K., Jaworski, B.J., and Kumar, A. (1993). MARKOR: A measure of market orientation. *Journal of Marketing Research, 30*(4), 467–477.

Krishnan, M.S., Kriebel, C.H., Kekre, S., and Mukhopadhyay, T. (2000). An empirical analysis of productivity and quality in software products. *Management Science, 46*(6), 745–759.

Lado, A.A., and Wilson, M.C. (1994). Human resource systems and sustained competitive advantage: A competency-based perspective. *Academy of Management Review, 19*(4), 699–727.

Laursen, K., and Foss, N.J. (2003). New human resource management practices: Complementarities and the impact on innovation performance. *Cambridge Journal of Economics, 27*(2), 243–263.

MacDuffie, J. (1995). Human resource bundles and manufacturing performance: Organizational logic and flexible production systems in the world auto industry. *Industrial and Labor Relations Review, 48*(2), 197–221.

Malik, A. (2009). Training drivers, competitive strategy and clients' needs: Case studies of three business process outsourcing organisations. *Journal of European Industrial Training, 33*(2), 160–177.

Malik, A., and Blumenfeld, S. (2012). Six Sigma, quality management systems and the development of organisational learning capability: Evidence from four business process outsourcing organisations in India. *International Journal of Quality & Reliability Management, 29*(1), 71–91.

Malik, A., Sinha, A., and Blumenfeld, S. (2012). Role of quality management capabilities in developing market-based organisational learning capabilities: Case study evidence from four Indian business process outsourcing firms. *Industrial Marketing Management, 41*(4), 639–648.

Mark, S.K.M., and Akhtar, S. (2003). Human resource management practices, strategic orientations, and company performance: A correlation study of publicly listed companies, *Journal of American Academy of Business, 2*(2), 510–515.

Mason, G. (2004). *Enterprise product strategies and employer demand for skills in Britain: Evidence from the employers' skill surveys.* SKOPE Working Paper No. 50. Warwick: University of Warwick.

Miles, B.M., and Huberman, A. M. (1994). *Qualitative data analysis: An expanded sourcebook* (2nd ed.). Thousand Oaks, CA: Sage.

Mudambi, R. (2008). Location, control, and innovation in knowledge-intensive industries. *Journal of Economic Geography, 8*(5), 699–725.

Mumford, M.D. (2000). Managing creative people: Strategies and tactics for innovation. *Human Resource Management Review, 10*(3), 313–351.

Narayanan, R., and Neethi, S. (2005). Creating human resources for information technology: A systemic study. Report submitted to NASSCOM IT Workforce Development Group, Version 2. Trivandrum: Tata Consultancy Services.

Narver, J.C., and Slater, S.F. (1990). The effect of a market orientation on business profitability. *Journal of Marketing, 54*(4), 20–35.

NASSCOM. (2014). *India IT-BPM Overview.* Retrieved from www.nasscom.in/indian-itbpo-industry

Nilakant, V. (2005, August). *Institutional dynamics in the evolution of the Indian software industry.* Paper presented at the Academy of Management Conference, Hawaii, USA.

Paauwe, J. (2004). *HRM and performance: Achieving long term viability.* Oxford: Oxford University Press.

Parzinger, M. (1997). A stage-wise application of total quality management through the product life cycle. *Industrial Management & Data Systems, 97*(3), 125–130.

Patibandla, M., and Petersen, B. (2002). Role of transnational corporations in the evolution of a high-tech industry: The case of India's software industry. *World Development, 30*(9), 1561–1577.

Paul, A.K., and Anantharaman, R.N. (2004). Influence of HRM practices on organizational commitment: A study among software professionals in India. *Human Resource Development Quarterly, 15*(1), 77–88.

Pettigrew, A., Sparrow, P., and Hendry, C. (1988). The forces that trigger training. *Personnel Management, 20*(12), 28–32.

Pfeffer, J. (1998). *The human equation: Building profits by putting people first*. Boston, MA: Harvard Business School Press.

Prajogo, D. I. (2007). The relationship between competitive strategies and product quality. *Industrial Management & Data Systems, 107*(1), 69–83.

Prajogo, D.I., and Ahmed, P. (2006). Relationships between innovation stimulus, innovation capacity, and innovation performance, *R&D Management, 36*(5), 499–515.

Prajogo, D.I., and Brown, A. (2004). The relationship between TQM practices and quality performance and the role of formal TQM programs: An Australian empirical study. *The Quality Management Journal, 11*(4), 31–42.

Purkayastha, D., and Fernando, R. (2007). *Some HR dilemmas in information technology and business process outsourcing firms. Case no. 407-080-1*. Hyderabad: ICFAI Centre for Management Research.

Rao, T.V., and Abraham, E. (1986). HRD practices in Indian industries: A trend report. *Management and Labour Studies, 11*(2), 73–85.

Reed, R., Lemak, D.J., and Mero, N.P. (2000). Total quality management and sustainable competitive advantage. *Journal of Quality Management, 5*(1), 5–26.

Ridoutt, L., Dutneall, R., Hummel, K., and Smith, C.S. (2002). *Factors influencing training and learning in the workplace*. Leabrook, SA: NCVER.

Schuler, R.S., and Jackson, S.E. (1987). Linking competitive strategies with human resource management practices. *Academy of Management Executive, 1*(3), 207–219.

Shipton, H., West, M., Dawson, J., Birdi, K., and Patterson, M. (2006). HRM as a predictor of innovation. *Human Resource Management, 16*(1), 3–27.

Sinkula, J.M., Baker, W.E., and Noordeweir, T. (1997). A framework for market-based organisational learning: Linking values, knowledge, and behaviour. *Journal of the Academy of Marketing Science, 25*(4), 305–318.

Sitkin, S.B., Sutcliffe, K.M., and Schroeder, R.G. (1994). Distinguishing control from learning in total quality management: A contingency perspective. *Academy of Management Review, 19*(3), 537–564.

Smith, A., and Dowling, P.J. (2001). Analysing firm training: Five propositions for future research. *Human Resource Development Quarterly, 12*(2), 147–167.

Smith, A., and Hayton, G. (1999). What drives enterprise training? Evidence from Australia. *The International Journal of Human Resource Management, 10*(2), 251–272.

Smith, A., Oczkowski, E., Noble, C., and Macklin, R. (2004). The impact of organisational change on the nature and extent of training in Australian enterprises. *International Journal of Training and Development, 8*(2), 2–15.

Stewart, G., and Brown, K. (2009). *Human resource management: Linking strategy to practice*. Hoboken, NJ: John Wiley & Sons.

Storey, J., Quintas, P., Taylor, P., and Fowle, W. (2002). Flexible employment contracts and their implications for product and process innovation. *International Journal of Human Resource Management, 13*(1), 1–18.

Wadhwa, V., de Vitton, U.K., and Gereffi, G. (2008). *How the disciple became the guru: Is it time for the US to learn workforce development from former disciple India?* Working Paper. Retrieved from www.kauffman.org/uploadedFiles/disciple_became_guru_080608.pdf

Watkins, K., and Marsick, V. (1992). Towards a theory of informal and incidental learning in organisations. *International Journal of Lifelong Education, 11*(2), 287–300.

Wozniak, G. (1984). The adoption of interrelated innovations: A human capital approach. *The Review of Economics and Statistics, 66*(1), 70–79.

Wozniak, G. (1987). Human capital formation and the early adoption of technology. *Journal of Human Resources, 22*(1), 101–112.

Yadapadithaya, P.S. (2001). Evaluating corporate training and development: An Indian experience. *International Journal of Training and Development, 5*(4), 261–274.

Yin, R.K. (2003). *Case study research: Design and methods* (3rd ed.). Thousand Oaks, CA: Sage.

7 Innovative people management approaches from three software research and product development firms

Ashish Malik

Introduction

In geographically dispersed networks, of which the offshore information technology (IT) service provision is a major part, integration and transfer of knowledge between users of a software product and the software development firm is critical to service delivery. In such offshore outsourcing IT firms, co-development of software work is carried out across borders and time zones leveraging the strengths of each co-development team. It is critical, therefore, to understand how the skills and human capital development formation occurs across co-development teams. The need to understand this is further accentuated by the inattention to skills development issues in the sector (Githens, Dirani, Gitonga and Teng, 2008; Lacity, Khan, Yan and Willcocks, 2010; Lacity, Solomon, Yan and Willcocks, 2011). Despite the timely contributions to the burgeoning body of knowledge on human resource (HR) and management practices in Indian firms, a quick review of special issues of *Human Resource Management* (2010), *International Journal of Human Resource Management* (2012), *Journal of International Business Studies* (2009), *Journal of Management Studies* (2010) and *Journal of World Business* (2012) reveals that little attention has been devoted to the mechanisms of skill formation in the Indian IT offshoring/outsourcing industry.

Research on human capital formation suggests that improvement in skill development and learning at a national level can be achieved by organisational-level training provision (Cappelli, 1994; Porter, Schwab, Sala-i-Martin and Lopez-Claros, 2004). The relevance of HRM and skills development, therefore, needs to be understood in the context of where skills are applied, that is, in the organisation. An increasing body of literature is highlighting the need to look at the 'soft' HRM aspects of technology and software product development, including aspects such as culture, change and learning rather than the 'hard' planning and technological factors (Heaton, 1998; Jenkin and Chan, 2010). Organisations engaged in software and IT product development are not only the end users of skills, but they also exercise strategic choices with regards to skills development (Kochan, McKersie and Cappelli, 1984).

The notion of strategic choice (Child, 1972; Kochan et al., 1984) is extremely relevant here as firms in the offshore IT outsourcing services sector have to balance the tensions between the key groups of dominant stakeholders such as the client, offshore product development subsidiary or provider and/or the parent organisation. It is through the interactions between the contractual and relational arrangements of key stakeholder groups that co-development of software and product development occurs. There has been a slow but steady stream of studies analysing the influence of client firms on the supplier firms' HRM practices covering a range of businesses from small and medium enterprises in manufacturing sectors (Rainnie, 1989; Valmasakis and Sprague, 2001), for example, to knowledge intensive services firms such as IT outsourcing services (Grimshaw and Miozzo, 2006, 2009; Swart and Kinnie, 2003).

While there is strong evidence of both direct and indirect forms of influence by client firms on supplier firms (Beaumont, Hunter and Sinclair, 1996), some researchers have highlighted the increasing role of the client's power (Harvard, Rorive and Sobczack, 2009) in shaping the HR practices of supplier firms. Still others have highlighted the need to reconceptualise the traditional concepts of 'actors in an industrial relations system' and rethink 'strategic choice' in these relationships by including clients and dispersed work teams as new actors in this new system of employment relations (Legault and Bellemare, 2008). To this end, this chapter argues that there exists negotiation between different stakeholder groups in determining an appropriate set of innovative HRM practices for carrying out outsourced/offshored IT and software development work. With this in mind, this chapter aims to answer the following research questions:

1   What are the key innovative HRM practices employed by software product development firms in India?
2   What are the key factors that impact on the development of these HRM practices?

The rest of the chapter is organised as follows. First, a brief review of India's software product development, research and design development sector is offered. Second, the theoretical framing employed by the chapter relevant for product development environment is presented. This is followed by the methodological and analytical strategies, discussion and conclusion.

The Indian IT sector

With revenues exceeding US$118 billion, the Indian IT industry has continued to post sustainable growth since the last three decades (NASSCOM, 2014a). Of the above revenues about US$31 billion (26%) are from software product development (15% or US$18 billion) and IT hardware products (11% or US$13 billion) and bulk of the above revenues are still from exports (NASSCOM, 2014a). Ethiraj, Kale, Krishnan and Sing's (2005) finding of the Indian IT industry's structure suggests that less than 1% of the total firms in the sector control close to 60% of the revenue are highly relevant. Even with the maturing of the sector, the above statistic of industry concentration has not changed much, though the concentration profile of firms by revenue has shifted a bit. For example, in terms of the industry's revenues, 11 large IT firms account for 40%, between 120–150 mid-sized IT firms account for 35%–40%, between 1,000–1,200 firms account for 10% and about 15,000 IT firms account for another 10% of the sector's revenues (NASSCOM, 2014a). Additionally, the increasing population of start-ups is unevenly distributed between software services, BPO and product development firms.

Within the engineering research and design product development firms, close to 50% of the revenues are from the semiconductor and telecommunications industry (NASSCOM, 2014b). The growth in software product development firms has been comparatively slow at about 8.8% and is mainly in the areas of enterprise applications, custom development, communication and collaboration, enterprise mobility solutions and research analytics (NASSCOM, 2014c). Nevertheless, there is an increasing level of trust in the product co-development and end-to-end development activities. A number of global IT product development firms are also testing the beta versions of their products in the Indian domestic markets before globally launching them (NASSCOM, 2014c). The Indian IT industry currently employs about 3.1 million people and is estimated to add another 166,000 employees in 2014 (NASSCOM, 2014d).

Literature review

Chapter 6 highlighted the role of work design and skills as key HRM practices that affect Indian ITSS firms' innovative capacity (Beugelsdijk, 2008; Ceylan, 2012; Jain, Mathew and Bedi, 2012; Laursen and Foss, 2003; Mark and Akhtar, 2003; Prajogo and Ahmed, 2006; Shipton, West, Dawson, Birdi and Patterson, 2006). Building on this aspect and employing a resource-based view (RBV) of the firm (Barney, 1991; Wright and McMahan, 2011; Wright, Dunford and Snell, 2001), the following section begins by reviewing the key theoretical arguments of the RBV and then provides a short review of the key factors affecting training provision in organisations. As product development often requires a collaborative approach, a brief review of literature on market-based organisational learning and quality management capabilities is offered.

Resource-based view

According to RBV theory, firms can be viewed as a collection of bundles of resources, wherein, if such resources (human resources or otherwise) are valuable, rare, inimitable and are organised in such a manner that is difficult for competitors to replicate, they can provide a source of sustained competitive advantage to the firms that semi-permanently control such resources (Barney, 1991; Wright et al., 2001). Boxall (1996, 1998) further argues that firms can achieve human resource advantage by making sustained investments in human capital and supporting human resource processes. These theoretical arguments were extended by Lepak and Snell (1999), wherein the authors presented four

HRM architectures of different configurations of internalising or externalising investments in human capital and processes by the firm. Depending on the strategic environment and the orientation of the firm in question they may choose a single, or a combination of one or more configurations to suit their business needs.

The above highlights the importance of human capital development at an organisational level. In a similar vein, a number of studies have found that for improving competitiveness, reducing unemployment and developing organisational capabilities for sustained competitive advantage, human capital holds the key (Felstead and Green, 1994; Pfeffer, 1998; Ployhart and Moliterno, 2011; Ployhart, Iddekinge and MacKenzie, 2011; Teece, Pisano and Shuen, 1997; Wright and McMahan, 2011). Despite the above, the debate over the relevance of knowledge, skills and abilities within policymaking circles and the academic and business communities continues (Felstead, Gallie and Green, 2002; Keep, 1999).

Factors affecting training provision

Numerous factors have been identified that influence provision of training in an organisational setting (Dostie and Montmarquette, 2007; Pettigrew, Sparrow and Hendry, 1988; Ridoutt, Dutneall, Hummel and Smith, 2002; Smith and Hayton, 1999; Smith, Oczkowski, Noble and Macklin, 2004). These studies reveal that research has, for the most part, focused on stakeholders within the organisation and thus have an *inward-looking* approach instead of adopting an *outward-looking* approach, which would also account for the influence of a firm's customers/clients on training provision (Bing, Kehrhahn and Short, 2003; Leimbach and Baldwin, 1997; Short, 2006).

At a macro-level, most studies on employer-funded training are often commissioned to address education and training policy issues. Finegold and Soskice (1988), for example, considered why the national skills and training systems had failed to raise the level of education and training of the British workforce to levels achieved by its international competitors. Smith and Hayton (1999) sought to clarify and demystify the low level of training provision by Australian firms. New Zealand scholars examined the *drivers* and *barriers* to training at the individual and organisational level (Blumenfeld and Malik, 2007; Bryson and O'Neil, 2008).

Evident in the above training demand models is extensive reliance on individual-level explanations and adherence to the predictions of human capital theory (Becker, 1962) or new technology-based human capital explanations (Acemoglu and Pischke, 1998a, 1998b; Bartel and Lichtenberg, 1987; Sparrow and Pettigrew, 1985; OECD/CERI, 1986, 1988; Wozniak, 1984, 1987).

While the above are useful theoretical lenses to understand how and why firms invest in training, the RBV relies extensively on the 'stickiness' of the organisational routines and the processes that embed and institutionalise learning in unique and inimitable ways to create barriers for replication. This is particularly relevant in product and R&D (research and development) firms as these firms are engaged in developing new products and intellectual property (IP) that needs heterogeneous resources and idiosyncratic modes of production to protect imitation. In some cases, firms have to access specialist knowledge from their external networks of clients and suppliers. To this end, this chapter considers the role of market-based learning (Sinkula, Baker and Noordeweir, 1997) and quality management capabilities (Malik, Sinha and Blumenfeld, 2012; Prajogo and Brown, 2004) as the former explains how an organisation can learn and share information and knowledge from external and internal sources and the latter allows for appropriate mechanisms for standardising and institutionalising organisation-specific developmental methodologies.

Methodology

An underdeveloped phenomenon, a relatively new industry and developing country context, and the complex nature of organisational decision-making makes qualitative case study methodology an appropriate choice (Eisenhardt, 1989; Yin, 2003). Case-study researchers emphasise that having a priori constructs and theoretical underpinning helps in shaping the focus of a study and enhancing the construct validity (Eisenhardt, 1989; Miles and Huberman, 1994; Yin, 2003). Following Yin, a multi-case site selection should aim at either a literal replication (one that predicts similar results) or a theoretical replication (one that predicts rival results but for understandable and predicted reasons).

The focus on software and IT product development firms reduces extraneous variation that may occur by researching firms from different sectors. Selecting organisations from a single industry sub-sector also assists in better cross-case comparisons and helps improve construct and external validity. A maximum variation purposive sampling (Eisenhardt, 1989; Miles and Huberman, 1994; Yin, 2003) was followed to observe the phenomenon in a diverse group of cases. Case selection criteria were developed using extant literature on enterprise training (Ridoutt et al., 2002; Smith et al., 2004), the structure of the Indian IT industry (Ethiraj et al., 2005; Heeks, 1998) and by following the NASSCOM's directory of IT and software product, design and development providers. In order to reduce single respondent bias, 20 respondents from functional responsibilities such as CEOs or country heads, HR managers, training managers, project or product managers, project or product employees and quality managers (see Table 7.1 for details) were interviewed following a semi-structured approach for a duration of 90–120 minutes.

Table 7.1 Key informants

Case organisations	CEO/ country manager	HR manager	T&D manager	Project manager	Quality manager	Employees	Business development manager	Total
PRODSERV 1		1	1	3	1			6
PRODSERV 2		2	1	1	1	1		6
PRODSERV 3	1	2		3		2		8
Total	1	5	2	7	2	3	0	20

Three case organisations from the software product development sector were selected based on (1) enterprise size, expressed in terms of employee headcount: medium (151–1,000), large (1,001–3,000) and very large (more than 3,000) organisations; (2) ownership: MNC and Indian; (3) the nature of product-market strategy: slightly differentiated and highly differentiated and specialised services. To maintain the study's reliability, a case study protocol containing semi-structured questions was developed after feedback from academic colleagues researching in similar areas. To ensure organisational confidentiality, pseudonyms are used and enterprise size has been rounded off. Firms are labelled as PRODSERV 1, 2 and 3. Of the three firms covered in this chapter, one firm, PRODSERV 1, also had a large IT software services business line. Descriptive details of the case organisations is provided in Table 7.2.

Analysis

Individual within-case reports were sent to organisations for their validation and any feedback. Numerous analytic strategies such as pattern matching and explanation building were employed. Miles and Huberman's (1984) suggestion of the use of visual displays and matrices (see Tables 7.1–7.3 and Figures 7.1–7.5) helped in strengthening the visualisation and validity of the data analysis. Analysis of the interview data points to three key innovative HRM practices employed by these firms to effectively deal with issues of exploration and exploitation of knowledge and resources. These are: work design; differentiated recruitment and selection; and learning and development approaches. The analysis and findings further suggest there were significant differences in the way each firm applied these HRM practices. While strategic orientation is critical in deciding the nature and extent of the role a firm's HRM practices may play in its production function, the final HRM practices were shaped by a range of internal and external influences. To this end, the analysis discusses how internal and external influences variously shaped the design and implementation of these HRM practices.

Work design and planning

A short discussion was provided in Chapter 2 (see Figure 2.1) of the typical steps involved in a software product development cycle. Typically, such an approach follows a set pattern of work activities that need to be carried out with strict adherence to best practice software development protocols and requires discipline to deliver timely and error-free staged deliverables at each stage of the development cycle. As in software development, the development cycle for semiconductor and integrated circuits also follows strict tollgates but is far more complex than developing software applications. It requires exacting standards of performance and verification at each of the following stages: system specification, architecture design, several design stages (e.g. functional, logic, etc.), physical verification, fabrication and then the chip manufacture stage. PRODSERV 1

Table 7.2 Case description and impact of key factors on training provision

Case organisations *Case description and impact of key factors on training*	PRODSERV 1	PRODSERV 2	PRODSERV 3
Ownership	Indian	MNC	MNC
Business model	Mostly third party	MNC subsidiary	MNC subsidiary
Nature of services and product-market strategy	Highly differentiated	Highly differentiated	Slightly differentiated
Number of employees (rounded)	40,000+	2,700+	150+
Industries served[1]	Automobiles, telecom, health, BFSI, defence, aerospace and education	Software solutions, mobile and semiconductor	Health
Key business lines[2]	Software products, AMS, BPO, consulting, reengineering, testing, product engineering and IT infrastructure	Microprocessor products	Health services, ERP product
Workplace change *(structural, ownership and technology)*	H, M, H[3]	H	L, H, H
Market orientation *(information sensing, dissemination and organisational response)*	H	M	M–H
Learning orientation *(commitment to learning, open-mindedness and shared vision)*	H	H	L
Quality management systems *(commitment, sharing information, continuous improvement and teamwork)*	H	H	M
Employee turnover	H	M–L	H
Enterprise size	H	H	M
Strategic HRM approach • *rewards and performance management systems* • *career planning* • *recruitment skills level and operating role* • *use of non-standard employment*	H H H L	H M–H M L	H L H N

Notes

1 BFSI: Banking, financial services and insurance; SAP: SAP is an integrated enterprise resource planning (ERP) software product developed by SAP-AG (Germany).

2 AMS: Application management and development services; ERP: Enterprise resource planning software; CRM: Client/customer relationship management.

3 H = High, M = Medium, L = Low, N = None, M–H = Medium to High, M–L = Medium to Low.

and 3 fall in the first category, software product development, whereas PROD-SERV 2 falls in the second category of semiconductor research and design and it requires exercise of high levels of control over the work activities.

In terms of similarities, PRODSERV 1 and 3 exercised high levels of control over the work design and activities of its engineers, whereas in the case of PRODSERV 2, given the extremely high levels of task complexity and technical skills needed for working in the semiconductor market, it realised that a control-oriented design was not conducive to innovative product development. As such, PRODSERV 2 allowed some leeway for experimentation and exploration of new ideas and knowledge through internal and external mechanisms. This does not suggest that PRODSERV 2's employees had extremely high levels of empower-ment and flexibility in scheduling their work tasks and activities. Rather, the nature of flexibility provided to employees was thoroughly tested in terms of improvements in the functionality and overall efficiency of the product's design. In instances where benefits realisation from new ideas was low, the dominant best practice and pre-decided workflow prevailed. The levels of product com-plexity and its impact on training seemed to be positively associated (see Figure 7.1). PRODSERV 2 limited provision of formal training to its employees; this can be explained by the standardised nature of work tasks it received from its US parent and an extensive reliance on informal learning, coaching and mentoring by senior developers.

Table 7.3 Nature and extent of training

	PRODSERV 1	PRODSERV 2	PRODSERV 3
Training characteristics			
Extent (volume)			
1 Induction (weeks)	15	2–4	2
2 Product/project specific (weeks)	2–3	4–6	1
3 MDP[1] (weeks)	2	2	0
4 Total (weeks)	19–20	8–12	3
5 Classification	H[2]	H	L
6 Expected annual training (for all staff, post-induction)	80 hours	80 hours	Need based
Training characteristics			
Nature (diversity)			
1 Internal resources	H	H–Mix (50%) each	M–H
2 External resources	L	M–H	L
3 Formalisation (assessment)	H	H	H
4 Delivery (formal/informal)	Mix	Mix	More informal
Training type:			
• Technical (%)	85–90	80	90
• Behavioural (%)	10–15	20	10

Notes
1 MDP = Management development programmes.
2 H = High, M = Medium, L = Low, N = None, M–H = Medium to High, M–L = Medium to Low.

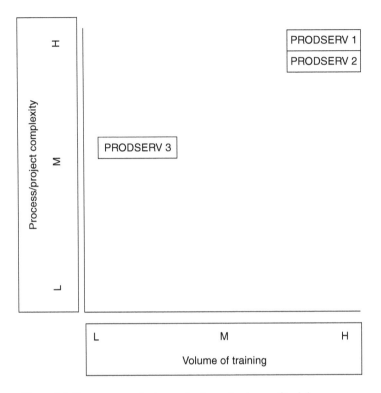

Figure 7.1 Process or project complexity and volume of training.

What appears from the above is that the parent organisations exercised excessive control over the subsidiaries' work scheduling. The parent firm's extensive forward planning of staged rollouts of new products and product enhancements was evident in the cases of both PRODSERV 2 and 3. Although none of firms had any accredited quality management frameworks, they all had developed their own 'proprietary' internal quality management processes, idiosyncratic development standards and 'best practices' to suit their own internal product environments (see Figure 7.2 for strength of quality management capabilities). For example, PRODSERV 2, a global market leader in the semiconductor market, had a set of global best practices as well as product development protocols that are considered as benchmarks by other chip manufacturers.

In the case of PRODSERV 1, the Indian MNC, although it had limited problems of inter-unit coordination in control of workflow, had significant influence from employees and customers in terms of suggestions for new product customisations and enhancements in product functionality. Each opportunity for expanding the product functionality was critically reviewed by the core product development team. Only where the changes enhanced the overall functioning of a product, did not compromise the product's functionality, and made it more

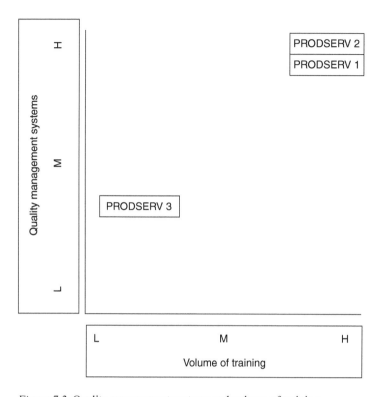

Figure 7.2 Quality management systems and volume of training.

efficient, only then were such changes allowed. In the case of significant changes, which usually resulted in additional resourcing decisions and acquisition of new skills and competencies, such decisions were evaluated based on potential benefits resulting from such changes. Thus, the workflow and planning was influenced by a number of internal (subsidiary and parent nation's employees) and external (clients and end users) stakeholders.

Differentiated recruitment and selection

While both PRODSERV 1 and 2 had developed highly formalised HRM processes for recruitment and selection, the actual emphasis on the levels and types of human capital varied significantly between the two firms. For example, PRODSERV 1, which sold enterprise software applications for the banking industry, relied extensively on recruiting large proportions of recent graduate engineers (up to 60%–70% of the total workforce) with up to two years of experience. High levels of entry-level hiring in the overall workforce composition helped PRODSERV 1 keep its costs down and it was able to reap benefits from the extensive investments it had made in its learning and development infrastructure.

PRODSERV 2 on the other hand needed high-end semiconductor and embedded chip design skill sets from the Indian labour market. Even though it relied on recruiting only computer science graduates from premier engineering institutes in India, its overall composition of recent college graduates was only 20%–25% of the total workforce due to poor skill matches (see Figure 7.3 for hiring strategy of these firms). The rest of its needs were met by poaching highly experienced engineers in this domain from the domestic and international labour markets. Its parent firm in the US, on the contrary, employed close to 70% of its workforce as recent college graduates, which is a reflection of the quality of the technology ecosystem in Silicon Valley and availability of large pools of engineers specialising in the semiconductor and embedded design technology segments. In terms of similarity, both PRODSERV 1 and 2 employed the extensive use of highly formalised screening processes to shortlist the right type of people needed for operating in a product and R&D environment. An extensive emphasis was placed on the right aptitude of independent problem-solving and the ability to think outside the box for developing innovative chips for various market segments such as enterprise, desktop, mobility and R&D.

PRODSERV 3, on the other hand, being a relatively smaller firm, had an extremely small HRM function (one HR manager), yet the level of formalisation

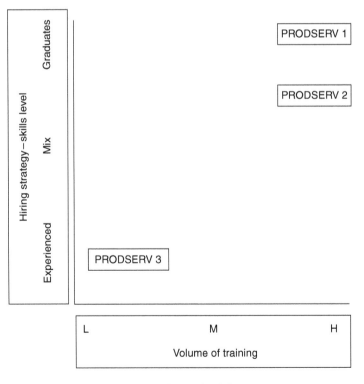

Figure 7.3 Hiring strategy and volume of training.

of its recruitment and selection practices was very high. PRODSERV 3 focused on hiring people with certain psychological traits using psychometric tools such as DISC profiling (*dominance, influence, steady* and *compliance*). Despite being an innovative product-development firm developing software products for the health-care sector, PRODSERV 3 selected employees who were high on *compliance* and *steadiness* scores and low on *influence* and *dominance* scores. The rationale behind such an approach was partly due to the nature of work sent to India and partly to exploit the existing product functionalities of its hospital enterprise resource-planning software product to promote structured and only incremental and disciplined suggestions. Employing staff who were too creative and dominating could potentially prove to be too risky as people with such personality types may adversely impact the core architecture of the product. Like PRODSERV 1, it trialled employing a significant proportion of its workforce from recent college graduates, but given the nature of high levels of skills needed and a very control-oriented work environment, this strategy did not deliver.

Learning and development

Relative to PRODSERV 3, PRODSERV 1 and 2 provided high levels of investment in formal training and mandated hours of annual training for ongoing employees (see Table 7.2 for details). The vast majority of training in all organisations was technical and project-specific. All the firms relied extensively on their in-house product manuals and directories for providing formal training to its recent college graduates. Although there were formal assessment tests undertaken by all three firms to assess employees' technical proficiency and understanding of key product functionalities, ongoing learning and development was delivered using a combination of formal and informal learning approaches. As such, PRODSERV 1 and 2 and to an even greater extent PRODSERV 3 relied on informal and incidental learning approaches such as learning by doing, learning through coaching and mentoring, and trialling parallel or dummy product development projects. Such an approach to learning can be largely attributed to the nature of the work and the need to protect the proprietary nature of product knowledge. Additionally, there was an expectation from employees working in product development firms to demonstrate independent problem-solving and self-directed learning skills, which is a critical skill for developing new products and bringing about product or architectural innovations.

Despite these similarities, there were remarkable differences in the extent to which the firms undertook exploratory or exploitative learning. PRODSERV 2 was the only organisation that encouraged *genuine* exploratory learning. The others focused more on exploiting their established product strengths and were reluctant to allow employees a free hand to tinker with the main product architecture. As noted above, PRODSERV 3's work design, product complexity, recruitment and selection approaches suggest that it allowed limited opportunities for exploratory learning as it received pre-specified development work from its US parent as part of its co-product-development methodologies. There were differences in the volume of training between firms owing predominantly to a 'make' strategy (PRODSERV 1 and 2) and a 'buy' (PRODSERV 3) strategy. PRODSERV 1 and 2's high levels of graduate hiring was complemented by their investments in learning and development. PRODSERV 1 and 2 allowed their employees to engage in higher levels of learning orientation (see Figure 7.4).

Because product firms had a product superiority mindset and were market leaders in their area of specialisation, none of the firms had high levels of market orientation. In particular, PRODSERV 2, being an undisputed market leader, had a medium level of market orientation. PRODSERV 1 and 3 still needed medium to high levels of market orientation as their software products needed customisation and post-sales installation support at the clients' locations (see Figure 7.5).

Moreover, the changing customer preferences meant that they had to reinvent their business logic and develop better market-information processing and dissemination capabilities. For example, at PRODSERV 3, the hospital operating room software application often needed interfaces with multiple hardware products from medical equipment vendors such as Phillips, Siemens and GE. As such, the compatibility required multiple customisation jobs from its hospital clients, which meant all project change information needed to be disseminated back to the development teams. Domain knowledge of both medical

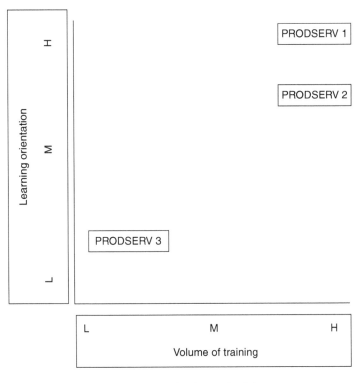

Figure 7.4 Learning orientation and volume of training.

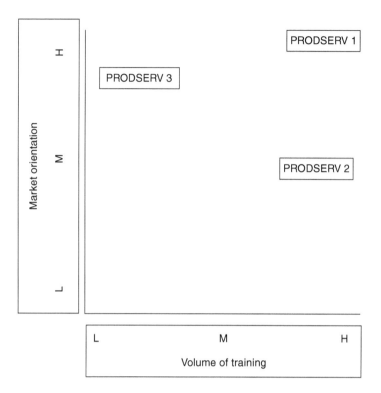

Figure 7.5 Market orientation and volume of training.

and health services was critical for employees to successfully execute such requests.

Discussion

The preceding analysis suggests that three key HRM practices – work design and planning, differentiated recruitment and selection strategy, and learning and development – are the key innovative HRM practices employed by IT product development firms and that these practices support organisational performance and growth. Barring PRODSERV 2, both of the other firms employed a control-oriented work design. All three firms employed differentiated recruitment and selection strategies and also completed this with the strength of the organisational learning and development capabilities. Further, in line with the extant training demand models (Dostie and Montmarquette, 2007; Smith and Hayton, 1999; Ridoutt et al., 2002), this study finds supports for some of the earlier relationships of technological change, product complexity, skills level and learning orientation and its impact on the extent and nature of training. Firms in this study measured training volume in terms of time spent on training (e.g. hours, weeks or days spent on training). This metric was particularly relevant as in the case of PRODSERV 1 and 3, clients' service level agreements required completion of 'training days' and 'formal assessments' for clients' employees. As a result, these firms needed to invest in some form of 'train the trainer' modules for imparting application training to their clients before the application was launched. This is a reflection of the nature of the clients' 'time and materials' service level agreements.

Similarly, the measures from the literature on the nature (diversity) of training arrangements, such as the extent to which firms relied on internal versus external, formalisation, assessment of training and the types of training (generic versus firm-specific or behavioural versus technical) offered, were problematic to operationalize in the Indian context. Client firms were provided with both forms of training and had an impact on the behavioural and technical skills training at both of these firms. A summary of the nature and extent of training provided by case organisations is presented in Table 7.2.

Investments in human capital were critical but, as mentioned earlier, for realising human resource advantage Boxall (1996, 1998) argues that it is how such resources are organised in a firm's production function that matters most. The unique organisation of internal and market-based learning capabilities (Malik et al., 2012; Sinkula et al., 1997) was critical in developing idiosyncratic routines. PRODSERV 2's unique routines for knowledge sharing and dissemination strategies to achieve skills development are examples of a RBV (Barney, 1991). For example, PRODSERV 2 used brown-bag lunch sessions, white paper competitions, peer review of new ideas, and other informal mechanisms of knowledge sharing and integration. In line with the tenets of the RBV, PRODSERV 2 also undertook high levels of customisations for implementing PeopleSoft's standard human resource information system, such that it changed each and every module of this application, thus making it extremely difficult and expensive for competitors to replicate. Given PRODSERV 2's focus in undertaking such high levels of customisation for its internal HR software, one can only imagine the extent of customisations and idiosyncratic design features it undertakes in designing and developing its semiconductor product markets.

Conclusion

The above discussion identifies a combination of control-, trust- and empowerment-oriented work design, long- to medium-term focus on human resource planning, differentiated recruitment and selection strategies, and embedding informal and incidental approaches to training and development in addition to the formal training approaches as the key HRM practices that HR managers must focus on for success in product and R&D firms. Additionally, the above analysis and discussion identified the range of internal and external influences that collectively shape the development of HRM practices. This has implications for how HR and business managers should engage with a range of stakeholders and actively pursue information-seeking behaviours for engaging in new learning from varied sources. Such an approach is highly desirable for the organisation's ability to simultaneously pursue exploration and exploitation of new and existing information.

References

Acemoglu, D., and Pischke, J.-S. (1998a). Why do firms train? Theory and evidence. *Quarterly Journal of Economics*, *113*(1), 79–119.

Acemoglu, D., and Pischke, J.-S. (1998b). Beyond Becker: Training in imperfect markets. *The Economic Journal*, *109*(453), 112–142.

Barney, J. (1991). Firm resources and sustained competitive advantage. *Journal of Management*, *17*(1), 99–120.

Bartel, A.P., and Lichtenberg, F.R. (1987). The comparative advantage of educated workers in implementing new technology. *The Review of Economics and Statistics*, *69*(1), 1–11.

Beaumont, P., Hunter, L., and Sinclair, D. (1996). Customer-supplier relations and the diffusion of employee relations changes. *Employee Relations*, *18*(1), 9–19.

Becker, G. (1962). Investment in human capital: A theoretical analysis Part 2 – Investment in human beings. *Journal of Political Economy*, *70*(5), 9–49.

Beugelsdijk, S. (2008). Strategic human resource practices and product innovation. *Organisation Studies*, *29*(6), 821–847.

Bing, J.W., Kehrhahn, M., and Short, D.C. (2003). Challenges to the field of human resources development. *Advances in Developing Human Resources*, *5*(3), 342–351.

Blumenfeld, S., and Malik, A. (2007). In through the out door: drivers of training supported by New Zealand organisations. *New Zealand Journal of Employment Relations*, *32*(1), 17–27.

Boxall, P. (1996). The Strategic HRM debate and the resource-based view of the firm. *Human Resource Management Journal*, *6*(3), 59–75.

Boxall, P. (1998). Achieving competitive advantage through human resource strategy: towards a theory of industry dynamics. *Human Resource Management Review*, *8*(3), 265–288.

Bryson, J., and O'Neil, P. (2008, May). *Developing human capability: Employment institutions, organisations and individuals*. Discussion Paper. Wellington: Industrial Relations Centre, Victoria University of Wellington.

Cappelli, P. (1994). *Training and development in public and private policy*. Brookfield, MA: Dartmouth.

Ceylan, C. (2012). Commitment-based HR practices, different types of innovation activities and firm innovation performance. *The International Journal of Human Resource Management*, *24*(1), 208–226.

Child, J. (1972). Organisational structure, environment and performance: The role of strategic choice. *Sociology*, *6*(3), 1–22.

Dostie, B., and Montmarquette, C. (2007). *Employer sponsored training in Canada: Synthesis of using data from the workplace and employee survey*. Quebec: Human Resources and Social Development Canada.

Eisenhardt, K.M. (1989). Building theories from case study research. *Academy of Management Review*, *14*(4), 532–550.

Ethiraj, S.E., Kale, P., Krishnan, M.S., and Singh, J.V. (2005). Where do capabilities come from and how do they matter? A study in the software services industry. *Strategic Management Journal*, *26*(1), 25–45.

Felstead, A., and Green, F. (1994). Cycles of training? Evidence from the British recession of the early 1990s. In A. Booth and D. Snower (Eds.), *The skills gap and economic activity*. Cambridge: Cambridge University Press.

Felstead, A., Gallie, D., and Green, F. (2002). *Work skills in Britain 1986–2001*. Nottingham: DfES.

Finegold, D., and Soskice, D. (1988). The failure of British training: Analysis and prescriptions. *Oxford Review of Economic Policy*, *4*(3), 21–53.

Githens, R.P., Dirani, K., Gitonga, J., and Teng, Y. (2008). Technology-related research in HRD publications: An analysis of content and metaperspectives from 2000 to 2006. *Human Resource Development Quarterly*, *19*(3), 191–216.

Grimshaw, D., and Miozzo, M. (2006). Institutional effects on the market of IT outsourcing: Analysing clients, suppliers, and staff transfer in Germany and the UK. *Organization Studies*, *27*(9), 1229–1259.

Grimshaw, D., and Miozzo, M. (2009). New human resource management practices in knowledge-intensive business service firms: The case of outsourcing with staff transfer. *Human Relations*, *62*(10), 1521–1550.

Harvard, C., Rorive, B., and Sobczack, A. (2009). Client, employer and employee: Mapping a complex triangulation. *European Journal of Industrial Relations*, *15*(3), 257–276.

Heaton, L. (1998). Talking heads vs. virtual workspaces: A comparison of design across cultures. *Journal of Information Technology*, *13*(4), 259–272.

Heeks, R. (1998). *The uneven profile of Indian software exports*. Development Informatics Paper No. 3. Manchester, England: University of Manchester, IDPM. Retrieved from www.sed.manchester.ac.uk/idpm/research/publications/wp/di/di_wp03.htm

Human Resource Management. (2010). Special Issue: Emerging patterns of HRM in the new Indian economic environment. *49*(3).

International Journal of Human Resource Management. (2012). Special Issue: Human resource management in the new economy in India. *23*(5).

Jain, H., Mathew, M., and Bedi, A. (2012). HRM innovations by Indian and Foreign MNCs operating in India: A survey of HR professionals. *The International Journal of Human Resource Management*, *23*(5), 1006–1018.

Jenkin, T., and Chan, Y. (2010). IS project alignment – a process perspective. *Journal of Information Technology*, *25*(1), 35–55.

Journal of International Business Studies. (2009) Special Issue on Offshoring Administrative and Technical Services (ATS). *40*.

Journal of Management Studies. (2010). Special issue: Offshoring and outsourcing. 47(8).

Journal of World Business. (2012). India Special Issue. 47(1).

Keep, E. (1999). UK's VET policy and the 'Third Way': Following a high skills trajectory or running up a dead end street? *Journal of Education and Work*, *12*(3), 323–346.

Kochan, T.A, McKersie, R.B., and Cappelli, P. (1984). Strategic choice and industrial relations theory. *Industrial Relations: A Journal of Economy and Society*, *23*(1), 16–39.

Lacity, M.C., Khan, S., Yan, A., and Willcocks, L.P. (2010). A review of the IT outsourcing empirical literature and future research directions. *Journal of Information Technology*, *25*(4), 395–433.

Lacity, M.C., Solomon, S., Yan, A., and Willcocks, L.P. (2011). Business process outsourcing studies: A critical review and research directions. *Journal of Information Technology*, *26*(4), 221–258.

Laursen, K., and Foss, N.J. (2003). New human resource management practices, Complementarities and the impact on innovation performance. *Cambridge Journal of Economics*, *27*(2), 243–263.

Legault, M., and Bellemare, G. (2008). Theoretical issues with new actors and emergent models of labour regulation. *Relations Industrielles/Industrial Relations*, *63*(4), 742–768

Leimbach, M.P., and Baldwin, T.T. (1997). How research contributes to the HRD value chain. In R.A. Swanson and E.F. Holton, III (Eds), *Human resource development: A research handbook*. San Francisco, CA: Berrett-Koehler.

Lepak, D.P., and Snell, S.A. (1999). The human resource architecture: Toward a theory of human capital allocation and development. *The Academy of Management Review*, *24*(1), 31–48.

Malik, A., Sinha, A., and Blumenfeld, S. (2012). Role of quality management capabilities in developing market-based organisational learning capabilities: Case study evidence from four Indian business process outsourcing firms. *Industrial Marketing Management*, *41*(4), 639–648.

Mark, S.K.M., and Akhtar, S. (2003). Human resource management practices, strategic orientations, and company performance: A correlation study of publicly listed companies. *Journal of American Academy of Business*, *2*(2), 510–515.

Miles, B.M., and Huberman, A.M. (1984). *Qualitative data analysis: An expanded sourcebook*. Thousand Oaks, CA: Sage.

NASSCOM. (2014a). *India IT-BPM Overview*. Retrieved from www.nasscom.in/indian-itbpo-industry

NASSCOM. (2014b). *Engineering & R&D services (ER&D)*. Retrieved from www.nasscom.in/indian-itbpo-industry

NASSCOM. (2014c). *Software products*. Retrieved from www.nasscom.in/indian-itbpo-industry

NASSCOM. (2014d). *Knowledge professionals*. Retrieved from www.nasscom.in/indian-itbpo-industry

OECD/CERI. (1986). *New technology and HRD in the automobile industry*. Paris: OECD.

OECD/CERI. (1988). *Human resources and corporate strategy: Technology change in banks and insurance companies*. Paris: OECD.

Pettigrew, A., Sparrow, P., and Hendry, C. (1988). The forces that trigger training. *Personnel Management*, *20*(12), 28–32.

Pfeffer, J. (1998). *The human equation: Building profits by putting people first*. Boston, MA: Harvard Business School Press.

Ployhart, R., and Moliterno, T. (2011). Emergence of the human capital resource: A multilevel model. *Academy of Management Review*, *36*(1), 127–150.

Ployhart, R., Iddekinge, C., and MacKenzie Jr., W. (2011). Acquiring and developing human capital in service contexts: The interconnectedness of human capital resources. *The Academy of Management Journal*, *54*(2), 353–368.

Porter, M.E., Schwab, K., Sala-i-Martin, X., and Lopez-Claros, A. (2004). *The global competitiveness report*. Geneva: World Economic Forum.

Prajogo, D., and Ahmed, P. (2006). Relationships between innovation stimulus, innovation capacity, and innovation performance, *R&D Management*, *36*(5), 499–515.

Prajogo, D.I. and Brown, A. (2004). The relationship between TQM practices and quality performance and the role of formal TQM programs: An Australian empirical study. *The Quality Management Journal*, *11*(4), 31–42.

Rainnie, A. (1989). *Industrial relations in small firms*. London: Routledge.

Ridoutt, L., Dutneall, R., Hummel, K., and Smith, C.S. (2002). *Factors influencing training and learning in the workplace*. Leabrook, SA: NCVER.

Shipton, H., West, M., Dawson, J., Birdi, K., and Patterson, M. (2006). HRM as a predictor of innovation. *Human Resource Management*, *16*(1), 3–27.

Short, D. (2006). The gap between research and practice in HRD: A summary of the discussion 1995–2005. In *Proceedings of the 2006 International Academy of HRD Conference*. Bowling Green, OH: AHRD.

Sinkula, J.M., Baker, W.E., and Noordeweir, T. (1997). A framework for market-based organisational learning: Linking values, knowledge, and behaviour. *Journal of the Academy of Marketing Science, 25*(4), 305–318.

Smith, A., and Hayton, G. (1999). What drives enterprise training? Evidence from Australia. *The International Journal of Human Resource Management, 10*(2), 251–272.

Smith, A., Oczkowski, E., Noble, C., and Macklin, R. (2004). The impact of organisational change on the nature and extent of training in Australian enterprises. *International Journal of Training and Development, 8*(2), 2–15.

Sparrow, J., and Pettigrew, A. (1985). Britain's training problems: The search for a strategic HRM approach. *Human Resource Management, 26*(1), 109–127.

Swart, J., and Kinnie, N. (2003). Knowledge-intensive firms: The influence of the client on HR systems. *Human Resource Management Journal, 13*(3), 37–55.

Teece, D.J., Pisano, G., and Shuen, A. (1997). Dynamic capabilities and strategic management. *Strategic Management Journal, 18*(7), 509–533.

Valmasakis, V., and Sprague, L. (2001). The role of customer relationships in the growth of small-to medium-sized manufacturing. *International Journal of Operations and Production Management, 21*(4), 427–445.

Wozniak, G. (1984). The adoption of interrelated innovations: A human capital approach. *The Review of Economics and Statistics, 66*(1), 70–79.

Wozniak, G. (1987). Human capital formation and the early adoption of technology. *Journal of Human Resources, 22*(1), 101–112.

Wright, P., and McMahan, G. (2011). Exploring human capital: Putting human back into strategic human resource management. *Human Resource Management Journal, 21*(2), 93–104.

Wright, P., Dunford, B., and Snell, S. (2001). Human resources and the resource-based view of the firm. *Journal of Management, 27*(6), 701–721

Yin, R.K. (2003). *Case study research: Design and methods* (3rd ed.). Thousand Oaks, CA: Sage.

Part II

Reflective practice

Practitioner insights

8 Managing people in an IT software services environment

N.R. Srikanth

Introduction

The spectacular performance of the Indian IT industry can be predominantly attributed to success in two sub-sectors of the industry: IT software services (ITSS) and business process outsourcing (NASSCOM, 2014). Relative to other sub-sectors in the industry, such as IT hardware and software product development, the above two sectors have reported a disproportionate share of revenues and employment for the last three decades (Arora, Arunachalam, Asundi and Fernandes, 2001; Ethiraj, Kale, Krishnan and Singh, 2005). In 2013–2014, the industry's overall revenues have exceeded US$83 billion (NASSCOM, 2014). Further, with less than 1% of large IT firms operating in India commanding a significant market share, there must be differences in the way these firms have organised their human resources, technology and business processes that are difficult for competitors to emulate and, thus, provide a source of sustained competitive advantage (Barney, 1991; Ethiraj et al., 2005). Development of such capabilities requires investment in human, social and relational capital for creating and integrating new knowledge into an organisation's daily routines (Becker, 1962; Porter, Schwab, Sala-i-Martin and Lopez-Claros, 2004; Grant, 1996a, 1996b; Nonaka and von Krogh, 2009), a view that has been reinforced in studies of strategic human resource management (Boxall, 1996, 1998).

Given the significant level of performance differences that exist in the sector, studying highly successful ITSS firms and the innovative people management practices (Ceylan, 2012; Jain, Mathew and Bedi, 2008) seems logical in understanding how firms develop their innovative capacity (Prajogo and Ahmed, 2006) and why the presence of certain resources and capabilities matter (Barney, 1991; Wright, Dunford and Snell, 2001; Wright and McMahan, 2011). A number of studies have argued that learning holds the key for developing critical organisational capabilities needed for a firm's immediate and future needs and in achieving high performance (Jarvenpaa and Mao, 2008; Malik and Blumenfeld, 2012; Malik, Sinha and Blumenfeld, 2012). Jarvenpaa and Mao (2008), for example, have found that the strength of HR capabilities is foundational in the development of other operational capabilities in offshore IT software services firms. Malik and Blumenfeld (2012) noted the presence of a strong improvement orientation is critical to the development of a learning orientation. Further, the levels of investment in large-scale quality management approaches can also help strengthen the market-sensing and internal learning processes (Malik et al., 2012).

The role of human factors in innovation was examined in a range of industry segments by Laursen and Foss (2003) who found that investment in learning and training and appropriate job design were the key practices common across manufacturing and services industries. Interestingly, the impact of learning and development was even more pronounced in the services sector. In line with some of the earlier studies on the role of skills in informing and supporting strategic HRM choices of firms, having a strategic approach to human capital management was evident (Ashton and Sung, 2006; Malik, 2009; Smith, Oczkowski, Noble and Macklin, 2003; Smith and Dowling, 2001). Thus, it is not surprising then to see an increasing number of organisations adopting a strategic approach to HRD (Garavan, 1991; Grieves, 2004; Hyland, Milia and Becker, 1991; McCracken and Wallace, 2000). By paying special attention to leveraging a firm's learning and development and knowledge management infrastructure, competitive advantage can be achieved. Yet, little is known of the nature and extent of human capital practices that are critical in ITSS.

In view of the above, this chapter highlights my experiences of skills development in the Indian IT services environment. It is critical to note at this point that skills development in a services environment is very different from the challenges involved in the high-end software and semiconductor product environments, a topic that will be examined in this chapter in some detail. Although I have experiences of participant observation in a product environment, this chapter will be confined to observations and analysis of how highly successful ITSS companies invested in certain learning and development systems and processes for exploring and exploiting human capital and process advantages for sustained growth and performance. Before delving into the unique and common approaches undertaken by firms in the IT services environment, one must understand the underlying logic of firms operating in the software services environment.

Uniqueness of the ITSS environment

The Indian ITSS industry has not been without challenges and numerous paradoxes. The story of its success, evolution and challenges is well documented in practitioner literature (Rahman and Kurien, 2007). Without repeating what is covered elsewhere in this volume, attention is drawn towards the most commonly noted software development steps identified in Chapter 2. While all these steps are critical, one key observation is that the evolution of the Indian software services industry began by undertaking the lower end and less complex steps of the software development cycle. Specialisation resulted in gaining efficiencies in the various steps of software development cycle. Further improvements and standardisation were possible through investment in project management skills and quality management frameworks such as the Capability Maturity Model, Malcolm Baldrige framework and ISO.

Methodology

My reflective account has been shaped by experience of more than two decades. To this end, this reflective ethnographic account outlines the strategies major domestic and multinational corporation (MNC) IT firms employed in the managing human capital. These reflections highlight the key lessons and the common pitfalls practitioners and decision-makers must avoid in the management of the IT software services professionals, dominating the Indian IT industry. Ethnography as a methodological choice seems appropriate (Van Maannen, 1988, 1998, 2006) as I have deep participant insights into the organisational settings creating new understandings of this phenomenon (Alvesson, 2003; Geertz, 1973). Using participant observation and being part and parcel of the experience, deep observations were possible. Detailed accounts of how strategy, skills and context interact with each other in the management of human resources in the ITSS sector offered here are not free from the limitations of my subjective interpretations of the experiences, however, there is comfort in these findings through my numerous engagements with ITSS firms (domestic and global MNCs) operating in India. To this end, the findings are close approximations of my subjective understanding of managing human resources in the Indian ITSS market.

Findings

What follows is a chronological account of how firms in the ITSS sector explored and exploited their human resources and human capital pools to develop distinctive capabilities for the sector.

Early days: individual contributors and generic technical skills investment

The function of the training department was essentially to provide specific skills and inputs to help a worker perform better on the job. Initially, the function did not adopt a strategic long-term approach in delivering the skills upgrade or inputs. Ironically, the function was always regarded as a hygiene factor and not a business imperative in most organisations until the second half of 1980s.

Specialised technical trainings were provided to the industry by the various industry-accredited bodies and government operated polytechnic institutions, which are generally regarded as being secondary to premier/professional education. Somewhere during the mid- to later part of the 1980s, a few skill building institutions emerged, operated largely by new age private sector companies that offered their services to the computer companies. The purpose of these institutions was to provide necessary workforce required for installation and maintenance of hardware (computers, desktop machines) that was being imported and sold in India. I recollects many of my peers enrolling in evening programmes, three to four hours a day for three days a week to upgrade their employability in areas such as word processing, spreadsheet creation and maintenance, database creation and management. A limited few who had the appetite for it and were devoid of other pressures also signed up for programmes such as C++ and COBOL. These folks were neither nerds nor geeks, they were looking at differentiating themselves well in a 'me too' job market. If you were a professionally qualified engineer, a two-year programme post your graduation would be sure to fetch you your prized visa to the West. The accountants or word processing specialists, too, had a greater say in picking their jobs in the more lucrative markets of Middle-East Asia and South-East Asia or even with the better paying multinational banks in India.

The story of the liberalised Indian economy with specific references to the Indian IT industry is well known and documented (Arora et al., 2001; Banerjee, 2004; Budhwar, Luthar and Bhatnagar, 2006; Budhwar, Varma, Malhotra and Mukherjee, 2009; Budhwar, Varma, Singh and Dhar, 2006; Malik, 2009). The increased number of engineering graduates entering the job market also provided the impetus to changing the demographics of the workforce in India – a more educated, professionally qualified workforce, and an extremely hardworking workforce. Being a witness and an active participant in such a shift does not happen very often. The dull, poorly resourced training department was gearing up for a makeover and the HR function was going through change to contribute directly to the necessary revenue model of an industry for generations to come.

As a witness to some of these changes happening in the world of IT services, to trade a job in an established institution for a role in the HR function of an IT services company back in early 1990s was considered risky. From moving out of the hustle and bustle of the financial capital of the nation to the then relatively laid back, pensioner's paradise called Bangalore had many a naysayer. The role of a training department in the IT services company for professionals aspiring to make their mark in the HR function was nothing more than a non-existent aspiration.

Training: from bridging 'skill gaps' to a 'revenue generator'

The IT services companies who saw ahead of their times were definitely keen on capitalising on the opportunity. While there was certainly an increase in the supply of students graduating in engineering degrees, the demand for employable people to take on jobs in software engineering and programming was always short. The training function therefore bridged the gap between what was available in the market to what was needed by the market.

Thus in the next stage, training as a function had to ensure that the people who were recruited could become productive fast and subsequently as a revenue-generating resource. Much of the training was on the job and with the support of the experts (Rahman and Kurien, 2007); machine time available back then was at a premium and hence the trainees were working through night and day to ensure that the new hires had learnt something new and that they were also getting geared for their visa interviews at the shortest possible lead times. The incentives were pretty much to make one readily acceptable to a customer, who would then sponsor their work visa.

Much of the curriculum then was tagged to the requirements of the customer and their work; hence people had very specific skills that they needed to focus on, for example, mainframe, db2, COBOL and so on. These were the most sought-after combinations. Of course, one needs a pleasing personality, reasonable communication skills and a clear criminal record. Owing to the demand, often a day or two before one boarded their 24-hour flight to the United States, they were given a crash course on culture and etiquettes. They were also provided with manuals of handwritten or photocopied notes that served as inflight reading material on COBOL and db2 technical sub-routines.

But this was also not seen as sustainable, particularly given the high degree of desire in the people travelling to the land of promises to switch jobs and stay there for the longer term. About the same time, people were building large capacities back in India to make sure that work got delivered out of India to the clients in the Western world, taking advantage of time zones. There was an emerging pattern of technology shift becoming visible and clients ranged from banking and financial services institutions to telecommunications and manufacturing.

Next, with increasing technological change and changing client requirements the HR developers were hearing technical terms like business applications, three-tiered architecture, Internet, object-oriented programming, relational database, customisation, packaged software and so on. All these were happening around the same time that the world was trying to solve the inevitable issue of Y2K. The year 2000 remediation or simply Y2K compliance was throwing up opportunities that were unheard of in terms of job creation and employability (Rahman and Kurien, 2007). Enterprising entrepreneurs set up training institutions to cater to the needs of the industry by offering specialised training for Y2K opportunities; some even had packages like Y2K on mainframes. The above phase suggests increased complexity and diversity in HR practices to deliver economies of scale and scope for realising sustainable levels of revenues from 'deployable resources'. As such this phase marked the beginning of a strategic role of HRM in the industry.

Training and learning as a business imperative

Given that there were no visible differentiators on the nature of work being delivered by most of the IT services companies then, clients were being warmed up to the idea of continuous learning and on-the-job training that was being provided as a tool to keep employees relevant to the shifting technical needs. Every new hire had to necessarily undergo training that was upwards of 400 hours or 10–12 weeks in the first year of their employment. This was a significant impetus to the training function. The move from consumable skills to focusing on providing a strong foundation of software engineering and programming skills led to the expansion of the training infrastructure. The training delivery stayed as close to the strategic needs as possible, also taking advantage of the numerous talents available to them (McCracken and Wallace, 2000; Malik, 2009).

The profile of people who were being hired into the organisations changed from specific technical skills to those with generic and strong analytical reasoning, mathematical problem-solving capabilities and ability to work on the changing technical skills. By offering simulation of real-life situations and work, trainers were tasked to deliver a 'ready to handle' attitude for any challenges that were being thrown at them. From training for specific skills, the training function was fast emerging as a learning department focusing on improving employees' desire to keep them relevant to the rapidly changing technical landscape. The differentiators were more in the form of providing opportunities to the existing workforce to equip themselves with more than one environment (mainframes or client server architecture), databases and new programming languages. At the same time there was the drive to push equal emphasis on non-technical skills, broadly classified as domain or industry knowledge. This served as an added advantage for the Indian IT services industry to move up the value chain.

With the emergence of training as a strategic business partner, the status quo in the training department was being questioned. Their new objectives were to create a framework in which any new or emerging software language could be rapidly industrialised to support the never-ceasing opportunities. Such an approach was critical as the academic curriculum that was being offered in most of the Indian engineering campuses did not seem to keep pace with the industry's needs. As a result, the training functions in most large organisations started reaching out to the larger talent pool by upskilling university academicians who, in turn, could impart the same to their students and make them industry-aware and acceptable.

One of the key areas in which the academic institutions needed to share their expertise was the area of research. This was lacking, particularly in preparation for the digital era. This gap was also seen as an area to fill in by the industry. Again, through social capital and innovative designs of collaborating with academia, the training departments in the IT services organisations were morphing rapidly into extensions of computer sciences departments of the universities, getting into education and initiating research. A well-known and respected IT services company had always called its training function as 'Education and Research'. The nomenclature made it clear that the focus was on the best knowledge that the organisation would need to stay ahead of the curve.

Training: morphing into continued education for engagement

With intensive competition in the factor markets in the IT services organisations in India and through Y2K remediation opportunities, the demand for new skills in all areas of package implementation of enterprise resource planning rose. In the telecommunications industry, the emergence of mobile telephony and an altogether new business market riding on the back of the Internet emerged. Around the same time, the war for talent forced organisations to retain their best-trained resources and offer them a career path that would make them re-energise themselves. Some organisations invested in continuing education programmes for their workforces, on the emerging technologies, albeit at different levels such as software engineer learned programming, a project manager relearned estimation techniques and a business manager learned to spell out the benefits of migrating to newer technologies.

At no time did such a training approach, of being a skills-impartment function in knowledge development, become a tool to counter attrition. The rapid demystification of technologies led to accelerated industrialisation and consequently deskilling of some of the roles for effective management of people, process and technology, the implications of the same being an ability to ramp up workforce in relatively lesser time to meet client needs. By now, the HR function had established a true role of a strategic business partner (Ulrich, 1997).

Consequently, with a renewed role of HR and training, large university-like campuses were created, so as to ensure little or no distraction to any newcomer to the organisation during their training period. The environment thus created offered the necessary stimulus required for employees to thrive in a learning culture. Increasingly, through the maturity of processes, the curriculum became more standardised and people undergoing specialisation were linked to further training once they completed their foundation programmes. These campuses always buzzed with energy and optimism. Classrooms were hi-tech in nature and access to information or experts was always made available. These campuses ushered in a transformation from an era of scarcity to an era of abundance. They still had their corporate objectives, but yet distanced from the day-to-day humdrum. It is through such significant investments in training that barriers to imitation and resource heterogeneity were created by large IT players (Barney, 1991).

The Omni 'E': E for Education, E for Enablement, E for e-Learning

The energy and enthusiasm of the classrooms could not remain sustainable. Learning content was being transferred on CDs and shared with people, a very early adoption of e-learning. However, in this situation, the content became of utmost importance and had to make up for the lack of an instructor beside you while you were reviewing or learning, the issues of copyright and patent were diligently looked into and safe harbour disclaimers were made mandatory.

The e-learning content in many instances only substituted for the print material and did not much negate the need for an instructor. However, here was a generation of the workforce that was already used to computers and some programming since their high school days and hence took to CD-ROM-based content like a fish to water. They certainly tool up learning at their own pace and the term 'Learn Anytime Anywhere' became a reality.

The flipside of e-learning though, was that the content was static and any ability to create content for the first time was quite laborious. Organisations necessarily needed to look at a different profile of people who often did not understand the content, to help support their needs. However, getting interdisciplinary experts ensured that e-learning modules were becoming multimodal in nature. The advent of multimedia also challenged the learning styles that were until then stereotyped. All e-learning or multimedia learning needed to be modularised quickly for effective industrialisation, thereby establishing differing levels of proficiencies – from basic to expert levels.

Content was still being transferred through CD-ROMs or external storage media or occupied a large amount of space of the enterprise servers, entailing the necessity of patented or confidential information still to be delivered through classroom sessions only. However, the static content being developed as e-learning modules was useful in the next stages of the evolution where learning moved from classrooms and CD-ROM to being delivered on to your desktop through the Internet.

What can be googled need not be learnt

This is a statement I heard from my son a couple of years ago. It is perhaps true to the extent that skills and knowledge that were being used for rapid industrialisation were no longer at the core of the organisations' objectives. The objectives have now moved to supporting adding new content to learning. Common skills that are required to perform a function efficiently have become a 'how to' and are readily available from the Internet. This resulted in massive content redundancies.

Improved Internet speeds and options have made learning move from classrooms to ready accessibility at your workstation. The invasion of the mobile spectrum has also altered learning away from a fixed place to being available on various mobile devices including phones. Now we are carrying our learning with us in our pockets. Such change has also altered the creation and dissemination of content. Expertise is made available offline and online and the learning styles of individuals are being customised by the learners themselves.

Beam me up, Scotty

The teleportation that we used to admire and dream as kids while watching *Star Trek* is real – the ability to harness experts and expertise across the world on your palmtop is real. Learning anytime, anywhere and winning your certification from a network of accredited, reputable institutions makes learning credible.

The certification process itself has become dynamic and provides relative data at the touch of a key to evaluate the proficiency levels of the participants. As we look into the future and sneak a preview, one gets a feeling that learning will no longer be limited to defined periods and timelines; as organisations are preparing for the future readying of their workforce we would see more telestration and learning through telepresence across the globe. Content needs to be relevant one more time.

Discussion

The development of an institutionalised training function proved to be a strategic HR business partner (Ulrich, 1997). The development of large corporate universities was a key innovative HRM practice implemented by large IT majors operating in the Indian context. This was made possible by the strategic choices exercised by key IT business leaders as the leaders could foresee the nature and extent of demand for skills and IT projects, and thus implemented proactive policy choices to deal with the opportunities and challenges presented by the changing global IT environment (Kochan, McKersie and Cappelli, 1984). The expanding skills infrastructure and subsequent benefits for revenue generation and profitability confirm the basic tenets of the human capital theory, high performance practices paradigm and strategic approaches to HRD (Becker, 1962; Laursen and Foss, 2003; Garavan, 1991; Grieves, 2004; Hyland et al., 1991). Such an approach required sustained levels of investment that are unique to each organisation's strategic needs (Lepak and Snell, 1999) and was not easily replicable by rival firms (Barney, 1991). There was an element of path dependence and social complexity that prevented resource mobility and transfer of knowledge. The path of the nature and extent of skills and capability development also varied due to the specific needs of the organisation and how investing in certain capabilities would help it sense new market information and develop efficient processes for delivering such services in a sustainable way (Malik and Blumenfeld, 2012; Malik et al., 2012).

Conclusion

In conclusion, what follows from the above account is that the Indian IT services firms' business model has evolved from a resource augmentation business to one that focuses on developing higher-order technical, process and project management capabilities for deploying IT services around the globe (Malik et al., 2012). Based on my experience of working in IT services, successful IT firms have continuously innovated in their learning and development approaches to maximise efficiency gains, reduce the time needed to make an employee productive and support the retention of key personnel by offering ongoing learning and development opportunities. One of the key strategic work innovations by large successful IT firms was the emergence of high-performance work and management systems, wherein strong recruitment and selection engines were complemented by capabilities such as a strong training infrastructure, quality and project management skills, and other technological and market- and business sensing capabilities. Collectively, these helped significantly to capture and realise value from the market opportunities that were presented.

References

Alvesson, M. (2003). Beyond neopositivists, romantics, and localists: A reflexive approach to interviews in organizational research. *Academy of Management Review*, *28*(1), 13–33.

Arora, A., Arunachalam, V.S., Asundi, J.V., and Fernandes, R. (2001). The Indian software services industry. *Research Policy*, *30*(8), 1267–1287.

Ashton, D., and Sung, J. (2006). *How competitive strategy matters? Understanding the drivers of training, learning and performance at the firm level*. Research Paper No. 66.

Oxford: Oxford and Warwick Universities, Centre for Skills, Knowledge and Organisational Performance.

Banerjee, P. (2004). *The Indian software industry: Business strategy and dynamic co-ordination.* New Delhi: Palgrave Macmillan.

Barney, J. (1991). Firm resources and sustained competitive advantage. *Journal of Management, 17*(1), 99–120.

Becker, G. (1962). Investment in human capital: A theoretical analysis Part 2 – Investment in human beings. *Journal of Political Economy, 70*(5), 9–49.

Boxall, P. (1996). The Strategic HRM debate and the resource-based view of the firm. *Human Resource Management Journal, 6*(3), 59–75.

Boxall, P. (1998). Achieving competitive advantage through human resource strategy: towards a theory of industry dynamics. *Human Resource Management Review, 8*(3), 265–288.

Budhwar, P., Luthar, H.K., and Bhatnagar, J. (2006). The dynamics of HRM systems in Indian BPO firms. *Journal of Labor Research, 27*(3), 339–360.

Budhwar, P., Varma, A., Malhotra, N. and Mukherjee, A. (2009). Insights into the Indian call centre industry: Can internal marketing help tackle high employee turnover? *Journal of Services Marketing, 23*(5), 351–362.

Budhwar, P., Varma, A., Singh, V., and Dhar, R. (2006). HRM systems of Indian call centres: an exploratory study. *The International Journal of Human Resource Management, 17*(5), 881–897.

Ceylan, C. (2012). Commitment-based HR practices, different types of innovation activities and firm innovation performance. *The International Journal of Human Resource Management, 24*(1), 208–226.

Ethiraj, S.E., Kale, P., Krishnan, M.S., and Singh, J.V. (2005). Where do capabilities come from and how do they matter? A study in the software services industry. *Strategic Management Journal, 26*(1), 25–45.

Garavan, T. (1991). Strategic human resource development. *Journal of European Industrial Training, 15*(1), 17–30.

Geertz, C. (1973). Thick description: Toward an interpretive theory of culture. In C. Geertz (Ed.), *The Interpretation of Cultures: Selected Essays* (pp. 3–30). New York, NY: Basic Books.

Grant, R.M. (1996a). Prospering in dynamically-competitive environments: Organizational capability as knowledge integration. *Organization Science, 7*(4), 375–387.

Grant, R.M. (1996b). Towards a knowledge-based theory of the firm. *Strategic Management Journal, 17*(S2), 109–122.

Grieves, J. (2004). *Strategic human resource development.* London: Sage.

Hyland, P., Milia, L., and Becker, K. (1991). Strategic human resource development. *International Journal of Manpower, 12*(6), 21–34.

Jain, H., Mathew, M., and Bedi, A. (2012). HRM innovations by Indian and foreign MNCs operating in India: A survey of HR professionals. *The International Journal of Human Resource Management, 23*(5), 1006–1018.

Jarvenpaa, S., and Mao, J. (2008). Operational capabilities development in mediated offshore software services model. *Journal of Information Technology, 23*(1), 3–17.

Kochan, T.A., McKersie, R.B., and Cappelli, P. (1984). Strategic choice and industrial relations theory, *Industrial Relations: A Journal of Economy and Society, 23*(1), 16–39.

Laursen, K., and Foss, N.J. (2003). New human resource management practices, Complementarities and the impact on innovation performance. *Cambridge Journal of Economics, 27*(2), 243–263.

Lepak, D.P., and Snell, S.A. (1999). The human resource architecture: Toward a theory of human capital allocation and development. *The Academy of Management Review*, *24*(1), 31–48.

Malik, A. (2009). Training drivers, competitive strategy, and clients' needs: Case studies of three business process outsourcing companies. *Journal of European Industrial Training*, *33*(2/3), 160–177. doi:10.1108/03090590910939058.

Malik, A., and Blumenfeld, S. (2012). Six Sigma, quality management systems and the development of organisational learning capability: Evidence from four business process outsourcing organisations in India. *International Journal of Quality & Reliability Management*, *29*(1), 71–91.

Malik, A., Sinha, A., and Blumenfeld, S. (2012). Role of quality management capabilities in developing market-based organisational learning capabilities: Case study evidence from four Indian business process outsourcing firms. *Industrial Marketing Management*, *41*(4), 639–648.

McCracken, M., and Wallace, M. (2000). Towards a redefinition of strategic HRD. *Journal of European Industrial Training*, *24*(4), 281–290.

NASSCOM. (2014). *India IT-BPM Overview.* Retrieved from www.nasscom.in/indian-itbpo-industry

Nonaka, I., and von Krogh, G. (2009). Tacit knowledge and knowledge conversion: Controversy and advancement in organizational knowledge creation theory. *Organization Science*, *20*(3), 635–652.

Porter, M.E., Schwab, K., Sala-i-Martin, X., and Lopez-Claros, A. (2004). *The global competitiveness report*. Geneva: World Economic Forum.

Prajogo, D., and Ahmed, P. (2006). Relationships between innovation stimulus, innovation capacity, and innovation performance, *R&D Management*, *36*(5), 499–515.

Rahman, W., and Kurien, P. (2007). *Blind men and the elephant: Demystifying the global IT services industry*. New Delhi: Sage.

Smith, A., and Dowling, P.J. (2001). Analysing firm training: Five propositions for future research. *Human Resource Development Quarterly*, *12*(2), 147–167.

Smith, A., Oczkowski, E., Noble, C., and Macklin, R. (2003). Organisational change and management of training in Australian enterprises. *International Journal of Training and Development*, *7*(1), 94–110

Ulrich, D. (1997). *Human resource champions: the next agenda for adding value and delivering results.* Boston, MA: Harvard Business School.

Van Maanen, J. (1988). *Tales from the field.* Chicago, IL: University of Chicago Press.

Van Maanen, J. (1998). *Qualitative Studies of Organizations*. London: Sage.

Van Maanen, J. (2006). Ethnography then and now. *Qualitative Research in Organizations and Management*, *1*(1), 13–21.

Wright, P., and McMahan, G. (2011). Exploring human capital: Putting human back into strategic human resource management. *Human Resource Management Journal*, *21*(2), 93–104.

Wright, P., Dunford, B., and Snell, S. (2001). Human resources and the resource-based view of the firm. *Journal of Management*, *27*(6), 701–721.

9 Managing people in an IT product and research and development environment

Amit Verma

Introduction

As per recent estimates from India's National Association of Software Services Companies (NASSCOM), the product and research and development sector (PR&D) has recently posted revenues of about US$18 billion (NASSCOM, 2014). This represents less than 12% of the industry's overall revenues. While over the last three decades this figure has more than doubled, nevertheless, there are only a few large PR&D firms that control a significant proportion of market share in this sub-sector of the Indian IT industry. Additionally, despite the spectacular growth rate of the overall IT services market in the Indian context, the PR&D sub-sector continues to post sub-optimal levels of growth rate and performance. This would suggest there may be some inherent barriers in the wider business ecosystem of the PR&D segment that pose challenges to this sector's growth rates. Although India as a destination for IT services and products has been highlighted in popular press, its growth rates would suggest that there is much more than the presence of technical, English-speaking and experienced human capital that is needed for the PR&D sector. Recent explorations have highlighted the need for a new approach (Aho and Uden, 2011), wherein firms are expected to understand the nature of their clients' needs and nurture the skills needed for both exploiting and exploring the human capital advantages in the marketplace (Aho and Uden, 2013). Thus, firms have to rely on resources that are internal and external to their resource architecture for managing sustained levels of performance, a view that has been shared by many in the field of strategy and HRM (Barney, 1991; Boxall and Purcell, 2003; Porter, 1991).

This chapter intends to highlight the differences that exist between resources and competencies needed in an IT product development environment in the context of high-technology semiconductor market as compared to the IT software services market. Given that the previous chapter highlighted the role of skills and recruitment in managing growth challenges in the Indian IT services market, this chapter will not restate these, rather it will particularly focus on the role of certain human resource and management practices that are conducive to meeting the demands of the PR&D sub-sector. Employing extensive and proximal experience of working in HRM and leadership roles in the semiconductor market in the Indian context, the author is able to offer a nuanced view of the key drivers and levers that are critical in shaping effective HRM practices needed by the industry's high-technology sector.

The rest of the chapter is organised as follows. First, a brief overview of the relevant theoretical framework is offered. Next, a short note on the methodological approach is provided. Third, a brief background of the semiconductor market's evolution in India is followed by the author's key findings and reflective accounts and experience of working in the IT PR&D's semiconductor market. Finally, a short note on the differences in managing innovation precedes the concluding thoughts.

Theoretical background

Strategic management scholars have long highlighted the importance of industry structure and a firm's internal capabilities, competencies and resources for achieving sustained firm growth and performance (Barney, 1991; Porter, 1991). Recent studies of the Indian IT industry covering both product and services environments have also highlighted the role of a firm's internal organisation of resources, capabilities and skills (Banerjee, 2004; Ethiraj, Kale, Krishnan and Singh, 2005; Malik and Blumenfeld, 2012; Malik, Sinha and Blumenfeld, 2012). Within this stream of research, there exist three sub-divisions focusing on: (1) the resource-based view (Barney, 1991); (2) knowledge-based view of the firm (Grant, 1996a, 1996b; Nonaka and von Krogh, 2009); and (3) dynamic capabilities for managing sustained growth and innovation (Helfat and Peteraf, 2003; Helfat and Raubitscheck, 2000; Teece, Pisano and Shuen,1997).

The resource-based view highlights the importance of a firm's internal resources and capabilities. Such resources should be valuable, rare, inimitable and organised in such a way that they create a barrier for imitation from a firm's immediate competitors. Only then can such resources create sustained competitive advantage. The knowledge-based view argues that firms need to invest in acquiring, developing, maintaining and renewing key knowledge (both explicit and tacit) that can potentially be a source of competitive advantage for firms. Grant (1996a) further suggests that knowledge integration is a key organisational capability that firms should develop as it allows firms to apply and integrate both common and specialist knowledge for meeting the firm's business needs. Finally, in relation to dynamic capabilities, while Teece *et al.* (1997) concur with the importance of developing valuable, rare, inimitable and well-organised resources and capabilities, and further argue that firms must also invest in new organisational routines and processes to support the development and renewal of existing capabilities. This may mean that firms develop new capabilities that are relevant to the market needs. Further, in the process of developing new routines and capabilities, firms may also discard old capabilities and/or recombine existing and new knowledge and skills in such a way that new capabilities thus developed are relevant to the market needs of the firm.

Following the basic tenets of the above three strands of literature, strategic human resource management scholars have applied the resource-based view to the strategic management of human resources (Boxall, 1996, 1998; Wright and McMahan, 2011; Wright, Dunford and Snell, 2001). Boxall (1996, 1998), for example argues that while an organisation can achieve human capital advantage by hiring appropriately qualified human capital with relative ease from external factor markets, for it to have distinctive human process advantage, however, it needs to invest and organise its human capital to explore and exploit the unique and common relationships that typically exist between different social sub-groups of an organisation. In a similar vein, Heaton (1998) found that appropriate organisational culture is critical to the success of high technology product design firms. Building on the differences that exist in the strategic orientation and milieus of an organisation, Lepak and Snell (1999) proposed human resource architectures suitable for various needs.

The above short review suggests that firms can organise their human resources and other complementary capabilities in a variety of innovative ways and generate sources of sustained competitive advantage. Such an approach has led to a growing academic literature focusing on the innovative designs and implementation of HRM practices in a range of contexts (Beugelsdijk, 2008; Ceylan, 2012; Jain, Mathew and Bedi, 2012). For example, Beugelsdijk (2008) found the presence of task autonomy and flexible working hours to be critical factors impacting product innovation. Similarly, studies from the Indian context have highlighted that while Indian multinational (MNC) firms have attempted to develop innovative sets of human resource management practices, a number of MNC subsidiaries operating in the Indian market have devoted a greater focus on managing the parent–subsidiary relations and the need for standardising parent country practices in the subsidiary operation (Jain et al., 2012). Overall, there appears to be a significant consensus that firms can build innovative capacity through a combination of social and human factors, with specific emphasis on work design and human capital interventions (Prajogo and Ahmed, 2006). To this end, this chapter will demonstrate through the author's extensive engagement within the PR&D sub-sector of the Indian IT industry, innovative human resource management and leadership designs relevant for exploring and exploiting human capital advantages in the Indian IT industry.

Methodology

Through the author's experience of working in the Indian IT industry for more than two decades, this ethnographic account reports on the successes and failures of the key human resource management practices and leadership interventions. This account highlights what worked or not in the PR&D sub-sector of the Indian IT industry. The use of ethnography in social sciences and management research as a legitimate approach for generating new knowledge is widely acknowledged in the literature (Van Maannen, 1988, 1998). The author's participant observations, and the notion of 'being there' and experiencing the phenomenon allows the researcher to make deep observations of the socially constructed phenomenon. By developing thick descriptions of the social and technical aspects of managing people in the PR&D sector, the interpretations noted here are subjective and based on personal observations of the author both as an observer as well as, in some cases, an active participant. These reflections are derived mainly from the author's engagement with two semiconductor MNC subsidiaries (one large and one medium-sized), operating in the Indian IT labour market.

Background of IT product development in an Indian context

Though hardware design as a skill has been in existence in the Indian hi-tech industry for almost three decades, its growth has been moderate when compared to the software services sector. Modern ICs (or semiconductors) are enormously complex large chips that are made up of more than one billion transistors. Owing to such high levels of complexity of modern ICs as well as market pressure to produce new designs rapidly, organisations have started to rely on to the extensive use of automated design tools in the IC design process. Semiconductor development is a long and complicated process that typically goes through the following stages: system specification, architecture, microarchitecture, design and implementation, bring-up, productisation and sustenance stages where the design is converted into a real physical product (often referred to as the chip in common parlance). For each of the typical process stages (see Figure 9.1) highly specialised technical skills are required.

Though there are inherent advantages of talent availability at a lower cost in India, a couple of key factors that have inhibited the growth of this capability are the fact that unlike software services market, the semiconductor development sector requires huge upfront investments in terms of physical infrastructure, especially at the fabrication stage, which have been wanting; and there is a lack of market for indigenously designed products. The lack of these two key ingredients in the Indian context essentially drove the development of this sector in a way where largely a services model evolved, for the small portion of product development work that was outsourced to India was largely in the implementation phase with very little higher-order competencies built around the architecture and the productionisation areas. In the next section, in-depth insights into the workings of human resource management (HRM) and design in this sub-sector are provided.

Reflective practitioner accounts

Most semiconductor companies in India started with a focus essentially on software or IT infrastructure services as India had established credentials around these competencies. Further, as a large part of these activities were being outsourced to and delivered from India, these companies established a direct presence in India. As a result, most of the HRM practices and strategies were built around the prevailing practices around these 'IT software services' demographics. For example, most PR&D companies in India would benchmark their compensation with software

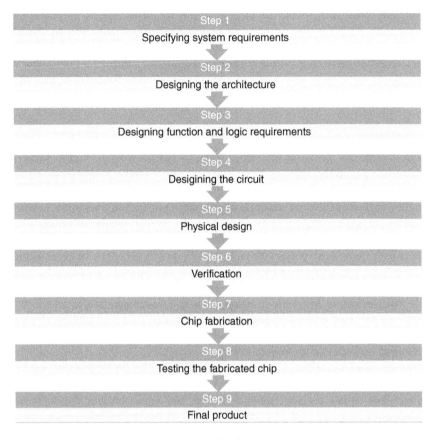

Figure 9.1 Typical development process of an IC.

service companies and developed their technical employees' salary ranges around software competencies. It was only in the late 1990s to the early years of the 2000s that the industry saw the first signs of a widespread intent to start investing in hardware capabilities in India. This change was largely driven by four key socio-economic events:

1   the global financial crisis and the meltdown that followed compelled corporations to look at more innovative ways to manage their costs. India was still coming up as a compelling destination with lower costs and availability of large pools of English-speaking and technically qualified talent;
2   the software and IT capabilities of a number of domestic IT firms and MNC subsidiaries were well established and provided confidence in the headquarters on their ability to start and ramp-up operations;
3   additionally, there was a change in the leadership pitch at Team India at most of these firms. The aggressive pitch by the local site management

teams to invest in India reinforced the parent firm's decision and confidence in the evolving technical and managerial capabilities of their Indian operations; and

4   a large base of Indian engineering talent in United States that was willing to return to India.

Over the last decade, the product ecosystem has developed significantly. As a result, there is substantive product development work that is now being done at hardware design centres in India though the ability to do complete end-to-end products out of India is still some distance away. Indian design centres have made significant strides in moving up the value chain and displaying ownership of product designs. As the author is an HR practitioner who has had an intimate view of product development initiatives in the semiconductor market in two multinationals albeit of different size, scale and culture, and has been involved through the entire product development and business life-cycle, some of the critical HRM imperatives that have enabled growth and innovation are explained in the findings and discussion section below.

Findings and discussion

Following are the key themes from an HRM and business model perspective that will be of value to practitioners as well as it has implications for theory development.

Start ahead of time

In the design and development of chips, the roadmaps are planned well in advance based on market need and segments, competitor plans, and fabrication technology advancements. It is very common in most companies to have a road map that typically covers at least two years or more in planning time. This is a departure from the literature regarding commonly misunderstood dynamism and short time-frames associated with product development firms. While it appears that product development firms have shorter product lifecycles through the frequent and sequential launch of new products, the reality is that there is a significant and often overlapping product ideation, design and development activity before the products are rolled out in the marketplace. The plan typically comprises significant architectural innovation and change followed by derivatives or variants that cater to different market segments or needs.

Reasonably well-defined roadmaps, a long lead time to production and derivatives of the main chip essentially mean that a there is a fair amount of reuse of existing design processes that happens even in a new chip. Nevertheless, the design and development team needs to spend a considerable amount of time learning and understanding the tools, methodologies and processes well ahead of time. Further, the teams need to be staffed, appropriately trained and integrated, and supported with the infrastructure way before the actual project kicks off.

This is vital to start way ahead as both these activities need considerable leadership investment.

The wired leader

Given the distributed nature of design and the interdependencies with other parts of the organisation, it is imperative to identify and onboard a leader who has the pedigree, experience, credibility and in-depth understanding of the organisation and its socio-technical dynamics. Ideally, this person is from within the organisation and is an executive sponsor who helps cut through the maze of processes that most organisations tend to have and provide quick decision-making. HR managers have to ensure that the leader is well educated and supported on the local culture and internal work practices.

The talent mix cocktail

As discussed earlier, chip development requires a multitude of skills covering architecture, frontend design, pre- and post-silicon validation and testing and back-end to name a few. The focus of talent is on the following activities:

1   *Build the core team* – Identification and onboarding of the key functional leaders is probably the most important element of the effort. Without the right functional leaders in place who not only are technically proficient but are committed and passionate about kick starting a new activity, are willing to 'get their hands dirty', and most importantly are willing to go above and beyond job descriptions. This core group needs to act as advocates, ambassadors and role models around which the team is built. The organisational leader has to be personally interested in hiring this core leadership team.

2   *Catch them young* – The talent mix that is needed in product development firms is very different as compared with IT software services firms. In more mature product development organisations, the ideal mix is around 30/40/30 – wherein 30% of the work force should ideally be at the early career individual contributors levels, 40% of the engineers should have intermediate experience, and the remaining 30% should have advanced technical and leadership skills in their domain. Given the talent availability challenges that are inherent in this sub-sector, especially where there is a broad base of engineers at the entry level but a severe paucity of experienced professionals, the organisation needs to redefine its strategy and invest heavily in high-potential new college graduates who can be moulded into the organisational requirements as against making a trade-off between capability and experience.

As one leader puts it: 'You do get 15 years' experienced engineers in India, but in most cases, it's one year of experience repeated 15 times over.'

While the above might be advantageous in exploiting existing strengths in a services environment, such employee profiles add little value to the exploratory and innovative learning designs that are typical in product development firms.

3   *Create what doesn't exist* – There would always be competencies that are non-existent in the local ecosystem and the organisation needs to do an early assessment of how to address those competency gaps. There are three strategies that the organisation can adopt based on the need, criticality and time available. These are:

   a   *Go out and create the skill* – Identify educational institutions that would be willing to work with the organisation and create programmes that would be tailor-made to building those skills e.g. Mask design or layout engineers who perform physical layout for mixed-signal, or work with application-specific integrated circuit (ASIC) and mixed-signal engineers to customise designs for integration floor planning, custom layout and verifying against design rules and schematics. These are all new skills and competencies needed in large numbers. All these skills were non-existent in India in the early 2000s. The organisation makes a conscious decision to work with local institutes to develop these skills by creating a curriculum, deputising internal organisational subject matter experts to teach pilot courses and work with teachers in these institutes to provide appropriate knowledge transfer and integration to create a sustained pool of layout engineers, and then hires them from that pool.

   b   *Hire adjacent skills ahead of time and train internally* – There would be skills for which the HR practitioners need to undertake careful HR planning and sourcing to avoid gaps in the workflow.

   c   *Hire an extended team in a location where it exists* – Where the need is highly specialised and the competency cannot be created in the medium run, hire where it exists, which is usually in the global design centre at the parent organisation's headquarters. However, it is essential to ensure that that there is a strong connection with the local team and knowledge transfer takes place.

Getting up to speed – the learning strategy

1   *Don't preach, teach* – Getting the newly formed energised team up to speed on tools, processes and methodologies is a critical imperative. Whilst formal class room training has some benefits, what really works is getting the team members to actually work on a live project that is in progress in the company. As mentioned earlier, most projects are derivatives and there is a fair amount of reuse, getting new engineers to work on existing projects is a very effective strategy as it not only provides hands-on learning experience but also helps them imbibe the development culture that exists in the organisation. The other significant benefit of the approach is that the parent organisation appreciates the help in the form of resources being developed, rather than looking at this as an overhead, which helps create independent relationships and networks that can be leveraged in the future. The members who go through the training also need to ensure that the engineers back home are also trained in real time and knowledge transfer and integration happens expeditiously.

2   *Bring in the experts* – The normal practice is to send engineers to the head-quarters for training and, while essential, it needs to be supplemented by bringing in the experts on-site and get focused learning from them. The benefits to the team are amplified with the experts spending time at the India development centres as against just sending a select group of engineers to the headquarters, as they tend to be a lot more focused and involved while they are on-site rather than at their home base.

3   *Systemise tribal knowledge* – Chip design is an art and a lot of highly specialised technical tacit knowledge exists within the minds of the experts. The organisation needs to develop a structured way in which this knowledge is extracted, codified and shared. Technical talks/tutorials and experience-sharing by experts is an effective way of knowledge dissemination but needs to be thoughtfully planned.

4   *Rinse and repeat* – Given the long development cycle, the teams go through a fair amount of transition where new teams are added and engineers are moved around within and across teams. To ensure that the basic foundational know-ledge is available and disseminated, the organisation needs to set up an informal knowledge management system. Contrary to most learning and development frameworks, ensuring that training is recorded, available and backed up by additional inputs if needed becomes vital for the effectiveness of the team.

It's in the mind – setting the culture

Product development by design is a long and arduous process that goes through multiple changes before fruition. The need to build and sustain the right organisation culture is the most crucial ingredient. In the Indian context, given the legacy of resource augmentation and the limited ownership model, most engineers are used to short and intense project lifecycles where they are working on a finite set of goals with clear deliverables and timelines, and interactions outside the team are largely driven by a few project leads, managers and programme managers. Product development teams work in a totally different environment with a lot of variables around schedules, features, and roles and responsibilities and therefore establishing the right culture and expectations within the team is a key requirement. Whilst there are many cultural attributes that fuel the product development teams, in the author's experience, the four defining ones are:

1   *Fuel the passion* – Rallying the team around the purpose of the project is the foremost priority of the leadership team. They have to ensure that they are able to communicate a vision that creates a sense of passion amongst the team. Usually the idea of being the first team to do something works as a great catalyst for creating the passions and smart branding helps e.g. the first processor to be done out of India or the first XYZ product for the company creates that emotional impetus that the team needs. Aligning the teams around the overarching goal sets the tone for how the team behaves.

2   *Break the silos* – Instead of focusing on organisational structures and clarity of roles and responsibilities, the team need to rally around goals and inter-mediate milestones. Hierarchies and silos can become the biggest barriers and there has to be a deliberate attempt to ensure that information flows seamlessly across the organisation. Indian engineers and managers tend to be extremely mindful of protocols and hierarchies. The leadership needs to consciously and continually dispel the mindset. One of the most effective techniques that helps in changing the mindset is the 'dungeon' approach or 'swarming the problem' where all engineers and managers who are working on a specific deliverable are huddled together in a conference room till the problem is resolved with a stated expectation that all members who need information and have dependencies are in the room and will interact directly, with limited email exchanges. Though not sustainable over long periods, it helps break barriers and creates a sense of ownership amongst the teams. Similarly, engineers need to be encouraged to reach out to their coun-terparts and communicate directly with them as against the hierarchical route. This also emphasises the need for ensuring that the teams are trained on how to collaborate effectively across various teams, levels and cultures.

3   *Engineers are THE leaders* – Engineers need to be a core part of the leadership team and be involved in decision-making at all levels, rather than it being the domain of managers only. The engineering leaders are not only the role models that inculcate the right behaviours but also represent the voice of engineering on all issues that impact the project. It is also important to ensure that the team that has the right communication infrastructure, visibility and recognition vehi-cles such as opportunity to interact with senior management, influence over the performance management and reward decisions and so on – to communicate that the organisation values engineers as much as leaders. Practices such as having manager-only meetings or leadership distribution lists that include only managers are not helpful. Similarly, we need to ensure that reward and recog-nition systems also comprehend this and are not biased towards managers.

4   *Breaking the rules* – As you build a product team, you have to be ready for excursions from current policies, procedures and practices. More often, a majority of these programmes evolved around the 'early movers', which in most cases were not core engineering teams. However, as the product teams come in, some of these programmes need a careful relook and modification to suit their needs. As an example, a product team would need its initial leader-ship coming in from the headquarters and that requires the Indian operations to revisit its expatriate and localisation programmes. Local HR teams need to be able to quickly identify the areas with different needs and present solutions to avoid a trust deficit that impacts the business and HR relationship.

Managing innovation: a different approach

One of the attributes that needs to be established upfront in the development team is the culture of innovation. Most offshore development teams have evolved through a process of staff augmentation capabilities to a small component owner-ship. The focus in PR&D is very different. Outlined below are some of the distinc-tive features in managing the innovation process. Start with the basics and educate the teams on the concept of intellectual property, the need to protect and, more importantly, not infringe it.

1   Top management champion within the team needs to drive the innovation programme, which includes working with global product development and legal teams to ensure that the infrastructure is replicated locally.
2   Establish the infrastructure to include a robust knowledge management system, which defines how information would be managed and shared within the team. This includes both document management and physical infrastructure, as at times the teams need to be physically separated from the rest of the organisation.
3   Clearly establish the process of managing new ideas and improvements. Innovation is a natural outcome of any design activity and the organisation has to clearly define a process by which these are captured, reviewed and presented with the organisation. Having functional czars within each of the functional groups who work closely with the Top Management Champion ensures robust evaluation of ideas.
4   Establish a recognition system that encourages innovation. Most global organi-sations have well defined patent/inventor programmes and while replicating these programmes is a given, supplementing them with local initiatives that encourage engineers goes a long way. Creating visible artefacts of success via recognition in team meetings, opportunity to present in all-hands meetings and walls of innovation where ideas are recognised spurs engineers to do more.

Conclusion

In conclusion, managing human resources for software PR&D firms in the Indian context is still in a nascent stage and will take a change in the current service mindset for it to mature and develop new products. This chapter identified a number of management and HRM practices that are necessary for managing human resources in a PR&D environment. In particular, this chapter identifies six key HRM and related management practices that are conducive to managing innovation and human resources in product environment firms. Highlighting the importance of a leadership style that empowers and excites staff, this chapter also emphasises the need to have an extensive focus on planning over the longer-term. HRM practices such as getting engineers with the right age and mix of skills, building a sustainable skills ecosystem, and engaging internal and external expertise in the technology domain through information sharing between suppliers and manufacturers are vital. Additionally, with the Indian market so deeply engrained in a services mindset, managing and creating a culture that supports product development and innovation is a key challenge. By breaking silos, recognising talent and allowing people to experiment and learn from their mistakes are critical practices for developing new products. The biggest challenge lies in whether the organisations have the ability and agility to identify the distinct and competing demands the two models: service delivery and product development. This places huge resource demands on its people management strategies and developing a culture that serves as an optimum model for straddling between these two IT services and PR&D sensibilities. Senior management and leadership play a critical role in managing this transition.

References

Aho, A.-M. and Uden, L. (2011, July). Value creation for software engineering in product development. In *Building Capabilities for Sustainable Global Business: Balancing Corporate Success & Social Good*. The 12th International Conference of the Society for Global Business and Economic Development, Singapore: Singapore Management University.

Aho, A.-M., and Uden, L. (2013). Strategic management for product development. *Business Process Management*, *19*(4), 680–697.

Banerjee, P. (2004). *The Indian software industry: Business strategy and dynamic co-ordination*. New Delhi: Palgrave Macmillan.

Barney, J. (1991). Firm resources and sustained competitive advantage. *Journal of Management*, *17*(1), 99–120.

Beugelsdijk, S. (2008). Strategic human resource practices and product innovation. *Organisation Studies*, *29*(6), 821–847.

Boxall, P. (1996). The Strategic HRM debate and the resource-based view of the firm. *Human Resource Management Journal*, *6*(3), 59–75.

Boxall, P. (1998). Achieving competitive advantage through human resource strategy: towards a theory of industry dynamics. *Human Resource Management Review*, *8*(3), 265–288.

Boxall, P., and Purcell, J. (2003). Strategy and human resource management. *Industrial & Labor Relations Review*, *57*(1), 84.

Ceylan, C. (2012). Commitment-based HR practices, different types of innovation activities and firm innovation performance. *The International Journal of Human Resource Management*, *24*(1), 208–226.

Ethiraj, S.E., Kale, P., Krishnan, M.S., and Singh, J.V. (2005). Where do capabilities come from and how do they matter? A study in the software services industry. *Strategic Management Journal*, *26*(1), 25–45.

Grant, R.M. (1996a). Prospering in dynamically-competitive environments: Organizational capability as knowledge integration. *Organization Science*, *7*(4), 375–387.

Grant, R.M. (1996b). Towards a knowledge-based theory of the firm. *Strategic Management Journal*, *17*(S2), 109–122.

Heaton, L. (1998). Talking heads vs. virtual workspaces: A comparison of design across cultures. *Journal of Information Technology*, *13*(4), 259–272.

Helfat, C.E., and Peteraf, M.A. (2003). The dynamic resource-based view: Capability lifecycles. *Strategic Management Journal*, *24*(10), 997–1010.

Helfat, C.E., and Raubitscheck, R.S. (2000). Product sequencing: Co-evolution of knowledge, capabilities and products. *Strategic Management Journal*, *21*(10/11), 961–997.

Jain, H., Mathew, M., and Bedi, A. (2012). HRM innovations by Indian and Foreign MNCs operating in India: A survey of HR professionals. *The International Journal of Human Resource Management*, *23*(5), 1006–1018.

Lepak, D.P., and Snell, S.A. (1999). The human resource architecture: Toward a theory of human capital allocation and development. *The Academy of Management Review*, *24*(1), 31–48.

Malik, A., and Blumenfeld, S. (2012). Six Sigma, quality management systems and the development of organisational learning capability: Evidence from four business process outsourcing organisations in India. *International Journal of Quality & Reliability Management*, *29*(1), 71–91.

Malik, A., Sinha, A., and Blumenfeld, S. (2012). Role of quality management capabilities in developing market-based organisational learning capabilities: Case study evidence from four Indian business process outsourcing firms. *Industrial Marketing Management*, *41*(4), 639–648.

NASSCOM. (2014). *Engineering & R&D services (ER&D)*. Retrieved from www.nasscom.in/indian-itbpo-industry

Nonaka, I., and von Krogh, G. (2009). Tacit knowledge and knowledge conversion: Controversy and advancement in organizational knowledge creation theory. *Organization Science*, *20*(3), 635–652.

Porter, M.E. (1991). Towards a dynamic theory of strategy. *Strategic Management Journal*, *12*(S2), 95–117.

Prajogo, D., and Ahmed, P. (2006). Relationships between innovation stimulus, innovation capacity, and innovation performance. *R&D Management*, *36*(5), 499–515.

Teece, D.J., Pisano, G., and Shuen, A. (1997). Dynamic capabilities and strategic management. *Strategic Management Journal*, *18*(7), 509–533.

Van Maanen, J. (1988). *Tales from the field*. Chicago, IL: University of Chicago Press.

Van Maanen, J. (1998). *Qualitative Studies of Organizations*. London: Sage.

Wright, P., and McMahan, G. (2011). Exploring human capital: Putting human back into strategic human resource management. *Human Resource Management Journal*, *21*(2), 93–104.

Wright, P., Dunford, B., and Snell, S. (2001). Human resources and the resource-based view of the firm. *Journal of Management*, *27*(6), 701–721.

10 Process consulting and adaptations of organisation development in the Indian IT industry

Joseph A. George

Introduction

In the first part of the century, as the Indian IT industry emerged prominently from engaging the Y2K crisis, several firms were consolidating service success with requisite organisational and people management processes (e.g. Arora, Arunachalam, Asundi and Fernandes, 2001; Athreye, 2004). From several hundred employees, firms began counting thousands of employees on their payrolls. In hindsight one may trace an institutional ecology effect to organisational forms, with business sector-focused 'verticals' on the one part, and, computing skill and technology platform-intensive 'horizontals' on the other part. In representational terms, overlay structures included profit and loss accountabilities along 'vertical' lines and cost management responsibilities across 'horizontal' lines. However, with scale-based growth these apparitions began to be challenged on complexity and strain on role and work relationships. The subtle interplay between individual cognition and organisational sense-making is not an obvious zone of attention for the growth and action focused business acumen in India's stabilized IT sector ecology. Design and development of firms have largely ignored elements of self-organisation or autonomous autopoetic (Krogh, Roos and Slocum, 1994) forms of responding to business environment challenge. Organisation development in its classical sense has much to offer that has only been partially leveraged by firms in the sector.

It is in the business environment, however, that the industry found its 'process' anchors. The American defence industry was particularly faced with quality issues from various software contractors. Anticipating the emergence of human capital, IT work force and workforce ageing issues, senior leaders in the Army's Chief Information Office and Office of the Assistant Secretary of Defense for Command, Control, Communications, and Intelligence sponsored development of the People CMM, an extension of Carnegie Mellon University's the Capability Maturity Model (CMM). (Curtis, Hefley and Miller, 2003).

Quality management and process approaches to change in the IT industry

A derivate of the CMM approach, the People Capability Maturity Model® (People CMM®) was established as a road map for implementing workforce practices that continually improve workforce capabilities. It establishes an integrated system of workforce practices that mature through increasing alignment with the organization's business objectives, performance and changing environmental needs. However, the word 'process' is a linguistic trap in which the business ecosystem may place transactions of commerce rather than the interactions of human beings. Over and above this, the socialisation of the word 'process' in the industry is premised by Software Capability Maturity models from the CMM suite of assessment models. Hence, the dominant references not only germinate from Carnegie Mellon's initial constructs of process, but also accentuate those elements that overlay project management structures of the work domains in IT.

Of the several firms world over that adopted the People CMM® route, Indian firms were the majority. Within these firms, even in linguistic terms, connotations and denotations of the word 'competency' ranged between technical, behavioural and face-valid descriptions of task demands, behavioural expectations or performance requirements. While 'development' became a buzzword for people in the Indian IT industry, the focus on business outcomes was kept alive by sponsors of such initiatives. In effect, People CMM® assessors verified the intent of the 'development' spirit, rather than the content of development itself. While the roots of the framework held the reference of organisational capability, the adoption of policies and practices to be assessed at respective levels of the People CMM® model ensured that individual employees in organisations at least got some incidental benefits of these organisational practices.

Organisation development approaches in the Indian IT industry

A smaller number of IT organisations began to see need to incorporate organisation development or OD cells in their organisations, largely within their human resources (HR) departments. However, they were formed as a 'pair of hands' to extend to business arms, the generic 'human' values treatment when it suited the design and implementation of changes that business or HR departments saw as feasible. Their mandates were to clearly earn respect from business for the HR department. However, it did not imply as a consequence that the content of practice approximated or mirrored the form of OD that its founders' – like Benne, Beckhard's or Argyris – tenets entailed (Hinckley, 2006, p. 30). The scope of OD in Indian IT firms was never organisation-wide, and seldom did the whole system participate in the problems they could solve through planned learning that could be applied for overall organisation effectiveness. Besides, in historical analysis, the label of OD could project the media-intensive promotion of HR functions with the 'feature'-laden mediation that could attract talent markets and capability.

This chapter begins with a brief review of why OD is critical in general and why it is a pertinent approach for understanding the key problems of organisation dynamics. This is useful to a process view of human interaction at the individual, group and organisational levels. Then it illustrates through several cases how lively the form of such dynamics could be in the eyes of the interventionist. For the limited purposes set out here, the diminutive form of a case description may be called a vignette, with no explicit coda as much as a limited description of main events and processes in the case. A cross-vignette and within-vignette analysis is presented thereafter via the lens of covert processes, a relatively post-modern view to organisation development.

In the vignettes, the skill intensity, the differentiation of OD roles in the HR function and the nature of practices purporting to be OD are depicted. While the vignettes are real, identities are protected so that those readers who wish to inform both practice and theorisation are not inhibited. There is therefore an assumption that the author makes, in the initiation of the reader to the distinction between OD-based organisation change vis-à-vis organisational change approaches in general. The consequential bias towards humanism, science and justice for participants in the process are values for the consultation process per se. The first set of vignettes is depicted through an 'inside' consultant perspective, followed by the 'external' consultant perspective. A 'separator state' is attempted for the reader, in the transition between the two sets of cases with a commentary on OD as a process in this context.

Vignette 1: business-process-led interventions

A qualified Lead Assessor for PCMM insisted that he could not be a judge in his own organisation's cause. Nonetheless, buoyed by the projected identity that his firm derived from CMMI assessments, he positioned the People CMM® route for a certain business unit of about 2,000 employees, so that growth could be managed at the scale of operations that the industry was witnessing. An internal team of business process leaders, functional leads from Quality and Finance, as well as HR professionals, were trained in the framework, to take up roles as internal assessors. They would work with the external Lead Assessor to carry out the assessment but it was the Lead Assessor who legitimised the exercise. When enlisting the support of a new recruit in the HR team, the internal Lead Assessor likened the activity to an OD intervention, as the top management was committed to the initiative, and put their money into consultation and assessment costs.

The new recruit, with relatively fresh eyes, asked his business unit HR head whether the assessment could verify the content validity of the competency model between selection and performance processes. The new recruit was told that the authors of the framework did not ask for it, and that the 'task' was to evidence documents of intent and documents of practice to be assessed for the People CMM® model, and that his performance evaluation would depend on it. Needless to add, the organisation was assessed to the highest level of the maturity model of the People CMM® for all its locations in India.

While the assessment provided a media-buzz and a professional buzz, employees' expectations did not ebb during the 'buzz' period: they anticipated more from the employer. In essence, the effectiveness criteria required to attract customer attention in competitive terms did not materialise and despite the chronicled legacy of this one-time assessment, the organisation could not match up to multinationals in the IT services businesses that did not even set up look-alike processes to entice their customers.

Commercially led frameworks could deliver bounded commitment for limited periods of time, without necessarily ensuring organisational transformation if the top management's commitment was only to pay lip service to these issues for the sake of marketplace positioning, rather than to sustain the spirit of human process interventions with renewal mechanisms that have equivalent if not greater resilience.

Vignette 2: outsourcer maturity

A very sensitive HR practitioner from a 48,000-member organisation wished that a bright and promising Programme Manager be successful in a client situation where the client (a 900-member organisation) felt let down by the service provider's marketing oversell. As first stated, the client wished to implement a greenfield Enterprise Resource Planning (ERP) system, after aborting its own internal attempts to do so. Personnel associated with the in-house effort were still on the payroll, when the decision to outsource the implementation was taken. Within months of the blueprinting process, process owners who needed to sign off on the process to be implemented deferred their decisions, and the delay was beginning to impact the costs of the implementation service provider. The resident personnel were frustrated, trying to contain the damage to the scope of the contract, without firm customer commitments across the manufacturing floor.

The service provider HR manager in charge of the business unit requisitioned the services of the resident consultant from corporate headquarters to salvage what seemed an impossible client situation. After hearing the client's version, the consultant used classical diagnostic skills. His aim was to understand the undercurrents that led to a choice-point that precipitated the need for this interaction. The client wished to roll back the contract and revert to an in-house solution or an alternate service provider.

After listening to key perspectives from process owners in the client organisation, the consultant rounded off the diagnostic phase with versions represented by the service providers module owners themselves. Much of the disclosures contained clues that were to do with the identity of the client. In accordance with the mindset of a rigorous manufacturing organisation, it was a pleasant discovery for the consultant to find that even members of the client's IT department regarded the service provider just as they would treat their parts suppliers on the shop floor.

The immediate rationale for decisions were not seen in light of the original executive decision of avoiding cost overruns in ERP implementation, but with an emotional anchoring of comfort by the internal people and a style of requisitioning stand-alone computing kit across different manufacturing processes. The behavioural outcomes were a result of having outsourced with a vendor frame of mind that treated the service provider as discrete parts manufacturer. Rather than dealing with knowledge workers on the premises for a specific period of time, the in-group phenomena of the client kicked in, unchecked by the nature of the outsourcing proposition. Besides, the blueprinting paradigm defeated notions of comfort that individual shops under the manufacturing roof had with vintage ERP and IT department personnel.

A design that addressed these two concerns was dealt with in a large-scale intervention involving 70 core personnel from both sides. They sat at circular tables in groups that resembled the eventual process team, each table having representation from both teams – client and service provider. Once the open format brought the sense of the organisation in the room, clarity towards the eventual ERP vision and related roles became clearer, with subtle facilitation of the nature of paradigms. Actions from commitments faced less resistance after bringing the entirety of the implementation team together. The client's implementation went on to become a manufacturing industry best practice case study for the ERP software vendor. The young Programme Manager became the unlikely hero, and the HR manager who pitched the corporate consultant from central HR development got a performance highlight. The consultant enjoyed the process of uncovering cues from business and client teams, and designing a learning process to nudge the overall team to progress from their stuck-points. The consultant's HR leaders at corporate HQ however, did not figure out what intervention skill or worth this intervention's impact was to the business. The consultant returned to base with a private satisfaction of having been useful to at least two organisational sub-systems, neither of which would bear upon his own performance rating or reward in his work unit.

Vignette 3: homesick, hair-oil sensibilities and hush-ups

In another episode of oversell, an Arab client ($9 billion in revenues) fiercely wanted to protect his own honour in defending a decision to move IT outsourcing from Western brands to an Indian company. Within the very first month of the engagement, the early recruits to the assignment were faced with what they would least expect in their own lands. Beside their compound, a large skyscraper, with several expatriates, was attacked by terrorists, and fear struck the area. In the arid, lonely desert, anyone used to social company and interaction with loved ones needed to take safety precautions – to the extent of appealing to their Indian HQ to repatriate them. The business leadership, HR leaders and process champions weighed in between the client and the employees (already about 40 in number within the first month of operations). A Western vendor seized the opportunity in the crisis to bid afresh to serve from a neighbouring nation, with intermittent travel to the client's headquarters to keep the engagement alive. The corporate

HQ of the Indian firm then decided to send in their in-house intervention specialist to salvage this impasse.

The interventionist had no experience of dealing with Arabs, and did what he
could to read up on the cross-cultural dimensions of working with Arabs. Upon
arrival in the country, he hurried to meet the principal sponsor and shared services chief of the Arab conglomerate. He was met by a matter-of-fact leader,
who wasted no time in spelling out his appraisal of the Indian IT services complement. 'First they showed us pictures of implementations in US stock
exchanges, and now we have guys you picked up from the street'. The parallel
between projected identity and experienced identity seems a hidden cost in many
an engagement. The Arab continued, 'They stink, they are no different from
labor. They do not drink tea with us. They huddle together. Anyone walking past
gets that odour of hair-oil, even if they have not shaven their faces'. The interventionist wondered how these were now relevant to the perceived and experienced threat from terror in residential neighbourhoods. 'The terrorist is not after
you. He is after my ruler, maybe me, but not you'. With a deep breath, the Arab
Shared Services Head now made his most operative request 'Train these people,
and let them know, despite how they have been, I'll protect them. I protect you.
But, I want to see intelligent people, like from the land of the guru'.

In the few days that were available, the interventionist worked on a plan to
facilitate at least two dimensions of employee behaviours based on extended
conversations with the client's operating managers. The first was for employees
to assume a consultative posture, vis-à-vis a service of menial nature. The second
was the contextualisation of this consultative stance in the Arab world. With the
interventionist role-playing the client's demeanour and possible objections, each
day, after work hours, employees got the chance to practise their interaction
skills in a relatively non-threatening environment. With so much done, the interventionist returned to HQ. Within a month the business leadership called the
interventionist to secure tickets for a fresh round of workshops on cross-cultural
alignments as the first workshops' participants seemed to show behaviours
desired by the client.

Vignette 4: I've got strategy figured, you figure the media to communicate

Post-merger integrations are some of the most unreported processes in popular
business literature. Partly because of sensitivities involved, and partly to do with
sequence and simultaneity in narrative, the dynamic involved is interesting, to
say the least. In this particular vignette, the title features the initial ask of the
host organisation's business leader who was given the responsibility to integrate
a large services organisation with the business process outsourcing entity it had
acquired. While the original founders of the acquired firm moved on, a few
senior leaders remained in significant roles on the top team of the merged organisation, working shoulder to shoulder with the larger services organisation. What
initially appeared as culture differences to these leaders soon became a matter of

protocol compliance that the service firm had required in terms of its financial and information technology reporting processes. Consequent to the void left by the founders of the acquired entity, a palpable sentiment of loss pervaded the surviving leadership. This had to do with the possibility of toning down a dearly cultivated employee-friendly work climate in deference to the formally distant process-oriented culture that the acquirer deemed necessary.

In the first meeting with the internal consultant of the large services firm, the head of the newly formed business unit was in determined mood, asserting: 'I've spent weeks figuring out what needs to be done. The strategy is pretty clear to me. We're bleeding at single digit operating margin, and urgency is required. I need your help in communicating the strategy effectively. This is a large workforce, and we must get it right.' The consultant offered the leader a reflective question 'So, what makes you think that the workforce will accept your strategy when communicated?' A deep silence of five minutes ensued. Pacing pensively in the large office room, the leader quipped 'You've got me thinking. Where were you going with what you said?' The consultant then mentioned that communication was an insurance policy for the leader, provided the ground was prepared right. If the leadership team knew what the climate for receiving the communication was, then the message content and the style of communication could be customised accordingly. 'In a communication such as this, you cannot retrieve once delivered. Yes, we need to get it right', said the consultant. 'So how have you been doing similar work elsewhere in the corporation?' The consultant then went to describe the process of diagnosis and feedback, and how it helped conserve resources, directing them more appropriately. In that deep listening the leader went with the consultant's flow and finally asked the operative question, 'So how long would you take to do this?' The consultant had no precedent for such a response, and went with his gut to say 'Six weeks'. A louder silence followed. 'Why so long?' asked the leader, wanting to know the method in bare detail. The consultant then laid out the diagnostic phase and mentioned how it would be shorter in the investigation phase and longer in the analysis and design phase. The leader, in a leap of faith as it were, consented to the consultant's process.

What followed was a deep listening from the leader to the findings after 26 hours of interviewing across a variety of roles and responsible positions. The frame from which the leader arrived at his original request was under scrutiny. But, to the leader's credit, his reframing of his post-merger priority ended in a targeted facilitation at the top management team, where goal and role alignment was incomplete post-merger. With personal disclosures of leadership lifelines and simulations that mimicked the operating rhythm of the workplace, neither the acquiring IT services organisation representatives nor the acquired BPO leaders had doubts that a new phenomenon of group learning had begun, wherein the integration of the two units flowed from the orchestration of leadership process in the top management team. Leaders reviewed their roles and responsibilities and their team role sacrifices resulted in a shift in operating margin from 4% to about 16% in the year since the integration began, without any external technology platform nor any radical business process re-engineering practices.

Conception of OD – similarities and departures

Let us pause here to see the commonalities and departures from patterns in the vignettes, thus far. First, the reader will note, that only portions of larger organisational units got the 'treatment' effect of an OD 'intervention'. Organisation Development is a practice approximating an art form, that premises values of humanism, participatory/democratic inclusion and justiciability (Fulmer and Keys, 1998) in that fairness in human interaction at workplaces are all ideals through which effective organisation follows. The conditions for the practice of OD include the following (Marshak, 2006; Marshak and Bushe, 2009; Worley, Hitchin and Ross, 1996):

1   The commitment of the top management to a long-term implication of planned intervention.
2   The agency of a third party – i.e. the consultant, between the sponsors and the larger organisation.
3   The use of behavioural sciences to inform the diagnostic, design and implementation of individual, group and organisational processes (whole system focus).

In the vignettes considered thus far, we have seen the consultant resides more distinctly within the third-party agency in Vignettes 2, 3 and 4; and implicitly in Vignette 1, where the internal Lead Assessor has advocated the view that the people process maturity framework adoption would be OD in itself for the HR leadership too.

In Vignette 1, the positioning of a process-led framework to affect the whole system could easily be explained away as OD, barring the scientific lens through which a few pertinent critiques are on offer. The principles of content validity and face validity do not hold for competency models alone, but for the essence of application. Beyond cognitive recall of an assessed organisation in commercial media, and content changes in policies and practices approximating the principles of justiciability and participation, the specific reference to individual, group and organisational theory as behavioural science was scant and indiscernible. Furthermore, as firms assessed under PCMM have the liberty of policies and practice implementation insofar as it is in the spirit of the maturity model, there is no adjunct provision in the model to verify content validity so as to offer predictive reliability of assessed units. The recourse to further assessments would be normally cost intensive, and yet not satisfy content and predictive validity of embedded units of analysis such as competency models and its aggregate impact in terms of organisational or group capability. In order that we get a schematic view of the issues being raised in this chapter, let us subject our frameworks to the role of the covert processes (Marshak, 2006) that engulfed these contexts, in Table 10.1.

In Vignettes 2, 3 and 4, the role of the HR function comes through as having a business operations-intensive, narrow role, thus obviating the need for a skilled

Marshak's dimensions of change	Vignette 1 – process maturity	Vignette 2 – outsourcer maturity	Vignette 3 – desert sands	Vignette 4 – frames to a view
Reasons – rational and analytic logics	• Commercial case for employer image and people process • Maturity in business growth phase	• Strained sales engagement from service provider and delayed delivery experienced by ERP customer	• Unexpected unknown in overseas location. Cost effectiveness logic under threat from overt behaviours	• Post-merger integration anxiety is projected through rationale of business analysis • A sound strategy would yield the desired organisational performance
Politics – individual and group interests	• HR leader cautions new HR entrant 'If founder of an assessment model says so, how can you oppose it?'	• Service provider projects capability that is distant from buyer's experience • Buyer's business users unwilling to recognise functional aspects of ERP	• Client segments socio-political boundary to further commercial objectives. Employees of Indian IT services firm put safety above job in foreign land	• The acquired organisation's leaders resisted overarching conformance to business process even as the acquirer wished to push through a deterministic 'strategy' as agenda to be implemented post-merger
Inspirations – values-based and visionary aspirations	• To be employer of choice with first mover advantage in assessment to standards	• For service provider to be the best among ERP vendors • For buyer to implement ERP at lower cost and quicker time than with internal team with most suited vendor	• Arab clients wish to unyoke from irrationally high cost Western IT service providers to near-shore 'guru'-like and cost-effective Indian firms	• An integrated services and BPO business proposition would be relatively unbeatable in combination
Emotions – affective and reactive feelings	• Engulfment to vision overpowering critical discernment of change	• Buyer firm's project manager caught between stakeholders and own reputation • Seller sulks from scene and positions HR as wedge to avoid embarrassment	• Arab clients wish to be respected on honour of their own commitment, without expressing much explicitly on internal socio-political strife • Indian service provider finds orchestrating employee commitment a challenge in adverse situations	• The denial of emotions in the integrated entity shone through the consultant's diagnosis • The salutary effect of top team dynamics told more than was considered collectively by the leader and the new team
Mindsets – affective and reactive feelings	• Business euphoric in support of employer image. Employees of longer-term sustenance	• Buyer deals with knowledge based vendor as they would with vendor of manufacturing parts • Seller treats greenfield ERP buyer as entity of lesser era	• Arab client uses positional authority to selectively convey perception of anger in the 'guys-from-the-street' depiction rather than Wall-Street facing suave executives, projected during sales cycle.	• The BPO firm was beginning to experience the relatively cold and distant approach to process integration • The execution focused, IT services firm was found wanting in matching the rapport that BPO executives exuded
Psychodynamics – anxiety-based and unconscious defences	• Business leaders aim for assessment as a 'prize' even as HR leadership gloss over ground level feedback on content validity of processes	• Buyer anxiety centred around judicious choice of vendor • Service provider's anxiety around marquee manufacturing industry case of ERP running aground	• The Arab client's pride was hurt in the role of the patron host of culture and expected transactional fidelity despite human tragedy • The Indian employees exerted moral obligation on their employer with regard to duty in hostile work destinations, even as the employer expected transactional fidelity from their employees in what they saw as a transient business exigency	• Irrespective of the primary background, employees demonstrated a common defensive pattern – of finding 'directional' guidance from their immediate superiors
Consultancy character	• Process template trumps personal employee insight	• Neutrality of facilitator critical to parties making headway from stalemate	• Cross-cultural assumptions critical to sensitising parties to the relationship	• Client's presenting statement only a symptom of a larger phenomenon in context

process consultant. The nature of adaptations of the OD art form used by the internal consultant is evident in the variety the vignettes represent. While the diagnostic phase was common to all the vignettes, the types of issues give a cross-sectional view to the range of problems that traditional HR departments would not typically 'solve'. The analysis in Table 10.1 is in most part a representation of group and individual dynamics that, when compared against consultative efforts, provides an overall texture to the similarities and departures from classical OD. While the vignettes hitherto have given an internal consultant perspective, it is useful to turn to the role of the external consultant in the same industry sector. The objective is to provide readers with a palette for the IT canvas, so that sketches may present visions that creative imaginations and emergent employee aspirations could benefit from.

Vignette 5: project teams' alignment

A client had first sought out an external consultant's facilitation for what would become the basis for operationalising strategic thrusts for the forthcoming financial year. The client was an offshore IT arm of an analytics firm. The process was carried out to the top management team's satisfaction, so much so that the senior leaders were able to see their priorities clearly enough to communicate them to the larger workforce in mnemonically cogent ways. This is the strength on which a Programme Manager with a large assignment wished to engage the consultant further to consider the dynamics and alignment of teams. The teams were reporting partly to her in the past and more fully in the course of the consultant's engagement period.

A senior top team participant who originally had accountability for the teams now under the Programme Manager was under the scrutiny of the local Managing Director. He was sensitive to the bad blood the former leader drew from his teams, through insensitive remarks and emails. The Managing Director advised his leadership to re-engage the consultant to see through the integration of the workforce – largely skilled engineers in data analytics, with the top management recast necessitated in the wake of the attrition and dissatisfaction identified in the erstwhile leader's team. The India unit was otherwise a consistent darling of workplace survey companies and HR management professionals' forums, due to the leadership's ability to enact an open knowledge friendly work atmosphere.

The design phase of the external consultant included conversations with the Programme Manager, to scope the nature of the intervention and the layered objectives she desired given her vantage point understanding from her previous role. Once comfortable with what she could expect from a potential intervention process, the consultant went on to encourage understanding directly from the team members whose response was critical to outcomes the US headquarters desired. With a final confirmation with the Programme Manager, the intervention was designed in two phases. The first phase would include an in absentia processing of feedback that the leader would walk in for. The second phase would include the larger workforce as in an open systems intervention. Hence, the consultant provided for interpersonal space first between the leader and her new direct reports. Each of them could then embrace the larger unit together as the focal unit responsible to the US headquarters for the success of a deliverable. The intervention design would also enable the leader to project her vulnerability in the challenge, and thereby earn the reciprocity that would enable forthcoming disclosures to make the analytic product more viable.

The larger group of about 70 technical staff from various work-streams were taken through the outlines of a World Café process, and values, issues and priorities critical to the team's context were known to all in the room. Each work-stream by role category then proceeded to provide the bare minimum actions in terms of initiatives and related measurable to make for alignment with their larger goal. The Large Programme Manager was now ready to re-engage the team members more confidently. The feedback from the teams regarding the intervention was positive, in that blocked energy was channelled into expression and new commitments were forthcoming from the participants in the change process. The Large Programme Manager took personal feedback for herself on how she might integrate direct report feedback and situate leadership imperatives in the knowledge that the former leader would continue to be part of the top management team. Beyond the immediate need for her to transition to the role, neither the top management team, nor the Large Programme Manager ever liaised back with the external consultant on the intervention. The Organisation Effectiveness Leader was, however, more acknowledging of the consulting effort and wrote a brief testimonial for the consultant.

Vignette 6: India and the rest of the world

A Japanese telecom network manufacturer with long-standing presence in the United States had commenced an India operations centre to complement a cost-based competitiveness strategy for the global market. The US team were not used to long-distance product development, especially across time zones. The India team were a few quarters into operation, settling down into a rhythm with R&D equipment, personnel and extended partnerships with product design and development partners in India. They were headed by a business development and strategy professional with a telecom services work experience.

In the presenting statement the India Development Centre Head mentioned to the external consultant the exigency was about establishing top team confidence that the India Development Centre was on its way to stable operations. The facilitation in the top team needed to bring US-based technical leaders to see the India development story as worthy of their emerging heritage. Conversations were arranged telephonically with the Senior Director in the US responsible for the India incubation period and it was followed by face-to-face ratification with the external consultant, on the US Senior Director's trip to India. Since the plan required approval from a distance, the consultant provided a session-by-session description of what the overall team assembling for the offsite work would get.

The Vice President in charge followed this up with a personal debrief on what he would most value in the outbound experience.

The design factored not only for the reported lines of interaction the individuals in the cross-border team were engaging in, but also embedded a constructive dimension to open up the participants to novel experiences. A simulation of the industry journal's future issue enabled participants to dissociate themselves from the problems they were engulfed in, and imagine a future they wished to see. They responded individually to the journalist's questions in the simulation, that would bring up the ongoing base and cross-border work structures in a connected yet peripheral manner. Beyond this subliminal anchoring from the present, the members' responses gave the consultant a quick window into the mindsets, rationale and aspirations from each participant's role perspective.

The following morning, the diverse leaders made up of four nationalities were paired in a scheme that would make for a peer-level mirror exercise on leadership and group process dimensions. The consultant played along as a peer with the views he accessed from each participant's simulation responses. With such enabling, each leader met with the other and they listened deeply to each other's narratives of their leadership philosophies and the situation they faced. The top leaders were now in a position to review each other's responses in a non-threatening and issue-based structure. The process by then had already relegated tensions caused by geographical divides to the resolved past, and brought forth opportunities that they could confront for a better future.

In keeping with what the consultant had heard in terms of interaction dynamics, the next process was to enable the participants with a personal and peer coaching theme, whereby psychological and social dimensions affecting progress could be explored. Polar preferences and conscious and unconscious derailers were brought to the surface to enable leaders to assume responsibility from a zone of shared awareness of personal and interpersonal tendencies. An example of the polarities conversed in pairs is:

> *Reciprocity is born of service and self-concern.* It generates obligation in others without having to resort to unethical or selfish aims.
> *Self-concern*: To relate to needs or interests of the self.
> *Service*: Being in helpful activity; aiding and being of use to others.

Thus, self-effacing and unduly selfish tendencies turned up as polarities that needed dexterous development toward a larger purpose for a healthy operating climate. In this manner, each participant developed a neutral vocabulary for interrelations on six pertinent polarities. The team set up peer coaching commitments which could then be reviewed every quarter. The Japan–US–India triumvirate was now only a pretext of investment in which several nationalities were impacted. Talent deployment came from various countries, and large investments came from economies that did not necessarily represent their nationalities. The facilitation closed out with the suggestion that the consultant be invited to

review the team's progress and consider being the team coach beyond the contracted intervention.

Vignette 7: strategic choices for a CEO

A manufacturer of printers and related hardware peripherals was struggling to
keep its business model viable. Its CEO knew an independent member on its
board to have a penchant for teaching issues to do with corporate financial
history and outcomes of strategic choice. When he got talking with the board
member, an authority on corporate governance and financial disclosures, he was
pleasantly surprised to learn that an opportunity existed to facilitate the top team
of the business and their direct reports through an experiential learning session
with an OD consultant.

The consulting model in this assignment had the financial expert taking on
the role of strategy content expertise, even as the OD consultant took the role of
a process facilitator to get the participants through in a humanistic way to participate in creating strategic choices for the company as a whole, cutting across
lines of businesses, if required. The duo took a typical debrief of the firm's
context from the CEO, and also from its founding chairman who chose to
witness the process as an interested observer.

The process began with a Lewinian de-freezing exercise. Every participant in
the group was involved in a planning and executing performance simulation.
This generated insights into information processing in the organisation as related
to translating business environment signals within the firm. With selective
nudges released as information by the strategy expert – typical terms like
strategy, competitive strategy, tactics, capability benchmarking and the like were
engaged with. The OD consultant also simulated for the participants select creativity thinking tools, which could aid in the non-prejudiced creation of strategic
choices. Four discernible strategy choice combinations were voted for in an open
space format. Later in the process, terms to do with execution were engaged with
in terms of a balanced scorecard approach. Ideas and insights from the participants' experiences made it possible to sift through the pros and cons of considered
choices, with the probability of catching the market unawares without unduly
high investment seen as a differentiating competitive advantage.

The CEO asked the OD consultant to document the process, and highlight
possibilities for group work in mission teams based on the four considered
choices of strategy. However, the CEO never got down to leading the groups to
the said choices of action and confessed, months after the event with the OD
consultant, that he took responsibility for the slack, and would require time to
review his own role in the situation the company was in. In a hierarchically
structured organisation, often the dynamics of involvement requires complementary support when democratic choice is to be followed through with consistent time and resource commitments. It also follows that without a
commitment structure that sees key roles beyond milestones in a designed intervention, relying on adages such as 'First do the possible, then the impossible

may also happen' is but a mindful check on positive psychology approaches that pervade neoclassical philosophies in OD consultation.

Process consulting in the IT industry

Stakeholders

The author has witnessed several forms of internal and external interventions in the Indian IT industry. For colleagues in the profession, who consult in their own individual capacities, often, OD is truncated in its potential, when the stakeholders erroneously negotiate their outcomes downwards with features like time and scope constraints brought to weigh in on the commercials. Nonetheless, as can be inferred from the vignettes in this paper, it is evident that skills of the OD consultant are in demand when there is no threat to the in-house HR organisation's or business sponsors' perceived power over outcomes in role and organisation design.

Chief Operating Officers, Delivery Managers, Business Unit Heads and HR managers often reduce consultancy in OD to a means of extending their own leadership style or to defend their stakes in a difficult situation for themselves. The size of firms in an IT service delivery business ecology is often accompanied by growth considerations. Adaptive differentiations made by Indian IT firms along lines of geography, business domain and skills of talent pools, often told of the scalar principles of span of control from a behavioural standpoint. Hence, leaders with a budget for OD consultancy services sized their scope to restrict the human element only to the extent their constituencies could be influenced for mutual advantage. OD consultants adapted to serve along these lines, rather than to refuse work because it did not span the 'whole system'. Often 'top team' interventions were seen as rare and quite the prize that OD interventionists in the IT industry could aim for.

On the other hand, the linguistic appeal of the term Organisation Development gave credibility to large HR departments. Specific processes such as competency assessment, performance management systems and the like were the routine of such OD departments, where neither theory, nor skill from the interventionist schools, were on trial for professional discharge.

Issue-mapping

As with the vignettes in this chapter, most presenting statements of clients typically undergo transformation with the participation of the third-party agency in OD consulting. The issues that get mapped in the contractual phase of an OD assignment are often steeped in human dilemmas, where values of respect and dignity stand implicitly challenged. In the Indian IT industry, for example, a starting place for considering issues arises from employee opinions expressed through surveys. However, the basis for action is, more often than not, oversimplified. The survey design, the findings and the scope for impact are seldom the result of a coherent interlinkage.

Bias for action often begets the act of survey events, and consequent action. Yet issues to do with the nature of the psychological contract and designing the employees' involvement in organisational effectiveness go undetected or lie oversimplified in action points. Peculiarly, for the most part of the industry's growth, despite progressive and employee-friendly policies at the workplace, business growth itself became an unconscious alibi for experiential dilemmas. A lack of method in enquiry and a lack of familiarity with the art in the design of interventions gave rise to some of the covert issues we have seen in this chapter.

Framing of outcomes

If the nature of the sought outcomes are analysed, the IT industry in India may shore up a topography of phenomena that represents latent interactions of organisation design elements seeking resolution through the singular personhood of the intervention sponsor. This aspect of process consultation is complexly poised – for it is at once consumptive in nature for the sponsor, and phenomenologically rich for the student of OD. As is typical in OD consultation processes, the client often discovers there is more to the dilemma under consideration, when analysed and/or framed by the consultant. To the extent that the client adapts its world view to the findings, one may hold up the soundness of the diagnostic methods. Development succeeds when feedback is sought with the intent to better one's skills and capabilities.

It is fair to ask a question here, especially in the context of the pace at which business success in the IT sector moves in comparison with other sectors of the Indian economy. The question is: Would feedback in a leadership development process be favoured over feedback in an organisation development process? This could be an operative issue with regard to how leaders may frame outcomes associated with group outcomes.

Prognosis and reflections

The march of rationality and the shadow démarche of the emotional being at workplaces may not be an organisation design factor per se. The human tendency to maximise economic gain has seldom run as high and far with ascendancy in career trajectories in any Indian economic sector. The preponderance of covert issues (not all of it being negatively poised) are there for us to see in real interventions. In a societal context, where honour, face and status can be perceived to be dented, the opening up to a comprehensive system-wide intervention may be only the tip of the issues that need human confrontation.

The rate at which newer implications of employee knowledge and aspirations need processing far exceeds the individual capacity of business or HR leaders. This in itself represents an opportunity for facilitating human interventions at all levels of the social system – individual, group and organisation. However, the rational tendency to objectify the elements of organisational templates such as roles, goals and procedures tend to obfuscate the emotional worlds of employees at the workplace. If we assume that employees equip themselves voluntarily and skilfully with emotional wherewithal, the focus on symbolic and instrumental elements may seem merely predicated on a group dynamic. The language and discourse within IT organisations speaks to a desire for efficiency more than effectiveness. Terms like utilisation, bench, factory-model, and billability, are also indicative of a self-regulatory environment for employees, where the minimisation of human intervention is sought. The movement from a logical corollary to a decisional reality in respect of OD in the IT industry may at first seem a non-rational discourse. However, as the vignettes inform us, there is an abject surrender of longer-term organisation effectiveness aims in favour of expedient performative agenda (Garrick and Clegg, 2001).

Newer forms of explanation emerge via social constructive phenomenology (Gergen and Davis, 2012), to accompany more positive approaches to human psychology at the workplace. Earlier forms of enquiry seem threatened in the practice of applied behavioural sciences. In the assiduous analysis of Burnes and Cooke (2012a, p. 1) on the state of OD practice, they argue that 'there are significant issues that it must address if it is to achieve the ambitious and progressive social and organizational aims of its founders'. It is this author's contention that, given the simultaneous demands that such practice places on cognitive, emotional and organisational resources of individuals in organisations, focus (Goleman, 2013) has been often the casualty in the scientific temperament of OD.

In the vignettes reviewed here, for example, despite the allure of available frameworks like that of covert processes, diagnostic schema often proceed in search of linear coherence. A dynamic simultaneity via richer teleological phenomenology eludes us, despite its centrality in human interaction processes. Initially conceived constructs like that of enabling and restraining forces as in a force field are overlooked in contemporary practice and theory integration, impoverishing the yield human process facilitation can potentially provide for practitioners and academics alike. While the prima facie conditions for OD interventions represent a modicum of complexity for cognitive appraisal of organisational phenomena, an abject neglect of the Lewinian field theory origins has probably been the loss of the practitioner community as well. Burnes and Cooke (2012b) argue that a return to Lewin's original conception of field theory, based on gestalt psychology and conventional topology, can provide academics and practitioners with a valuable and much-needed approach to managing change.

It can be argued, for example, that among the restraining forces for OD itself, the heightened opportunity and relevance for employees in a developing world like India is bound by its socio-economic context. Pronounced financial and economic security that prevails over psychological and social network security may have diminished the expression of OD's ideals among agencies of process and sponsors of change, both. However, such a proposition, even if it is to be proved tenable, does not find mention even in the covert process diagnostic units of Mindsets and Psychodynamics in the cited vignettes (see Table 10.1). Gestalt-based 'holism' (Carter, 2004) may at times be reduced to a conception of organisations as mere 'information processing' units. Its inherent sub-systems with their requisite complex nature make amenability to linear, three-stage interventions – as in diagnosis, intervention, evaluation stages – perceptually and phenomenologically incomplete due to an attentional bias of oversimplification.

Implications for the IT industry

Role of leadership

It would appear that OD's classical tenets find adaptive departures and in such adaptations one can find evidence of leadership response, assumptions about the essence of human presence in the workplace, and how language is used to communicate these adaptations. The case for collective leadership is subsumed often by the linearity assumed in power structures of IT firms.

The ecology of career systems is defined by standard role templates; so much so that for a majority of IT business roles, reductionary techniques suited to financial planning have banded employees in compensation worth, irrespective of accurate predictors of individual worth or reliable indicators of adaptability in knowledge-based performance contexts. Scale in the business economy has also meant scale in standard role designs with variations on the role left largely to operational processes of the business. Hence, leaders whose reward systems are cued on financial impact tend to contain their aspirations to the immediate expediency of performance goals textured by dimensions of cost, quality (conformance to specifications than service quality per se), risk management, schedule conformance and attrition control. The tendency for firms in the sector has been to aggregate these measures, despite variations in context from project to project. Hence, in the absence of operative methods to account for variations in context, performative logic of a financial nature pervades the nature of accountability that role holders subject themselves to. This is in the nature of a transactional employee contract (Rousseau and Wade-Benzoni, 1994), which biases justice principles affecting issues like resource availability, talent readiness and scope or effort variances during the execution of projects in the sector.

Model of human being

Shorn of differentiated identity of a teleological nature (Tenkasi and Boland, 1993) leaders or people in positions of power and authority over resources, possibly trade-off between the economic return on their effort and the side-bets they may place on opportunities for alternate private gain. Thus, to galvanize groups in the classical ideals of internal commitment in the OD sense would seem Herculean effort devoid of financial specification and bereft of reductionary symbols of individual achievement. To shift from a behaviourist response of reward to an altruistic or relatively humanitarian reciprocity is cognitive shift and, perhaps more crucially, an emotional upheaval for which leaders may not be equipped through formal means of corporate activity.

While there has been considerable consternation at failure to achieve the requisite balance between the economic identity of the firm and the more generative and human-transformation capacity of firms (Beer and Nohria, 2000), there is also a crisis in the meaningful contributions that employees at various levels could make in the IT sector. Progressively, therefore, the model of the human being is signified most by the term 'resource', exemplifying a fungible, replaceable and objectified commodity, as if their supply were perennial or granted. Attempts at normative re-education have only been made at the level of the individual, and the leader or manager who receives young and fresh talent has also had to cope with generational differences in approach to work and life in general. A Chief Technology Officer had this interesting observation 'Fresh from college engineers today live their private lives in public spaces', exemplifying social media technologies challenging the world views of managerial talent. Regressive control is perceived by young talent when their company intranet policies restrict access to personal email and social media exchange.

Conclusion

In conclusion, the findings suggest that unconscious tendencies are likely to be stressful to the longevity of the industry and that the resilience of its workforce springs not only from the pace at which the external environment shapes human preferences through the Internet and telephony; but also from infrequent review of extant work practices and deferred emphasis on the emotional content of workplace decisions. Irrespective of the global reach of Indian IT firms, cultural learning and transfer is left unmanaged beyond the customs and taboos of foreign lands. Similarly, in merger and acquisition activity, the joining of forces is relegated to the synchronisation of financial books and information technology platforms, despite caution from past experiences and frameworks (Marks and Mirvis, 2010). While the larger local market for IT services consolidates incrementally, the seller is yet to bear the value of intangible learning from overseas to set expectations with uninitiated clients in India. Such tendencies are symptomatic of a lack of institutional learning or its poor management. To expect unconscious competence from a less complex organisational form to a more differentiated organisational form is also indicative of inept management of organisation design, where structural features are a poor substitute for requisite human and organisational processes. Each such tendency is opportunity for OD to make inroads, with its generative, social-constructive and appreciative enquiry philosophies. However, the constraint has seldom been the philosophical root as much as its critical discernment and the comprehensive system-wide application it entails.

References

Arora, A., Arunachalam, V. S., Asundi, J.V., and Fernandes, R. (2001). The Indian software services industry. *Research Policy*, *30*(8), 1267–1287.

Athreye, A. (2004). The role of transnational corporations in the evolution of a high-tech industry: The case of India's software industry – A comment. *World Development*, *32*(3), 555–560.

Beer, M., and Nohria, N. (2000). *Breaking the code of change*. Boston, MA: Harvard Business School Publishing.

Burnes, B., and Cooke, B. (2012a). The past, present and future of organization development: Taking the long view. *Human Relations*, *65*(11), 1395–1429.

Burnes, B., and Cooke, B. (2012b). Kurt Lewin's field theory: A review and re-evaluation. *International Journal of Management Reviews*, *15*(4), 408–425.

Carter, J.D. (2004). Carter's cube and a Gestalt/OSD toolbox: A square, a circle, a triangle, and a line. *OD Practitioner*, *36*(4), 11–17.

Curtis, B., Hefley, B., and Miller, S.A. (2003). Experiences applying the people capability maturity model. Retrieved from www.crosstalkonline.org/storage/issue-archives/2003/200304/200304-Curtis.pdf

Fulmer, R.M., and Keys, J.B. (1998). A conversation with Chris Argyris: The father of organizational learning. *Organizational Dynamics*, *27*(2), 21–32.

Garrick, J., and Clegg, S. (2001). Stressed-out knowledge workers in performative times: A postmodern take on project-based learning. *Management Learning*, *32*(1), 119–134.

Gergen, K., and Davis, K. (Eds.) (2012). *The social construction of the person*. Chagrin Falls, OH: Taos Institute Publications/WorldShare Books.

Goleman, D. (2013). *Focus, the hidden driver of excellence*. New York: NY: Harper Collins.

Hinckley, S.R. (2006). A history of organisation development. In B.R. Jones and M. Brazzel (Eds), *The NTL Handbook of Organization Development and Change, Principles, Practices and Perspectives*. San Francisco, CA: Wiley.

Krogh, G.V., Roos, J., and Slocum, K. (1994). An essay on corporate epistemology. *Strategic Management Journal*, *15*(S2), 53–71.

Marks, M.L., and Mirvis, P.H. (2010). *Joining forces: Making one plus one equal three in mergers, acquisitions, and alliances*. San Francisco, CA: Jossey-Bass.

Marshak, R.J. (2006). *Covert processes at work: Managing the five hidden dimensions of organizational change*. San Francisco, CA: Berrett-Koehler Publishers.

Marshak, R.J., and Bushe, G.R. (2009). Revisioning organization development diagnostic and dialogic premises and patterns of practice. *The Journal of Applied Behavioral Science*, *45*(3), 348–368.

Rousseau, D.M., and Wade-Benzoni, K.A. (1994). Linking strategy and human resource practices: How employee and customer contracts are created. *Human Resource Management*, *33*(3), 463–489.

Tenkasi, R., and Boland, R. (1993). Locating meaning making in organisational learning: The narrative basis of cognition. *Research in Organisational Change and Development*, *7*, 77–103.

Worley, C.G., Hitchin, D., and Ross, W.L. (1996). *Integrated strategic change: How OD builds competitive advantage*. Reading, MA: Addison-Wesley Publishers.

11 Senior management mentoring and coaching for exploration and exploitation

J. Karthikeyan

Introduction

This chapter provides an ethnographic account of the author's experiences of coaching senior executives in India's IT and business process management (IT/BPM) industry. The author's reflective account highlights how certain behaviours can be developed through executive coaching and that these are critical in supporting explorative and exploitative forms of learning (March, 1991) necessary for developing innovative capacity. Research on organisational ambidexterity has tended to focus on the ability of firms to simultaneously engage in new learning through exploration, risk-taking, autonomy and innovation in their products and services on one the hand, and *exploiting* their existing knowledge, learning and resources for gaining efficiencies through appropriate task structures and work cultures on the other (March, 1991; O'Reilly and Tushman, 2008; Raisch, Birkinshaw, Probst and Tushman, 2009; Tushman and O'Reilly, 1996). Innovation requires change and in such a context, the role of leadership and senior management teams in implementing such change is widely acknowledged in the literature on organisational ambidexterity (Smith and Tushman, 2005; O'Reilly and Tushman, 2007; Jansen, George, Van den Bosch and Volberda, 2008). As such, this chapter demonstrates the key leadership behaviours developed through coaching that are critical in exploring and exploiting the human capital opportunities in the Indian IT industry. Developing such behaviours and learning capabilities is critical for a leader's self-exploration and an organisation's creativity and innovation processes.

The Indian IT industry has proven its mettle in the highly competitive global outsourcing market for IT/BPM services. Despite a slowdown in the global economy with overall revenue contribution of US$118 billion demonstrates signs of resilience and agility in the IT/BPM industry (Malik, 2013; NASSCOM, 2014). The growth rate of exports is estimated to be between 12%–14%, whereas, the domestic market is expected to grow between 13%–15% per annum (NASSCOM, 2014).

While India remains a key contributor to the global IT market, there are trends that suggest that further growth will come from new and disruptive technologies. There is a growing understanding of a clear shift in customer procurement preferences for the IT/BPM industry that demands the industry transformation for the next wave of growth. Research suggests an increase in global technology spending and opportunities created through adoption of disruptive technologies are expected to propel growth in 2014 and beyond (NASSCOM, 2013). NASSCOM's report further indicates that while the first US$100 billion landmark can be attributed to the cost arbitrage, process and service quality advantages, the next US$100 billion will be through a combination of higher-value services and an increasing proportion of non-linear growth strategies.

The rest of the chapter is structured as follows. The author begins by outlining the changes in the Indian IT industry's innovation landscape. Next, a brief review of the coaching and mentoring literature is offered, followed by the methodological approach adopted for this chapter. Finally, the empirical evidence from the author's executive coaching consulting experiences from nine cases is presented. These individual cases are analysed using the analytical framework developed by the author through decades of coaching and consulting experience. Finally, the chapter concludes with implications for practitioners and policymakers for the new, technologically disruptive, and innovative IT landscape that is set to unfold and shape future growth trajectories.

India: a changing innovation landscape

Some of the key drivers for this growth in addition to the existing offshore delivery business model will include innovative offerings in SMAC (social media, mobility, analytics, and cloud) technologies to fuel growth. Moreover, the future of the industry will be a transformation leading to a complete blend of services, products, solutions and platforms. An IDC worldwide estimate suggests that of the total ICT spend of about US$5 trillion by 2020, nearly 98% of growth will be driven by platform technologies and SMAC (IDC, 2014). In summary, there are indicators that future growth will be fuelled by disruptive technologies such as SMAC technologies and changes in the IT services, wherein strategic business intelligence will be more critical than the current focus on process automation and will involve collaboration with and increased use of customer facing technologies (IDC, 2014).

In view of the above technological driven disruptive change and innovations, the Indian IT industry can no longer sustain the efficiency model of exploitation of resources and process capabilities. Senior leadership has to recognise the need for the simultaneous use of exploitative and exploratory learning mechanisms, or ambidextrous learning mechanisms, and embed these mechanisms in their daily routines, renewing the resource architectures to make the most of the next wave of growth, fuelled by disruptive technological innovations. To this end, this chapter focuses on case studies of coaching nine senior leaders from four case organisations in the Indian IT industry, highlighting the benefits coaching can bring in developing organisational ambidexterity. Through in-depth one-on-one coaching of these leaders, the author developed – through constant iterations and negotiations with the clients – the key leadership behaviours necessary for engaging in exploitative and/or exploratory forms of learning.

With the accent on non-linear growth and the faster application of SMAC and other disruptive technologies, organisations are finding it relatively easy to invest in innovation platforms. For example, between April 2013 and March 2014, the IT Industry added only 13,000 employees for every billion dollars in revenue (Alawadhi and Mendonca, 2014), as compared to 2003 when the industry added nearly 40,000 employees for every billion dollars in revenues. This change marks the increasing efficiencies and the need for new and innovative ways of reconfiguring resources and technology. A country's innovation capabilities have long been central to its competitive advantage. The recent review of innovation rankings from Bloomberg Business Week indicate that India is not amongst the top 50 most innovative nations (Bloomberg, 2014). A similar and worrying trend has been identified by data from Dutz (2007) wherein, only 16% of Indian manufacturing firms offer in-service training, compared with 92% in China and 42% in the Republic of Korea. Indian firms that do provide in-service training are 23%–28% more productive than those that do not. The gross enrolment in higher education is only 12% in India, compared with 90% in Korea and 68% in the Russian Federation and the aggregate domestic R&D spending has never exceeded 1% of the GDP, of which, 75%–80% comes from the public sector. However, between 1998 and 2003, multinational corporations spent $1.3 billion on research and development (R&D) in India – showing that its valuable assets could be exploited more effectively.

More recently, there are signs of some comfort emerging with the increase in the number of intellectual property applications in IT up from 76 in 2008 to 858 in 2012 (KPMG, 2014). The investments by large IT players in SMAC technologies has significantly increased and has proliferated to both large and small to medium-sized enterprises. These investments vary from US$100 million in the case of Infosys Technologies and US$50 million for Tech Mahindra. There are signs of an increasing shift of the centre of gravity for innovation to emerging markets such as India. GE and Phillips have relocated a significant proportion of their innovation labs to India and have produced totally new products from their India innovation centres for both Indian and emerging markets. The concept of *Jugaad* or frugal innovation and reverse diffusion from emerging markets is gaining momentum (Cappelli, Singh, Singh and Useem, 2010; Govindarajan and Trimble, 2012; Kumar and Puranam, 2012; Radjou, Prabhu and Ahuja, 2012). GE's development of an electrocardiogram (ECG) device suited for the Indian market is an example of frugal innovation. The ECG product, MACi (wherein the 'i' represents India), was launched in 2009 with a price tag of US$535.The product was conceived and developed in India and contextualised to meet the demands of the Indian market. A lot of thinking went into to (1) reducing the complex functionalities in the existing product; (2) increasing the ease of use to support the low-skills user ecosystem in India; (3) creating a reliable and serviceable ecosystem; (4) developing a product–environment fit, for example, with power, dust and heat; (5) developing local access and familiarity through awareness; and (6) achieving cost effectiveness and clinical efficiency.

A recent report by KPMG (2014) highlights investment in R&D, ideation culture, knowledge centres and continuous improvement groups among the many approaches adopted by firms in the Indian IT industry. Given the importance of leadership identified in change and innovation management literatures, the following section provides a brief review of the coaching and mentoring literature in general, with a specific focus on the coaching of senior leadership, leading to the development of an analytical model.

Literature review

In recent years, an increasing number of individuals and organisations have started using coaching (ICF, 2012). Essentially coaching involves a coach helping a person (coachee) build their effectiveness through an effective coach–coachee relationship (Heslin and Vandewalle, 2006). At this stage it is critical to differentiate the two terms of mentoring and coaching, as often they are used interchangeably. While it is understood that a mentoring relationship has an active component of learning from a mentor, a coach is a person with whom the coachee learns with (O'Connor and Ertmer, 2006). Mentoring is generally much more long term and open ended (Burdett, 1998), than coaching and is usually carried out by a senior employee who acts as a role model for a subordinate and perhaps less proficient employee (Megginson and Clutterbuck, 2006). Thus, coaching is a short-term engagement and with a very specific brief, which is delivered by establishing a close relationship with the coachee thus making it easier for the coachee to learn, develop and improve their personal effectiveness (Ellinger and Hamlin, 2008).

The study and practice of coaching emanates from a number of disparate disciplines. The most dominant among these disciplines are: psychology, management, education, health, sports and sociology. Of more interest to us is the increasing importance of coaching in the field of human resource (HR) management or workplace coaching, as an applied field of practice. The largest contributions come from the discipline of psychology and as Berg and Karlsen (2007) suggests, psychological approaches to coaching broadly fall into the following sub-domains of learning at individual levels: behavioural, cognitive, humanistic, cognitive-behavioural and existentialist philosophies. In this tradition, often the most common approach adopted by coaches typifies operant conditioning to influence behaviour (Hackman and Wageman, 2005). A number of other psychological theories underpin the practice and content of coaching. Of relevance here is self-regulation theory (Grant, 2001; Du Toit, 2006), wherein individual behaviour can be directed towards a particular objective. This approach can be applied to a range of learning outcomes such as emotional, motivational, and cognitive dimensions of learning.

The affective domain is particularly relevant to understanding the coachee's underlying values and goals and how they may be affecting the individual's effectiveness at an individual, group or organisational levels (Abbott, Stening, Atkins and Grant, 2006). Coaching can add value in the above scenario as it helps the coachee to manage the workflow demands by focusing more on a directed behaviour (Bachkirova and Cox, 2007). In a similar vein, the cognitive domain focuses on building an individual's meta-cognition abilities and how that can be effective in a range of contexts (Abbott *et al.*, 2006). A coach can facilitate the client to explore and develop their reflective thinking skills as well can engage them at an affective and cognitive level thus impacting their personal and interpersonal effectiveness.

A number of contributions from the field of management confirm the role coaching plays in an organisational context (Berglas, 2002; Coutu and Kauffman, 2009; Ket De Vries, 2005; Goldsmith, 2008).

The origins of coaching in management, according to Grant and O'Hara (2008), dates back to the early 1930s; nevertheless, most researchers and workplace coaches often rely upon theoretical lenses from psychological, educational or other disciplines, and often pay little attention to management and organisational settings (Butterworth and Linden, 2006; Bartlett, 2007; Gray and Goregaokar, 2010). In management coaching, the use of external coaches has far exceeded the use of internal workplace coaches. External executive coaches are often employed by an organisation for a short- to medium-term engagement to coach leaders and executives on very specific aspects of their personal ineffectiveness (Diedrich, 1996;

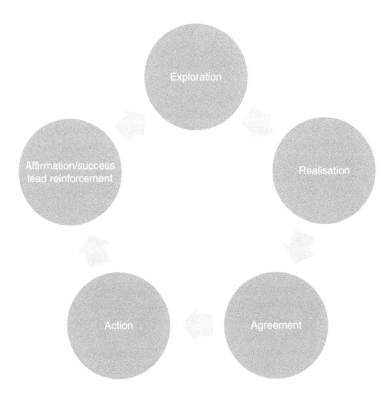

Figure 11.1 Managing a coach–coachee relationship (source: author).

Berman and Bradt, 2006; Freedman and Perry, 2010). What follows from the above is that coaching can improve personal effectiveness in a range of workplace contexts, through quick fixes by the coach and overcoming the active resistance of the coachee to undergo personal reflections, which often involve emotional stress and passive behaviours.

Methodology

This chapter provides an ethnographic account of the insights, experiences and reflections of the author's engagement with senior executives in the Indian IT industry. The following is a reflective ethnographic account of select cases that focus on senior executive coaching engagements for developing innovation capability and capacity. The most common problem presented in the author's experience was an extensive focus on a resource exploitation mindset. The coach's challenge was develop and instil behaviours and values that support exploration and alternative ways of delivering services or designing products. Similarly, a somewhat less-presented problem in these cases was that of excessive exploration and experimentation by leaders at the expense of execution and exploitation of current strengths. Again, the focus was to get a balance or develop leaders who can be ambidextrous. The case studies are of nine senior executives from four firms operating in the Indian IT industry. As such an ethnographic approach is an appropriate methodological choice in capturing the author's experiences (Van Maannen, 1998, 2006). Ethnographic accounts are increasingly being used in management studies (Alvesson, 2003) and are relevant for developing new insights to support development of innovative behaviours. By being actively engaged with one-to-one discussions as a participant in facilitating the decision-making, this approach can yield extremely nuanced and valuable insights of specific instances that may be generalised to a broader set of circumstances. Table 11.1 provides a descriptive account of profiles of senior executives coached.

Table 11.1 Descriptive details of the senior executives coached

Case	Designation	Area(s) coached for personal effectiveness
1	Director	Risk-taking ability, strategic planning
2	Product director	Planning skills, personal leadership
3	Vice president	Avoid judgements and develop influence
4	Vice president	Leadership style exploration, planning style, strategic orientation
5	Director	Communication, collaboration, feedback
6	Director	Leadership style, engagement skills, risk-taking
7	Director	Leadership style, candour, overanalysis, personal effectiveness
8	Director	Team engagement and communication, judgemental, personal style
9	Director	Leadership style, team effectiveness and client engagement

By its very nature, this approach is limited due to the subjective nature of interpretations of the author and the overarching influences the author has had through a range of life experiences. Nevertheless, through these deep and extensive engagements with a range of IT firms in India (domestic and global MNCs), the author has confidence that these accounts can offer valuable insights to managers seeking solutions and change through coaching in the Indian IT industry.

Analysis and findings

As indicated above, the executive coaching assignments covered herein show a number of areas for improving personal effectiveness. The details of individual coaching processes are provided in Tables 11.2 to 11.10, but here an analysis is presented of the key leadership behaviours that support exploration and exploitation of new knowledge for building innovation capacity and capability amongst senior leaders. In addition to areas of personal effectiveness of senior leaders, much can be learnt from the services and product environment firms about the needs of their leaders for exploitative and explorative learning.

After undertaking a content analysis of the key themes emanating from the nine cases, it became apparent that some senior leaders needed more support for developing how to engage in exploitative learning behaviours than explorative learning behaviours. Cases 2, 7, 8 and 9 had a greater need to develop their skills of exploitation. Cases 1, 3, 4, 5 and 6 on the other hand had a greater need to develop their skills of exploration. The cases are summarised in Tables 11.2 to 11.10.

Even though the leaders belonged to information technology services and product development firms, the need for exploitative behaviours was evident in both. This finding concurs with the literature on organisational ambidexterity (O'Reilly and Tushman, 2007, 2008; Raisch *et al.*, 2009; Smith and Tushman, 2005; Tushman and O'Reilly, 1996). The exploitative behaviours were replicated as key issues at a within-case level as well as came out strongly across the above four cases (2, 7, 8 and 9). Similarly, within- and cross-case analysis of Cases 1, 3, 4, 5 and 6 revealed the need for developing exploratory behaviours.

Behaviours conducive to exploitative learning

The behaviours conducive to exploitative learning are: action orientation, task and resource planning, active engagement, valuing metrics, managing emotions, delegation, candour, clear communication and information sharing, tough love, and celebrating wins and achievements. The presence of these behaviours is logical for developing exploitative routines in organisations. Organisational members are expected to maximise resource utilisation and efficiency through delegation, clear planning of tasks and responsibilities, very clear performance expectations of their employees, often specified to a very granular or metricised level. Where issues of poor performance exist, managers must develop the skills of candour and clear communication, and actively engage with employees and

Table 11.2 Case 1 – A director working in product and platforms groups

Exploration	Realisation	Agreement	Success lead reinforcement
High need to be correct and is risk-averse	1 Being self-critical impacts innovation 2 Can sometimes make him follow up without being asked 3 Realises that when things are not closed it can worry him	1 Take more risks 2 Agreement that excessive follow-up can be seen as interference 3 Agreement that he cannot plan for all eventualities specially in when new models are emerging	1 'Let's go' at home and similarly at work does not volunteer help 'where not needed' 2 Does not over analyse his ideas, lets ideas crystallise 3 Uses his logical thinking approach to focus with a re-adjustment on what is the best possible outcome than what is the worst outcome 4 On follow-ups he agrees that he will share benefits or reasons for his follow-up e.g. to ensure success with the teams 5 Taken some risk intentionally e.g. cloud platform and 'not plan it to the nth level' since new models will emerge
Management's perception that he: 1 is not proactive; and 2 can be more strategic	1 Others may sense lack of confidence if he does not contribute 2 Realises that he too can share in forums 'I often realise. I could have said more or less the same things my peer said after the meeting is over'	1 Contribute more in meetings, 2 Build his own personal brand where he would need to show: a clarity in communication b conviction in his ideas c confidently present the ideas	1 Did a presentation on vision for platform group with coach, using 'Rule of Three' Framework, the risk-free environment with the coach helped coachee to practice and present to team 2 Success has made coachee seek opportunity to contribute in peer forums
He needs: 1 to be innovative 2 to be seen as take-charge person	1 Overanalysing gets in the way of being innovative, take risk 2 Plan for a meeting where he pushes for discussion that is little 'Outside in'	1 Not focus on outcomes and try and generate scenarios 'What if I did this… What if I did that…' 2 Use of humour	1 Took initiative and sought to understand client requirements 2 Said that he will continue to seek more opportunity for customer interactions 3 Spotted opportunity for quick deployment mode on automation, only 5/6 of 130 customers are automated on cloud 4 Now increasingly uses Outside In/Reasons To Innovate and customer views to push innovation in platforms

Table 11.3 Case 2 – A product director in product development group

Exploration	Realisation	Agreement	Success lead transformation
1 Managing emotions, anger management 2 Needs to demonstrate consistent style in managing himself	1 Leader's (his) moods changes can be picked by team 2 Nonverbal behaviours impacts teams 3 Emotions impacts leaders ability to communicate with clarity	1 To manage emotions better	1 Shares with spouse happenings in office 'it helped me empty out and get balance back' 3 Now calmer with everyone at home and work 4 Coachee has joined gym as well

Needs to plan better since his manager does not like last-minute surprises	1 Realises that others get stressed as much as him when new items come onto the agenda
	2 Realised the need to develop next line by delegating more
	3 Realise that he cannot be a crisis manager all the time
	4 To operate at higher role will need to:
	  a streamline work/standardise/templatise processes
	  b manage more products
	  c lesser involvement in day to day
		1 To call for meeting with agenda
		2 Strive to stick to agenda
		3 He would define expectations with team and roles in advance and
		4 Increase frequency of reviews to prevent last-minute surprises
			1 Started sending agenda in advance to team
			2 He has started conducting meetings in regular frequency to avoid last-minute surprises
			3 Leader started delegating more
			4 Increased the frequency of reviews on key elements

1 He is keen on creating a personal brand as a thought leader/role model to other leaders 2 He will need to demonstrate clarity, communicate with confidence where it matters (in peer/customer interaction)	1 Awareness that was he was tentative in peer/customer interactions 2 He possesses significant product knowledge, with more than nine years on the product 3 He will think long term and innovate, where delegating will free his time	1 Adapt leadership style in line with the situation 2 Show leadership in product and peer interaction 3 Expand portfolio and add newer products 4 Explore active customer-facing role (consulting)	1 Works with team on general direction of approach (what needs to be done) rather than micromanage and instruct team on 'how' it needs to be done 2 Work to simplify operational complexity 3 Stood ground with product management team on e.g. new product release date 4 Challenges customer in customer interactions 5 Product integration with his suite e.g. logistics

Table 11.4 Case 3 – A vice president in product management group

Exploration	Realisation	Agreement	Actions
Not to prejudge people	1 His role demands that he attend meetings where there might be a need to go with flow and not necessarily give a point of view 2 Realisation that he needs to overcome the aloofness built as a result of concentrative work and analytical style, both at work and home 3 Realisation that overanalysis has diminishing returns after a point and leads to analysis paralysis	1 To listen/make notes to focus on what is being said than to analyse it 2 To record and reflect own views/opinions and its valence (positive or negative to what he hears from others 3 Reflection on own mindset/orientation after the meeting	1 Started going to meeting without opinions 2 Asked questions to understand others point of view anyone rather than get upset 3 In follow-up session shared felt good about using this approach 4 Now has started writing mails without overanalysing reactions from others, sends out decisions as well
Do I need to be an expert in all areas?	1 While he enjoys the technical component of the job, realisation that he cannot be the expert in all areas 2 Add points and value only when needed and not get pressured to contribute	1 Worked on the analogy of an Indian administrative services/general management person 2 Agreement that General Manager works with the strengths of team 3 Agreed to ice breakers, basis common areas of interest, and use them while meeting peers	1 Ask questions with some preparation and connect and build rapport with other party on telephone calls 2 Started asking team leading questions naturally 3 Used this approach to meet one-on-one with peer after office meeting 4 Coachee reported that meeting went fine 'no fuss', minimal adjustment with confidence realisation that coachee can do non-work-related socialising
1 Being assertive versus being consultative 2 Impact and influence others 3 Build executive presence	1 Sometime being consultative will lead to having no decisions from meetings 2 I need to invest time in relationships and not only interact professionally/business-like 3 Reflection that while he was in Korea on site was only focused on work and never interacted socially with team	1 Use the agenda to reiterate decision points 2 Role model behaviour where coachee discards own ideas to accelerate meeting progress 3 Have simple conversation openers, studied in the US, hence can relate to cultural milieu, popular culture	1 Shared an agenda with leaders/peers before going to the meeting, sent material and highlighted items for closure 2 Used letting go/spirit of give and take to drive outcomes from each meeting 3 The fact that we had spent time with each other given frequency of calls also helped

Table 11.5 Case 4 – A vice president who is handling a fast-growing 'cloud portfolio'

Exploration	Realisation	Agreement	Success lead transformation
Exploring leadership journey and own leadership style	1 While he has been shaped by the heroic style of leadership needs to lean on others and seek support from others where needed 2 Reflection of the high need to win	1 Pace-setting heroic style (lead by example) of leadership has a place, but perhaps not sustainable; team works long hours and in area that is new 2 Agreements that he will need to build others capability 3 He needs to make the shift and needs to let go and delegate	1 Identify areas where maximum time is spent people, escalation and operational work etc. 2 Involve team in escalations, and slowly disengage (where possible, set up escalation matrix 3 Hire team including senior team that can objectively spot areas for improvement and not be operational 4 Hire for thinking/ideation problem-solving skills as much as execution
How to free up time	1 Realisation that while the nature of (cloud service operations/support) work demands resolution, there is a need to segment customers and make better use of his time 2 Realisation that he need to let go and not micromanage or show that anxiety	1 Agreed to segment customers so that his time is spent on the key accounts 2 Agreed that his style may put pressure of team, since everyone has different levels of tolerance for stress	1 Put team in front of key customer to handle issues 2 Resist the urge to problem-solve all issues himself, with the incentive to focus on key accounts
How to be more strategic	1 He needs to enable team to generate priorities 2 Modulate leadership approach with direct reports 3 To wear a business hat in view of elevation in role 4 To look at root causes and generate long-term solutions	1 He will create forums to formally signal that his direct reports will take larger roles and accountabilities 2 Manage/temper his approach for overbearing verification 3 To focus on newer measures of performance beyond utilisation 4 Work on long-term solutions 5 Show sponsorship/visible support for employee engagement and opinion surveys	1 Took team for an offsite where team generated priorities; coachee only acted as sponsor 2 Customer case, use of root cause analysis, including a how to speed up system (architecture) b realisation when we correct we can create problems, (third-party upgrades need to sync up with upgrade from coachee firm) c need to ring fence/isolate
Reflection on leadership styles and role demands	1 Need to build team capability 2 Reflection that others can benefit from coaching as approach	1 He has to make adjustments in his natural communication style with teams and be directive than influence teams	1 Earlier operational to strategic content ratio in role was 80:20 and now has moved to 50:50 2 Shared experience where employee negligence led to: customer escalation. After proper due diligence we fired the person, since the process adherence was not followed 3 Now no room for mistakes (stakes are high) 4 Reflection was earlier influencing type, now has to be a little directive given the bet on cloud services, moved from ASK to TELL approach and need to balance back

Table 11.6 Case 5 – A director who is managing the transition of products in a critical M&A context

Exploration	Realisation	Agreement	Success lead transformation
Explore with leader basis incidents his own leadership style and communication	1 He may come across as a little heavy handed on account of his communication style 2 Needs to invest time to understand why people take positions	1 To pause and listen to others 2 Use of humour to lighten the message and reduce intensity 3 Agreed to map they stakeholders to see if they are FOR, AGAINST or NEUTRAL to an initiative	1 In team meetings asked questions 'What will you do…?' Instead of jumping in to participate and lead team 2 Teams were happy from this new approach and worked on their individual commitments on time
Work on feedback on the need to prepare himself and team for meetings and be specific on feedback	1 Of the need to inform team of an agenda and their role 2 Realised that to help his team will need to prepare for meeting 3 Realised the need to provide specific feedback to team	1 Provide team opportunity to present to global vice president from region 2 Agreed to provide specific sharper feedback to team to improve on specific areas to set them on path of improvement	1 Run agenda driven focused meetings helped him focus and provide specific feedback to team 2 Coachee's team valued specific feedback to improve
How to be more collaborative with peers	1 Realisation on the interdependent nature of his role 2 Realises that to transition product from acquired company, he need to assure the anxiety in incumbent product owner 3 Realises the need to skilfully work with relationships and not be pushy in approach	1 Consciously take a facilitator role and let others take a decision 2 Agreed to spend time one-on-one as an option to addressing people in groups 3 Invest time to build consensus with peer, Sometimes 'slow is fast'	1 In team recognition process played the role of a facilitator rather than advocate his views 2 Met each member in the team (40 plus on-site to ensure he spent time with them and involved them to be party to the decision to move account to India office 3 With team reorganisation realised the need to inform teams to extent possible to of impeding change: a spent time with team lead one-on-one b then addressed whole group of changes without personal specifics
Need to be more innovative basis 360 feedback	1 Realisation that products can be disrupted 2 He as a leader can facilitate forums to promote innovation	1 Work on creating time/a day for yourself 2 Create culture of problem-solving with code jam festival 3 Agreed to put a business case challenge for team and prove it as viable with ROI	1 Change/reorganisation in team has impacted this plan 2 However planned to work on mobility solution

Table 11.7 Case 6 – A director consulting who needs to let go on need for control

Exploration	Realisation	Agreement	Success lead transformation
Of leadership style and its impact on others	1 Shared that he uses a differentiating (accent on performance) approach, he consciously manages the teams, till he can trust their capability 2 Basis coach conversation 360 feedback reflected on statement where teams report he as their leader needs to trust teams capabilities more	1 Indicated that he asks teams to lead conversations and presentation and play a lower key role 2 Agreed to not only engage with top performers but with all	1 Shared that this approach has helped him turn around performance of his team 2 Team presented the associate survey results after he did the initial presentation 3 Some of the lower-performing direct reports are doing better
Create engagement and connect with teams with larger goals	1 Need to connect with the needs and motivations of team 2 Update/communicate with filters/ appropriate screening 3 Engage well with teams and is approachable	1 Reflection that he was doing this a lot/ connecting with teams and later tempered his approach since he got feedback that he was overcommunicating, 2 Heard feedback from team that he is not very voluble in contrast to past behaviour 3 Agreement that he perhaps has overcompensated	1 Communicates more frequently with teams 2 Observes closely what interests and motivates them and provides them support in this direction
Raise the bar and innovation quotient with teams	1 Realisation that he can be enthusiastic and can overpromise and work on the fly 2 Has a strong need to lead the change with a visible role and be in control	1 Basis coach observation agreed that he needs to be conscious of teams need for certainty, while he is gung-ho and has a 'let us do it' approach 2 Also realise that sometimes when he is not leading change, needs to give in to others' point of view	1 Shared the outcomes and the big plans for new product suite and renewed new product focus with teams
Need to unlearn and take a few risks	1 Realisation that he needs to be totally sure before he commits to change 2 Can be practical in his world view than work on abstract 3 Leverage his strength to be relaxed (almost bravado) in challenging situations	1 Shared that he prefers to work on areas that he is familiar 2 Agreed with coach that his way of learning is by doing. He needs to have a concrete experience, reaffirmed that in 7 Habits workshops he prefers to share his own work–life examples to drive a point	1 In the annual global offsite meeting was able to share concrete experiences form is experience in client sites A and B etc. 2 Explore other approaches e.g. share vulnerability with audience to connect with them when in unfamiliar areas

Table 11.8 Case 7 – A delivery director who had to build a culture of performance

Exploration	Realisation	Agreement	Success lead transformation
What is his usual style and how it impacts his interactions	1 He needs to be more assertive with counterpart and teams when there are code breaks 2 Realised that being non-assertive is hampering him and his team's productivity	1 Agreed not to provide 'escape' button 2 Be forthright in communication and hold his ground	1 Wrote a direct mail to the client to share code break and need to follow agreed processes and methods 2 Earlier would have worked himself or with team to clean up
Have difficult conversation with underperformers	1 Need to review the productivity of team 2 Differentiate good and poor performers since it impacts overall team engagement scores	1 Agreed that he can be diplomatic and that being diplomatic gets in the way of delivering a performance improvement message 2 Agreed that he should focus in conversation on the specific expectations at one time and not leave mixed messages for the team so that underperformer walks away assuming all is fine/hunky-dory	1 Called the underperformer for a joint conversation with his direct reports 2 Clarified the need to improve performance in a specific areas 3 Put the person on performance improvement plan, not to 'sugar coat' feedback 4 Planned to prioritise with team and direct reports' actions to increase engagement scores
Tendency to overanalyse things	1 His comments on the fly can impact his reputation 2 He needs certain direction/clarity from his supervisor to be comfortable	1 Agreed that he need to temper his communication 2 Seek clarity form boss 3 Realise to work on plan in case clarity is not available	1 Shared conversation with his leader helped him get comfort to deal with planned changes for team 2 Since supervisor is in another location need to seek time with him beyond calls
Need to build personal brand and visibility	1 Realisation that he has great domain and product development expertise 2 Is able to problem-solve to satisfaction of client 3 Has good credibility with his team on his mastery in the subject	1 Need to showcase his achievement with clients in appropriate forums 2 Seek client testimonials 3 Play to his strengths, if he feels he is 'in a rut' and show passion and commitment that his work stands out and seek clarification	1 Share capabilities 2 Plan to seek product development leadership role for products #1 and #2 since the platform will change, has a good chance given his experience and expertise

Table 11.9 Case 8 – A project director who needs to collaborate with others across borders for new product development under demanding time-lines

Exploration	Realisation	Agreement	Success lead transformation
What is his usual style and how it impacts his interactions	1 Realised that he needs to communicate more often with team 2 Shared that he can and does roll up his sleeves to speed up work that gets in the way of team communication	1 Agreement to spend more time with the team one-on-one 2 Support new team and demonstrate patience to build their capability	1 Spent time on finding out what motivates team member 2 Analysed if it is a skill or will issue 3 Shared with team their individual responsibilities
Work on unresolved issues with counterpart	1 Realised that since issues were unresolved with peer counterpart it was hampering his team interactions and coming across in his demeanour (pressure and stress) 2 When coach pointed out to his demeanour realised that he needs to take a pause and use other approaches	1 Agreed to work with peer to close on issues on priority 2 Realised that peer has a different personality and communication approach and the need to modulate his approach in accordance and 3 Build trust with peer	1 Sought meeting with peer 2 Opened channel of communication with others apart from the peer, especially those his peers trust to build credibility 3 Shared with peer that the can only work when there is some clarity on, for example, which platform to work for the product 4 Had an open/'hot' conversation that settled the loose ends that helped him progress on his tasks in hand
Need to have regular team engagement and communication	Understood the need to maintain high level of engagement with team, especially the new team given long time-frame of product development	Agreed to work on a frequency and process of communication with teams	1 Shared with team on what information he needs in a review meeting 2 Built consistency in approach where he and his counterpart peer shared about empowerment of next line 3 In which specific areas will he and the peer be involved 4 With this trust-building approach peer also seeks his views before taking decision
Need to build personal brand and visibility	1 Realisation that he is seen as a person who can solve complex problems 2 Realisation that he needs to add additional dimensions to his brand	1 Agreement that he seeks information and certainty to take decisions rather than use an intuitive approach 2 Understood of the role of intuition in decision-making and judgement	1 Started reading blogs to find other points of view 2 Commitment to seek a larger volunteer role to build his personal brand
Need for control and its impact on decision-making and judgement	1 Realises that he needs to free his time for long-range thinking, and also broaden his horizons 2 Realisation that he seeks information and certainty to take decisions	1 Agreed that he will need to also work with team by being less combative/forthright and be facilitative and generative so that he can focus on long term 2 Was reading and reviewing information to be able to spot opportunities	1 Agreed to work on a plan where he can accelerate decision-making (basis: his experience with peer): a work to his strengths (use of data) b present the information and attendant risks c close with a compelling reason to act (go to market first, likely revenues over product lifecycle etc.) 2 Enthuse team to plan: a use a theme song b use of an interesting project story or incident to get team's attention

Table 11.10 Case 9 – A director who handles strategic services for clients

Exploration	Realisation	Agreement	Success lead transformation
What is his usual style and how it impacts his interactions	1 Realised that his communication style and approach may hamper his impact on the other party, e.g. in a 10-day engagement he may only share his views very much later 2 Realisation that while he has the experience and expertise and confidence he may need to be more visible when needed and take charge	1 To share his point of view and not hold back 2 To steer the agenda when needed and not be passive	1 Shared a related experience where sales lead did not read client needs. The client was more keen to know the ROI but colleague was selling benefits and features 2 Coaches intervened for client 3 Made an affirmation to stay in touch and mine existing client where his company has delivered value
Need to balance focus for clients (as specialist) with task to develop overall team capability	1 Realised the need to build team capability given the reorganisation 2 Realises that with his ambition need to work/scale up in terms of revenues/sales, impact will need a strong next line	1 Agreed that he has to build specialised skill sets in team 2 Agreed that he will find time and pay specific attention to interests and motivations of team 3 This will help him move team in roles that fit their unique gifts and abilities 4 Agreed that this approach differentiates a good and great manager	1 Has basis reorganisation relooked at team, spoke to counterpart to create a structure for field support organisation in addition to consulting 2 Building team capability will help him in being in front of the client more often 3 Provide regular feedback to team on the job, of specific areas
Tendency to be mild	1 Realisation that he inherently respects people at all levels/show grace in interactions 2 Realisation that holding back, not disagreeing visibly, is not seen as strength	1 Agreed that sometimes 'niceties are best left at home' and he will need to push back 2 Agreed that candour has its place in communicating at work 3 In developing his team he agreed he will need to take some tough calls through difficult conversations if the teams do not fit role in strategic services	1 Had a difficult conversation with a team member 2 Since has data and was observant, shared that data the conversation 3 Having the conversation was a relief and it went okay (reiterated for him that he can be tough yet fair) 4 Hold his ground and square up with peers (work in progress)
Need to build personal brand and visibility	1 Realisation that he has a good image with team, colleagues, client, across his company 2 Is able to problem-solve to satisfaction of client and a role model Subject Matter Expert	1 Agree to build a broaden his impact and network with clients 2 Add other elements to his personal brand 3 Agreed that decision makers across the globe need to know him	1 Seize the moment/opportunity to showcase his unique abilities and not stay in sidelines 2 Track wins in clients where Strategic Services played a key role

teams. The behaviours are extremely relevant in cases of IT services and product outsourcing where co-development teams have to work across geographical boundaries and time zones. The presence of such behaviours supports both the exploitation of resources and managing innovation and work outcomes effectively. Most of the above learning behaviours can be classified at cognitive and affective levels (Delahaye, 2005) and are known to be effective professional competencies for managers.

Behaviours conducive to explorative learning

The behaviours conducive to explorative learning are: facilitation, strategic analysis, outside-in orientation, scenario planning, open-mindedness, tolerance/trust, patience/letting go, focus on effort and outcomes, peer interaction, extensive information sharing, wider involvement, delegation and empowerment, collaboration, collective problem-solving, non-judgemental, seeking feedback, reflection, and humour. When an organisation wants to develop new knowledge internally through its employees and teams, or externally through its clients or through networks of open innovation, the leaders and managers tasked with this responsibility must undertake strategic analysis with an eye on external market strengths whilst also keeping in mind the organisation's internal strengths and capabilities. The leaders engage in scenario planning and demonstrate open-mindedness to new ideas. To foster free flow of ideas and evaluation, they must act as facilitators, often letting go of established positions that are acting as potential barriers. Realising that innovative solutions do not rest with one individual, managers and leaders need to adopt an approach that values extensive information-sharing, frequent and open peer communication, often delegating tasks with authority, and empowering employees to take risks and reflect upon the learnings from potential failures. In cases where there are timelines to be met and deliverables to be reviewed an outcome based approach and seeking feedback from the group on the success and reflecting on both the achievements and failures creates an environment of trust.

Learning from the cases

1   *Experimentation, by its nature, will inevitably result in failures* (Lee, Edmondson, Thomke and Worline, 2004). Yet, without these failures, learning cannot occur. The coaching cases indicate that leaders need to allow for small failures and use a style to promote the team to take charge, refraining from solving the problems for the team. Small failures arise not only in the course of purposeful experimentation, but also when daily work is complex and interdependent, as exemplified in Coaching Case 4. The case shows (1) need to be mindful of customer load/season when upgrading software, (2) need to sync the upgrade with other software vendor ecosystems. The coachee was using heroic style of leadership and not reaching to the larger organisation to find others who can help to correct the problem. Case 1 indicates low orientation to risk taking.

Compensating for problems can be counterproductive if doing so isolates information about problems, or one plans conservatively and never fails. Both cases suggests limited or no learning.

2   *Delegate.* Groups that improve more over a fixed time-frame or that take less time to improve must be learning faster than their peers. Short learning cycles will translate into superior future performance. The cases indicate the need for leaders to delegate, to be supportive than being highly evaluative and to generate learning in teams.

3   *Design for flexibility and fail fast.* Rather than seeking to prove what they already believe, exploratory leaders seek discovery through creative and iterative experimentation (Garvin, 2000). As Cases 1 and 3 suggest, planning to the *n*th degree can be counterproductive. Setbacks occur, especially if the leader is security minded and prevents risk-taking, as they check minute details and worry over success. Creating a detailed plan and being emotionally attached to it can be also a significant financial waste.

4   *Diversity promotes learning.* Learning about complex, interconnected problems also suffers from ineffective discussion among parties with conflicting perspectives. As Case 3 indicated, creating an agenda, learning to concede and maintaining a spirit of give and take could promote discussion. Sometimes it is just a matter of understanding that your peer has unique style that is different from your own approach. As Case 8 indicates, this helps leaders realise the reason for conflict.

5   *Create safe psychological spaces.* Status differences, a lack of psychological safety, and lack of inquiry into others' information and experiences related to substantive issues can combine to ensure that a group as a whole learns little. As indicated in Cases 6 and 8 there is a need to focus on an inquiry-based approach than advocating one's point of view. As Case 3 demonstrated that meeting others without an agenda and in a social setting can also build on the inquiry process.

6   *Show genuine interest in others.* People in disagreement rarely ask each other the kind of sincere questions that are necessary for them to learn from each other (Argyris, 1985). People tend to try to force their views on the other party rather than educating the other party by providing the underlying reasoning behind their perspectives. Cases 2 and 3 show the need for leaders to be self-aware of own emotional state and engage meaningfully with others. Home and personal relationships is a good place start as Case 2 indicates. Cases 7 and 9 indicate the need to be more assertive and push back where needed.

7   *Learning is richer with multiple perspectives.* The ideas, experiences and concerns of others are valuable when facing uncertainty and high-stakes decision. Multiple perspectives are critical to making appropriate choices of new possibilities and filling gaps in knowledge through combining information sources. As Case 3 points out, leaders need to realise they cannot be expert in all areas and must accept this reality. Leaders also need to explore other leadership approaches and styles of decision-making to build a more

holistic response, as shared in Case 8. When leaders follow an exploratory approach and take risks, they embrace ambiguity and acknowledge openly gaps in knowledge, they can promote learning, as validated in Cases 1 and 2.

8   *Learning comes from small problems or process failures.* Exploitation requires eschewing quick fixes and workarounds, and instead stopping to take the time to analyse and seek to address root causes of the problem. Therefore, resolving problems to prevent recurrence is likely to take longer than working around the problem, harming efficiency in the short-term. These short-term costs of learning are particularly problematic when workers face fragmented tasks or heavy workloads that preclude the necessary slack for learning. As Case 5 illustrates, separating the operational teams that support customers 24/7 to work on customer escalations and a problem-solving team to focus on root cause analysis supports learning. As the case indicated, a senior leader could facilitate investigation and implementation of solution efforts worked in this case.

The human desire to 'get it right' rather than to treat success and failure as equivalently useful data greatly impedes learning. This is true in routine work contexts, but it is particularly problematic when facing novel and unknown situations in which no one can know in advance all that is needed to perform well. Individuals prevent learning when they ignore their own mistakes in order to protect themselves from the unpleasantness and loss of self-confidence and self-esteem associated with acknowledging failure (Taylor and Brown, 1988).

Conclusion

This chapter highlights the importance of senior executive coaching in the Indian IT industry. Noting the Indian IT industry's transition from excellence in exploitation to exploring new forms of learning, this chapter highlights the importance of developing behaviours that are conducive to dealing with disruptive and discontinuous change. Using data from the author's senior executives' coaching experiences from Indian IT industry, this chapter developed a framework for coaching executives and identified behaviours that are critical in supporting exploratory and exploitative learning, as both these forms of learning are necessary for maintaining and managing growth and innovation. Further, findings reveal the importance of exploration behaviours in IT services firms as well as exploitation behaviours in product environment firms.

In addition to the behaviours identified in the case analysis, the findings from the cases also indicated a number of key elements that can drive innovation in firms. First, internal governance is a critical element and requires instituting formal structures, principles and decision rights that enable agreement and alignment with strategy. Second, relationship management amongst organisational members and clients for resolving tensions needs corporate coordination. Third, programme management is critical in complex initiatives in IT development environments where coordination of objectives, resources and interdependencies is required. Fourth, the architecture of the technology infrastructure and information flows is critical for knowledge integration. Fifth, strong process skills need to be developed in the talent. Sixth, change leadership should be provided where necessary to ensure team/project/business unit integration. Seventh, the leadership has to be such that it supports disruptive change. Emerging leaders are often best suited to this role. Eighth, these elements require high levels of emotional commitment for all the people involved. Finally, organising to learn and organising to execute are two distinct management practices, one suited to exploration and the other to exploitation respectively (Argyris and Schön, 1978). Developing such behaviours is critical for improving the personal effectiveness of senior leaders. The author believes they will be critical in positioning the Indian IT industry in the next era of its growth.

References

Abbott, G., Stening, B., Atkins, P.W.B., and Grant, A.M. (2006). Coaching expatriate managers for success: Adding value beyond training and mentoring. *Asia Pacific Journal of Human Resources, 44*(3), 295–317.

Alawadhi, N., and Mendonca, J. (2014, 16 July). Automation in IT companies reducing space for employees; puts question mark on future of IT grads. *The Economic Times.* Retrieved from http://articles.economictimes.indiatimes.com/2014-07-16/news/51600564_1_vineet-nayar-hcl-technologies-ganesh-natarajan

Alvesson, M. (2003). Beyond neopositivists, romantics, and localists: A reflexive approach to interviews in organizational research. *Academy of Management Review, 28*(1), 13–33.

Argyris, C. (1985). *Strategy, change, and defensive routines.* New York, NY: Harper Business.

Argyris, C., and Schön, D. (1978). *Organizational learning: A theory of action perspectives.* Reading, MA: Addison-Wesley.

Bachkirova, T., and Cox, E. (2007). Coaching with emotion in organisations: Investigation of personal theories. *Leadership and Organization Development Journal, 28*(7), 600–612.

Bartlett, J. (2007). Advances in coaching practices: A humanistic approach to coach and client roles. *Journal of Business Research, 60*(1), 91–93.

Berg, M., and Karlsen, J. (2007). Mental models in project management coaching. *Engineering Management Journal, 19*(3), 3–14.

Berglas, S. (2002). The very real dangers of executive coaching. *Harvard Business Review, 80*(6), 86–92.

Berman, W., and Bradt, G. (2006). Executive coaching and consulting: 'Different strokes for different folks'. *Professional Psychology: Research and Practice, 37*(3), 244–253.

Bloomberg. (2013). *50 most innovative countries.* Retrieved from www.bloomberg.com/slideshow/2013-02-01/50-most-innovative-countries.html

Burdett, J. (1998). Forty things every manager should know about coaching. *Journal of Management Development, 17*(2), 142–152.

Butterworth, S., and Linden, J. (2006). Effect of motivational interviewing-based health coaching on employees' physical and mental health status. *Journal of Occupational Health Psychology, 11*(4), 358–365.

Cappelli, P., Singh, H., Singh, J., and Useem, M. (2010). *The India way: How India's top leaders are revolutionizing management*. Boston, MA: Harvard Business School.

Coutu, D., and Kauffman, C. (2009, January). *The realities of executive coaching*. Harvard Business Review Report. Boston, MA: Harvard Business Review.

Delahaye, B.L. (2005). *Human Resource Development: Adult learning and knowledge management* (2nd ed.). Brisbane: John Wiley & Sons (Australia).

Diedrich, R. (1996). An iterative approach to executive coaching. *Consulting Psychology Journal: Practice and Research, 48*(2), 61–66.

Du Toit, A. (2006). Making sense through coaching. *Journal of Management Development, 26*(3), 282–291.

Dutz, M.A. (2007). *Unleashing India's innovation: Toward a sustainable and inclusive growth*. Washington, DC: World Bank. Retrieved from www-wds.worldbank.org/external/default/WDSContentServer/IW3P/IB/2007/10/17/000310607_200710171451 09/Rendered/PDF/411750IN0Unlea101OFFICIAL0USE0ONLY1.pdf

Ellinger, A., and Hamlin, R. (2008). Behavioural indicators of ineffective managerial coaching. *Journal of European Industrial Training, 32*(4), 240–257.

Freedman, A., and Perry, J. (2010). Executive consulting under pressure: A case study. *Consulting Psychology Journal: Practice and Research, 62*(3), 189–202.

Garvin, D.A. (2000). *Learning in action: A guide to putting the learning organization to work*. Boston, MA: Harvard Business School Press.

Goldsmith, M. (2008). *What got you here won't get you there: How successful people become even more successful*. London: Profile Books.

Govindarajan, V., and Trimble, C. (2012). *Reverse innovation: Create far from home, win everywhere*. Boston, MA: Harvard Business Press.

Grant, A. (2001). Grounded in science or based on hype? An analysis of neuro-associative conditioning? *Australian Psychologist, 36*(3), 232–238.

Grant, A., and O'Hara, B. (2008). Key characteristics of the commercial Australian executive coach training industry. *International Coaching Psychology Review, 3*(1), 57–73.

Gray, D., and Goregaokar, H. (2010). Choosing an executive coach: The influence of gender on the coach–coachee matching process. *Management Learning, 41*(5), 525–544.

Hackman, J., and Wageman, R. (2005). A theory on team coaching. *The Academy of Management Review, 30*(2), 269–287.

Heslin, P. and Vandewalle, D. (2006). Keen to help? Managers' implicit person theories and their subsequent employee coaching. *Personnel Psychology, 59*(4), 871–902.

ICF (2012). *ICF Global Coaching Study*. Retrieved from http://coachfederation.org/prdetail.cfm?ItemNumber=1970&_ga=1.51456298.2063038318.1417825105&RDtoken=2 3075&userID=

IDC (2014). *IDC Predictions 2014: The Battle for Dominance on the 3rd Platform Heats Up*. Retrieved from www.idc.com/getdoc.jsp?containerId=prUS24417213

Jansen, J.J., George, G., Van den Bosch, F.A.J., and Volberda, H.W. (2008). Senior team attributes and organizational ambidexterity: the moderating role of transformational leadership. *Journal of Management Studies, 45*(5), 982–1007.

Ket De Vries, M. (2005). Leadership group coaching in action: The Zen of creating high performance teams. *Academy of Management Executive, 19*(1), 61–76.

KPMG (2014) *Innovation Transforming the Growth Landscape: Capitalising IP in Indian IT-BMP*. Bangalore: Author.

Kumar, N., and Puranam, P. (2012). *Inside India: The emerging innovation challenge to the West*. Boston, MA: Harvard Business Review Press.

Lee, F., Edmondson, A.C., Thomke, S., and Worline, M. (2004). The mixed effects of inconsistency on experimentation in organizations *Organization Science, 15*(3), 310–326.

Malik, A. (2013). Post-GFC people management challenges: A study of India's information technology sector. *Asia Pacific Business Review, 19*(2), 230–246.

March, J.G. (1991). Exploration and exploitation in organizational learning. *Organization Science, 2*(1), 71–87.

Megginson, D., and Clutterbuck, D. (2006). Creating a coaching culture. *Industrial and Commercial Training, 38*(5), 232–237.

NASSCOM. (2013). *Report on Indian IT and BPM Industry*. New Delhi: NASSCOM.

NASSCOM. (2014). *NASSCOM Annual Report, 2013–14*. Retrieved from www.nasscom. in/sites/default/files/NASSCOM%20Annual%20Report%202013-14.pdf

O'Connor, D.L., and Ertmer, P.A. (2006). Today's coaches prepare tomorrow's mentors: Sustaining results of professional development. *Academy of Educational Leadership Journal, 10*(2), 97–112.

O'Reilly, C.A., and Tushman, M.L. (2007). *Ambidexterity as a Dynamic Capability: Resolving the Innovator's Dilemma*. Working Paper No. 07-088. Cambridge, MA: Harvard Business School.

O'Reilly, C.A. III, and Tushman, M.L. (2008). Ambidexterity as a dynamic capability: Resolving the innovator's dilemma. *Research in Organizational Behavior, 28*, 185–206.

Radjou, N., Prabhu, J., and Ahuja, S. (2012). *Jugaad Innovation: Think frugal, be flexible, generate breakthrough growth*. San Francisco, CA: Jossey-Bass.

Raisch, S., Birkinshaw, J., Probst, G., and Tushman, M.L. (2009). Organizational ambidexterity: Balancing exploitation and exploration for sustained performance. *Organization Science, 20*(4), 685–695.

Smith, W.K., and Tushman, M.L. (2005). Managing strategic contradictions: A top management model for managing innovation streams. *Organization Science, 16*(5), 522–536.

Taylor, S.E., and Brown, J.D. (1988). Illusion and well-being: A social psychological perspective on mental health. *Psychological Bulletin, 103*(2), 193–210.

Tushman, M.L., and O'Reilly, C.A. (1996). Ambidextrous organizations: Managing evolutionary and revolutionary change. *California Management Review, 38*(4), 8–30.

Van Maanen, J. (1998). *Qualitative studies of organizations*. London: Sage.

Van Maanen, J. (2006). Ethnography then and now. *Qualitative Research in Organizations and Management, 1*(1), 13–21.

12 The world's largest *'ideapreneurship™'*

Putting employees first so the customer never feels second!

Prithvi Shergill and Kapil Notra

Introduction

In recent years, the uniqueness of the Indian managerial and leadership style has attracted immense practitioner and academic interest leading to several studies examining the distinctive Indian approach with a global business reach (Cappelli, Singh, Singh, and Useem, 2010; Govindarajan and Trimble, 2011, 2013; Radjou, Prabhu, and Ahuja, 2012). These studies have also highlighted the importance of managing people for both, exploiting the current business models as well as exploring new models and knowledge for achieving sustained levels of growth (Govindarajan and Trimble, 2011). The importance of managing growth through innovation has been a core theme in the above collections. In this chapter the authors discuss how HCL Technologies implemented its journey in a post-*Employee First Customer Second* era popularized by its ex-CEO, Vineet Nayar (Nayar, 2010a, 2010b, 2010c). The new approach for managing people has been well documented by Harvard Business Press (Nayar, 2010a, 2010b) and has been taught at numerous business schools (Hill, Khanna, and Stecker, 2009). This chapter begins by setting out the background to this journey, highlighting the learnings from the approach and the subsequent strategies introduced to sustain the momentum generated by this approach in 2005.

The journey

Back In 2005, HCL believed that all was well and perhaps rightly so! The company was growing at 30% compound annual growth rate (CAGR), with 18,000+ employees, operations in 18 countries generating US$700 million in revenues.

While this presented an excellent picture, in reality, all was not well. The HCL Leadership was struggling to answer what happened to the pioneer in the Indian IT industry, any which way one looked at it:

- the company that was number one in almost all the portfolios managed;
- the company that introduced many technologies and service innovations to the industry; and
- the company whose innovations, combined with an entrepreneurial culture, attracted the best and brightest to work at HCL.

What went wrong?

Consider yourself driving a car with your family on a highway to a picnic spot. You are relaxed as you are on vacation. In all likelihood you would be driving at a comfortable speed of 60–70 kmph, notwithstanding others who sped by. You are comfortable in that speed and choosing not to pay attention to others racing ahead of you.

That was exactly how HCL felt during the years 2000 through 2005. The company was indeed growing in 2005 with a 30% CAGR to boot. But when compared with our competitors, who were outgrowing us at a faster rate, we were not only losing market share, but mind share as well. While attrition increased, the rate of attracting and retaining talent decreased.

Many in the HCL leadership were in a celebratory mood. Most felt good with the company's performance. Very few were investing time to envision the flip side of the coin. No one was ready to acknowledge the competitive challenge looming large on the horizon. It was at this point of time that Shiv Nadar, our founder and chairman appointed Vineet Nayar to be the CEO of HCL Technologies.

The initial analysis he was asked to do indicated that during 2000–2005, the company was offering a dated service mix to a changed market place resulting in slower than market growth.

Emergence of start-up behavior

Over the years, the four tenets of EFCS – Mirror Mirror; Trust, Transparency and Flexibility; Inverting the Pyramid; and Recasting the Role of CEO – became the currency of practice of all managers in the organization. What this led to was a noticeable change in employee behavior – one that was akin to the origins of HCL as a garage startup. However, this time it was a grassroots movement.

The entrepreneurship in our history reflects in a commitment of the employees to enhance the value zone created every time they interact with their clients and stakeholders. From being advocated and being management-led, we saw the shift to employee-led, management-embraced way. We also discovered the emergence of Grassroots Intrapreneurs, a DNA distinctly embedded in every employee – seeking the license to ideate, decide, and act every day!

Evolution of organic creativity

The way any employee creates change is through the power of translating information, insight into innovation. The consistency of belief in employees at HCL in value centricity and the license to ideate and take advantage of the freedom to decide and act using programs and platforms that captured these small but powerful ideas has led to institutionalization of a grassroot employee-led culture.

Stories where ideapreneurs demonstrated creativity abound in HCL, which demonstrate the sustenance of our entrepreneurial history as India's original garage startup, in our DNA. Deeper research revealed that the continued business growth of HCL, even during turbulent economic times, was a resultant of an unique combination of this intrapreneural DNA and the freedom to ideate, that returned value to customers which were beyond what was the contracted. There are many instances of how employees went out of their mandated work to create processes that helped the customer save millions of dollars, without being asked for it. It was also observed that such actions were characterized by three key employee behaviors:

- *Need to Seed*: Independently seeking alternatives to the norm, generating and fostering ideas that promise incremental, progressive shift from the status quo.
- *Desire to Nurture*: Evolving networks that nurture these ideas to realization; providing flexibility in work, encouraging and mentoring to up-skill talent, evolving ideas in scope toward implementation, and garnering ambitious scale.
- *Commitment to Harvest*: Recognizing results, rewarding business outcomes, and generating ideas to renew enterprise shift, incubating an intrapreneurial ecosystem that self sustains growth from "initiative" to "*finitiative*."

The impact of these behaviors is further multiplied by programs that enable HCL ideapreneurs to SEED their innovative ideas across a range of platforms. All SEED platforms are designed to capture customer centric innovations that make a difference to their business, thus laying the cornerstone of "Relationships Beyond The Contract."

1 MAD JAM

This event celebrates the most outstanding ideas from all HCLites, MAD JAM, or the Make A Difference Jamboree, reflects the vibrancy of the culture at HCL – the culture of ideapreneurship™, where ideas are seeded, nurtured, and harvested; and every employee is an idea-led intrapreneur, an *ideapreneur*.

At HCL, we empower and enable individual employees at all levels of the organization to shape innovative solutions that address operational and customer challenges. MAD JAM is a platform for identifying business-centric innovation emerging from employees across the organization for organizational leaders to nurture and harvest. A jury of senior leadership shortlists the best ideas, which are turned into videos and hosted on the HCL intranet and on YouTube, and employees vote for their favorite entries.

Till now, MAD JAM has helped many outstanding innovators launch their ideas and be acknowledged as the best-of-the-breed at HCL. We engaged with more than 50,000 HCLites through the MAD JAM portal; 1,500 innovators sent in 647 ideas; 36 of the best ideas were turned into short films; and finally, 16 ideas made it to the grand finale in MAD JAM 2011 and 2012.

MAD JAM 2013 helped *ideapreneurs* take their ideas to the next level – convert them from concept to reality with the help of MAD VC fund of US$250,000. The funding is available not only for the winning ideas, but the ones which have the potential to scale-up and be harvested for benefit to clients and HCL.

2 Value Portal

The Value Portal is an HCL platform that has been designed to record, facilitate, manage, assess, and share customer-focused innovations. The basic concept took shape when we realized that within day-to-day work, teams were innovating and sharing suggestions with customers, which were being extensively appreciated.

To capture our employees' ideas in a structured manner, we built an application called the Value Portal. HCLites post their ideas on the portal to get them reviewed and enhanced by senior HCL leaders, and showcase these ideas to the customer, once they are endorsed. Proposed ideas are adopted by customers if they feel convinced about the idea, which is when the value of the idea is certified as delivered. We see this end-to-end employee-driven customer-centric innovation as an outcome of the "grassroots movement" within HCL.

Today, we engage with more than 18,000 employees through the Value Portal, and have so far generated over 32,000 grassroots-driven innovative ideas for 380+ customers on process improvement, cycle-time reduction, tool development, technical solutions, and cost optimization. Over 7,000 of these ideas have been approved by customers and implemented by HCL, to deliver over US$600 million of value to customers. These ideas didn't just deliver one-time value to clients; they have become a part of HCL's overall solution set with limitless potential to add value every time they were used for other projects and clients

The Value Portal is a real example of how our culture of *ideapreneurship™* encourages crowd-sourcing at work; leveraging collective ideas of thousands of *ideapreneurs* to deliver value to customers, beyond the contract.

3 Lead Gen

Lead Gen is a program to capture untapped business demand through employees who directly interface with customers. Employees use the Lead Gen site hosted on the company intranet to log in any information that they think will lead to a an opportunity for HCL to create value for the client. An employee lead is defined as the "knowledge of a business pain point, or a customer requirement, which can be addressed by HCL's portfolio of IT Services." The employee capturing the lead will be eligible for a reward if the lead results in a successful deal closure.

4 Patent Office

A comprehensive HCL patent process that allows rigorous evaluation of patentable ideas by a decentralized patent office aligned to different lines of business. Ideapreneurs are rewarded both at the filling and granting stage. These programs had a direct co-relation with meaningful business outcomes, and therefore, form an innovation ecosystem that is self-supported. It all started from our values, which led to desired behaviors, and an increase in participation in the programs that led to meaningful business outcomes. Hence, our values led to behavior patterns that leverage programs to deliver successful outcomes in a virtuous cycle, making HCL as one of the world's largest *ideapreneurships™*.

Entrepreneurial freedom

"HCL employees have the freedom to develop their own ideas, decide and act," says Prithvi Shergill, Chief Human Resources Officer, "and the role of line leadership is to ensure there is a sense of purpose and autonomy experienced by our people as they exercise their mastery."

The strategy involves staff having candid conversations to decide if they need to change their own working practices, those of the team or the organization as a whole. Everyone is expected to highlight their perspective on individual and organizational strengths and weaknesses so the necessary changes are then enacted with the aim of making everyone accountable for their own performance. "Highlighting what they are good at helps employees to create an environment of collaboration in which colleagues can achieve an objective together, while identifying areas that can be developed further results in advice and support from others," explains R. Anand, Vice President, People Programs.

The company operates an internal social platform, Meme, featuring a discussion forum through which employees can blog, raise issues, share views, and engage in dialogue with senior management.

A self-assessment metric called EPIC (Employee Passion Indicative Count) has been introduced to help employees identify their "passion drivers" because these are what keep people engaged. "By understanding what they are passionate about and what their strengths are as well as their potential, we gain sufficient insight to ensure that we deploy our people in the most effective and most productive way," says Prithvi. "This drives enhanced contributions and innovation, which is of great benefit to the organization and in turn helps each individual's personal growth. By advocating consistency in belief and adoption of tailored programs and practices, we focus on making HCL people 'ideapreneurs' who seed, nurture, and harvest ideas for the benefit of the customer, the organization, and themselves as individuals."

One example of that is Anupam Anand, a project manager at HCL who noticed that the search engine of a major US client was only configured to its own Web browser. He therefore installed a default pack in all of the client's products so that its search engine would become the default one in all users' systems. He also suggested the use of a universal installer, which is a file that installs the customer's search engine as the default search engine in all Web browsers to maximize their user base. These initiatives were expected to generate US$15 million of business for the client in 2013, and the universal installer resulted in 758 million unique clicks by customers worldwide in just one year.

Another HCL success story is employee and avid blogger Vineet Bhatt. He came up with the innovative idea of inviting active bloggers to post their experiences of a global security software client's products on either their personal blogs or the customer's own blog channel. Bloggers whose posts drove traffic to the customer's website and resulted in a purchase were rewarded. The idea was warmly welcomed and initiated by the client, resulting in US$2 million of additional revenue.

Culture as our employee value proposition

In a hyper-competitive market, businesses today are under immense pressure. This pressure stems from the emergence of various trends in the business eco-system – the "Millennials" are changing the workforce mix, and technology advancements are impacting how business connects to its customer. These factors exert pressure as organizations look inwards to drive process efficiencies and maximize business levers to extract more bang for the buck. Therefore, the role of a function like HR increasingly impacts business outcomes.

In our view, a progressive HR organization is distinguished by its ability to design and deploy practices that exponentially impact benefits of *Work* – by multiplying value for customers; *Workplace* – by multiplying the impact of the ways of working and environment; and *Workforce* – by multiplying the productivity and performance of our people.

HR continues on this journey of evolution at HCL Technologies – it is therefore, not a surprise that our business priorities are shared responsibilities that we pursue together with line leadership. Our strategic priorities focus on influencing Work, Workplace, and Workforce, are seen as an accountability that is co-owned by all HR and line leaders. Initiatives across these three areas of focus provide clarity on their execution. For instance, optimizing agility in our talent acquisition function will help impact economic fulfilment, which has a direct correlation to our revenue goals. As we traverse across the planning year, we continue to review and evaluate these initiatives that act as proof points. The entire HR team partners and works collaboratively to accomplish these shared (long-term) goals, which are articulated as our strategic intent.

The focus of our people practices is to strengthen the sense of purpose, enhance autonomy, and build mastery. This resonates with our workforce and reinforces the confidence that is seen in our HR team's capabilities to execute to the business strategy.

Our approach to ensure line leaders engage, enable, and empower HCLites is tailored to address each stage of the employee lifecycle (plan, join, learn, deploy, perform, engage, grow):

- By connecting through:
  - *Meme*: HCL's in-house social networking platform, that provides access to a social network while at work. Conceptualized to enhance

collaboration, build trust and transparency, and invert the organizational pyramid. It can facilitate discussions, engagement, and collaboration all to multiply innovation across geographies, time zones, and employees.

- *Dialog*: A platform to enhance face to face employee-leadership communication, it assists employees to understand the line of sight of their work to business performance and raise questions and concerns with ways of working.
- *Live Connect*: It serves as a virtual vehicle to share information and feedback between employees and the leadership and preserves the HCL culture of personal interaction and open communication that allows leaders to have real time virtual interaction with their teams spread across geographies and time zones.
- *Employee Connect*: This is facilitated actions taken based on information captured on a portal of the one-to-one meetings completed between HR team members and employees to understand their professional and personal goals.

- By enabling employees to live their passion with initiatives for their professional benefit:
  - *The Toastmasters Club:* For the employees to develop leadership and communication skills.
  - *The Polyglots' Corner:* To give HCLites an opportunity to learn a foreign language by registering for classes organized at the workplace itself.
  - *Stepathlon:* A unique race through a "virtual world" for 100 days.
- By making employees' life easy by:
  - *Assisting HCLites Anytime (AHA):* An employee-driven program that integrates employee services under one platform selected democratically by employees themselves.

    Through AHA, we offer differentiated employee services (deployed via policies and/or support processes that are co-created with location specific Employee First Councils) while keeping in mind the demographic factors of age, gender, location, family size, skill, interests of each individual. Through AHA, we reach out to employees on a regular basis with a set of proposed services that are perceivably beneficial to them. Employees can choose all services on offer, or à la carte. Once a significant number of employees have expressed their interest in a proposed service, we will offer it to eligible employees after consulting with the Employees First Councils.

AHA offers services classified under four categories – Work, Self, Family, and Life:

- *Work:* This category offers policies and benefit programs that assist employees to deliver better on the job. At HCL, our constant endeavor is to provide a work environment where our employees are encouraged to explore new horizons, and are given access to best-in-class facilities that help them deliver their best. We also realize that while managing their professional and personal priorities, they need support systems in place that would enable them to balance both without compromising on either front. Towards this, under this category, we offer a range of policies and services which would help them in work–life continuity, like Tuition Assistance, Sabbatical, Come Home, Valet Parking, and Nursing Station

- *Self:* This category has initiatives that focus on employee well-being and are designed to reduce day-to-day stress/hassles. "Self" is all about oneself. It is about the "me" space, where everyone wants to invest in but which is forgotten most of the time because of our hectic work and life schedules. Under this category, there is a range of offerings starting from health through to financial advisory services – all of which is intended to help our employees put themselves and their needs first, like 24/7 Emergency Support, Financial Planning Workshops, and Health Check Camps
- *Family:* This category includes benefit programs that enable employees and their families to enhance the comfort in their lifestyle. After a charged-up day or week at work, ensuring projects are delivered and time-lines are met, we realize the importance of personal time when our employees are unwinding or spending quality time with their family. We want to ensure they get ample opportunity to relax and rejuvenate without being concerned by the cares of day-to-day living. Hence the services offered under this category ensure that they have more time in hand for themselves and their loved ones, like Home Care, Travel Packages, and Railway Ticket Booking.
- *Life:* This category includes de-stressors that help employees manage work pressure better. The final category under AHA intends to help make employees' lives smoother and less stressful, and also gives them a chance to explore their interests beyond work. These are offered through Stress Management, Safety Training, Dining Discount, and Music Classes.

By engaging families through:

- *HCL Jamboree:* A family carnival organized for employees and their families, with various stalls, talent shows, and at recognition ceremony.
- *SUNSHINE:* A summer camp exclusively for the children of HCL employees in the age groups of four to 15 years. It is a week-long event and various children-related activities are organized at the venues.
- *Bring your Kids To Work Day:* A special day where we invite the children of our employees to accompany their parents to work.
- *Day Care Centers*: We have centers in-campus and near-site available for the very young children of our employees.
- *Mobius*: This is a concierge service providing health support available for employees and their families.

By rewarding and recognizing with:

- *On the Spot Awards:* Under categories of:
  - *Above and Beyond:* For employees who perform tasks that are clearly above the normal duties assigned to the individual's role.
  - *Achievement:* For high levels of teamwork, results, and/or customer service.
  - *Catalyst for Social Change:* For outstanding contribution to sustainability, diversity, and CSR initiatives.
  - *Client Appreciation:* Appreciation received from the client for a job done exceptionally well.
  - *Collaboration:* For those who demonstrate outstanding teamwork in the achievement of the goals of the project.
  - *Exceptional Participation:* For high participation by an employee as a member of the employee resource groups such as Chargers, EFC, and Youthopia.
  - *Initiative:* For HCLites who demonstrate extraordinary resourcefulness and the ability to act and make sound decisions without direction from others.
  - *Results Orientation:* For employees who go the extra mile to meet critical deadlines or deliverables.
  - *I love my work*: For employees who feel passionate about working with HCL and enthuse the team at the workplace.
  - On average 500+ employees gets recognized every month.

- *Ideapreneurship Awards:* To encourage and recognize ideapreneurs who have:
  - Contributed the highest number of qualified leads through Lead Gen.
  - Highest value delivered through implemented ideas in Value Portal.

- *Infinity:* Initiative to applaud employees who have made an impact on the organization on a sustained basis and demonstrated outstanding performance in consecutive years:
  - Number of people who have accomplished this two years in a row has increased by 31% in 2013.

- *Extra Miles:* A peer-to-peer recognition program to enable people to recognize efforts of subordinates, managers, colleagues, and peers across the organization.
  - Miles are then converted to points which the employee can exchange for goods and services of value to them.

By empowering using information from:

- *360 Degree Feedback Reports:* Highlights perceived strengths and blind spots.

- *Passion Report (Team and Individual):* Highlights top passion areas, the extent to which they're being leveraged, and the dominant theme.

We are committed to co-creating these practices by embedding democracy in the way in which we operate by involving Employee Resource Groups and networks to give shape to our workplace policies and programs so as to create an inclusive environment. This is done by investing in:

- *Employee First Councils:* To act as the sounding board for HCL as we look to keep our policies and practices relevant and support HCL in cascading information and decisions related to various operational activities.
- *Youthopia:* To identify and promote practices for HCL to ensure practices resonate with our multigenerational workforce.
- *Chargers:* To facilitate self-interest groups and a vibrant platform that keep our employees engaged.
- *Women Connect:* Work along with HR and line leaders to shape policies that enhance our gender inclusion quotient.
- *Heritage Networks:* A network of employees from different nationalities to discuss cultures, and help each other understand cultural differences to enhance productivity on the job.

By enabling growth and mastery by investing in job-based integrated technical, professional, and domain-learning curricula we invest in increasing proficiencies as demonstrated by the:

- *Disciplined Ideapreneur* who is knowledgeable and, generates ideas himself/herself or by encouraging others in the team. Recognizes the inadequacies of self and the team, seeks most effective and efficient methods in carrying out tasks. May have difficulty in implementing solutions with this limitation. She/he is able to evaluate potential ideas that can impact business outcomes and is also able to reward and recognize the idea generators.
- *Emerging Ideapreneur* is in an evolving stage of skill development and is uncomfortable in attempting to break away from the norm. Believes in collaborative work and adds value to teams' abilities. She/he may be able to generate ideas, but may not be able to generate business outcomes.
- *Operational Ideapreneur* is introspective, extremely confident, believes in self-development, and always moves toward personal growth. She/he is open to feedback and takes charge to seek knowledge, information, and resources to implement the generated solutions. This person follows the policies strictly and may not be efficient at measuring business outcomes.
- *Inspiring Ideapreneur* is aware of team and organizational needs, takes responsibility of mistakes and accepts consequences. She/he has absolute trust in supervisors and subordinates, is open to feedback and criticism, and believes in information transparency. The person does his/her absolute best and sources knowledge, skills, and resources needed for completion of tasks

and takes pride in achievements. She/he rewards idea generators for achievements and contributions made towards business.

Future-proofing our practices

During 2013, a change program known as Program FIRST enabled us to introduce and invest in institutionalization of the Future-Ready Initiatives for Results and Smart Transformation we see the need for. Designed to provide our employees the autonomy to contribute; the mastery to build required skills; and clarity of purpose to contribute towards organizational and personal growth. It introduces practices that strengthened capability for line leaders to enable, empower, and engage HCLites. Program FIRST upgraded our human capital processes in areas of career, performance, rewards, talent, and learning management:

- *Career management* reflects the tenets of our business philosophy Employees First, Customers Second, enabling realistic discussions and building trust transparently with an extended network, and puts decisions in the hands of employees.

  How this translates to an employee is that they can now select their aspired roles on the existing social media platform in HCL and leverage it to help get better advice on his or her career through peers and managers using Role Referrals (peer channels) and Path Recommendation (manager group channels).

  In addition, employees can schedule counseling discussions and provided they meet criteria, can expect to be considered for opportunities they aspire to in line with their progress articulated in their career development plan.
- *The performance management* process provides clarity around goals/expectations and encourages people to provide timely feedback.

  How this translates to an employee is that he or she takes the lead in seeking timely clarity on expectations and performance against these – to absorb/reflect and course correct. Role-based expectation-setting levels their contribution with those of peers effectively increasing the transparency of performance assessment and talent segmentation. Mid-year/periodic feedback becomes an opportunity to identify areas of improvement for mid-course correction and receive performance coaching, especially if performance is lagging. For leading performers, it becomes an opportunity to get re-assessed for progression.
- *Rewards practices* differentiate pay for position and distribute rewards relative to performance against expectations.

  What it means to employees is that their reward quantum and distribution is now changed based on performance. We provide the opportunity to individuals who improve performance to 'earn back' the rewards they did not receive in the previous year.
- *The talent management* process is designed to enable our employees to realize their potential.

This translates into processes that will help the organization identify top talent and support their success by enhancing the quality of decisions related to deployment and development. We may be one of the only organizations in the world that assesses potential for 100% of our people every year.

- *Learning programs* support employees to enhance current role performance and enable them to build skills for future aspirations.

  Now the employees can view and apply for all the learning offerings related to their role and job family across technical, domain, quality, and behavioral courses, and will have opportunities to self-learn and learn what to learn through the help of career counselors.

The next generation

HCL invests in the communities it operates in and has consistently encouraged self-starting businesses, partnerships with companies, educational institutions, and its clients, all of which has contributed to its culture and ways of working.

To engage with new talent, HCL Technologies has set up a program called Make A Difference, Lead The Difference (MAD LTD), which involves students from all over the world submitting innovative ideas to the scheme's website. Senior leaders from within and outside HCL evaluate these submissions. "We take the best idea, and that person is then mentored and funded to develop it to its full potential," says General Manager Kavita Khushalani. "They work with us for six months as CEOs of their own platform to bring their business idea to fruition."

A similar initiative called Ideathon involves students blogging their ideas to HCL, with the top few getting to engage and discussing these with HCL Technologies senior leadership.

Outreach programs

HCL employees also give back to the community through outreach programs anchored by the HCL Foundation. There are HCL Youth Centers set up across deprived areas of India where volunteers teach subjects such as English, maths, and sciences. "Thanks to our virtual learning platform, even HCL staff in England can contribute towards improving the English of the children in our Youth Centers online," says Srimathi Shivashankar, Head of Diversity & Sustainability.

Increasing revenues

HCL's investment in this company culture, along with the initiatives and programs it instituted, has resulted in having consolidated revenues of US$5.5 billion for the year ended FY2014, while revenue generation per employee rose from US$48,600 in 2007 to US$60,500 in FY2014. Customer satisfaction indices have also jumped by 200% from FY2008 to where it stands now in F2014.

This approach has also impressed competitors, the media, and the academic world, alike. It has earned the company numerous awards, including being named one of 'Britain's Top Employers' by the CRF Institute in 2014 for eight years running. The award recognizes the outstanding working conditions created by the company at its London office. HCL has also been acknowledged by *Fortune* magazine as the 'World's Most Modern Management', while Harvard Business School teaches its students about HCL as a case study on business transformation. Anant Gupta, President and CEO, HCL Technologies has received the '2014 Women's Empowerment Principles (WEPs) Leadership Award – 7 Principles' from United Nations. As a proof point of delivering differentiated customer value, 26 of HCL's existing customers have won one of the industry's premier awards 'Value Honors 2012'. Held in conjunction with the InformationWeek 500 ceremony, these awards recognized the unique value created between service providers and customers in transforming customer businesses. HCL is one of only 11 Indian companies to make it to the Forbes's prestigious *Asia's Fab 50* list of the 50 best publicly traded companies in the Asia-Pacific and among only four Indian companies to be part of this group for the past three years. HCL is also one of only two IT services providers to appear in this prestigious listing in 2011 and 2012, as well as the only Asian company featured on *Fortune*'s Dream Team of senior executives. Our HR team being recognized in multiple forums is also a proof point of the ability of the function to create differentiated value created for employees. HCL has been conferred with the 'Asian HR Leadership Award 2012' for 'Innovative HR Practices', as well as won the 'NASSCOM HR Award' in the 'Glocalisers' category for 'successfully driving an integrated global employer brand while balancing the need for localization'.

With HCL seen as an innovative and successful organization with a value system that attracts people who demonstrate the required entrepreneurial energy, it has enabled the company to reinvent itself in a challenging environment and create a reputation for being a place of work that values change and growth.

Conclusion

In conclusion, this chapter highlighted the three critical behaviors of seeding, nurturing, and harvesting that are critical to fostering creativity and growth in global IT firms. Although values drive behaviors and actions, the organization initiated several supporting programs for institutionalizing these behaviors. Employing the guiding principle of co-creation of ideas and value with the customer and initiative being led by the employees, three key supporting programs that supported the new approach are: MAD JAM, Value Portal, and Next Gen. Through these programs the organization generated, selected, shared, and implemented ideas that can be implemented with the customer's involvement. Through these and other employee-centered programs, the organization increased its employee engagement and commitment, critical for sustaining creativity and innovation in the workplace. By developing a supporting framework for various types of ideapreneurs, HCL Technologies created a competency curriculum for ensuring the momentum can be sustained into the future. The Future-Ready Initiatives for Results and Smart Transformation (FIRST) program is an approach to achieve just this goal.

References

Cappelli, P., Singh, H., Singh, J. V., and Useem, M. (2010). Leadership lessons from India. *Harvard Business Review*, *88*(3), 90–97.

Govindarajan, V., and Trimble, C. (2011). The CEO's role in business model reinvention. *Harvard Business Review*, *89*(1/2), 3–8.

Govindarajan, V., and Trimble, C. (2013). *Reverse innovation: Create far from home, win everywhere*. Boston, MA: Harvard Business Press.

Hill, L. A., Khanna, T., and Stecker, E. A. (2007). *HCL Technologies (A). Case 408-004*. Cambridge, MA: Harvard Business School.

Nayar, V. (2010a). *Employees first, customers second: Turning conventional management upside down*. Boston, MA: Harvard Business Press.

Nayar, V. (2010b). A maverick CEO explains how he persuaded his team to leap into the future. *Harvard Business Review*, *88*(6), 110–113.

Nayar, V. (2010c). Employees first, customers second. *Chief Learning Officer*, *9*(10), 20–23.

Radjou, N., Prabhu, J., and Ahuja, S. (2012). *Jugaad innovation: Think frugal, be flexible, generate breakthrough growth*. San Francisco, CA: John Wiley & Sons.

13 Towards an integrated model of human capital development for business model innovation

Synthesis and new knowledge

Ashish Malik and Chris Rowley

Introduction

The success of the Indian information technology (IT) industry can partly be attributed to its ability to constantly adapt to the changing business environment. Change often involves an element of learning and the firm's ability to integrate common and specialist knowledge into their production routines (Grant, 1996a, 1996b). Such changes often require organisations to explore new knowledge and exploit existing knowledge and resource bases (March, 1991). More recently, scholars have suggested that the ability of organisations to simultaneously explore and exploit new learning, or ambidexterity, is a key dynamic capability for ensuring sustained growth and performance (O'Reilly and Tushman, 2008; Teece, Pisano and Shuen, 1997). As evident in Chapters 1, 2 and 5, firms in the Indian IT industry undertook significant changes to their operations and business models for solving their clients' business problems by developing sustainable value propositions. Such a view is common in research on business models, which suggests that successful firms create and realise value by offering solutions that fulfil a customer's latent or expressed needs at effective prices (Zott, Amit and Massa., 2011; Johnson, Christensen and Kagermann, 2008). Reinventing business models requires attention to four key areas: customer value proposition, resource architecture, profit formula and underpinning processes (Johnson et al., 2008). Human resource (HR) and HR management (HRM) practices can and do support the management of change, developing new learning and knowledge resources and, through appropriate policy choices, firms can develop robust process management (Caldwell, 2001; Ulrich, 1997; Ulrich and Brockbank, 2005).

Building on our organising framework developed in Chapter 1, this chapter synthesizes the evidence from practice and research from the Indian IT industry's dynamic context for developing a better understanding how certain HRM practices contribute to business model innovation. Again, the rationale of the 'Working in Asia' series comes through in terms of 'voice' for organisations and practitioners.

Revisiting the organising framework

Figure 13.1 builds on the organising framework developed in Chapter 1. Following our analysis of the contributions in this book, we found two sets of practices: HRM and development (HRM/D) and management practices that support high performance and business model innovations in the Indian IT industry. The opportunities and challenges for profitably managing people in the industry's two key sub-sectors: IT software services (ITTS) and IT product development contexts, are indeed very different. Finally, in our review of the underpinning contributing useful and core theories employed by researchers in studying HRM/D issues and business models in the Indian IT industry, we note that four key theoretical perspectives dominate: the resource-based view (RBV); transaction-cost economics (TCE); HR development (HRD); strategic HRM (SHRM) approaches, including predominantly the best-practice approach, High-Performance Work Practices (HPWS). Though the HPWS approach typically includes HRM practices, in some cases inclusion of several other management practices, such as market-information sensing, quality management practices and senior executive coaching and mentoring, was also part of achieving high performance.

Finally, the literature makes implicit and explicit references to the development of management and HRM/D practices in a business model. Table 13.1 provides further details of the key themes we have covered.

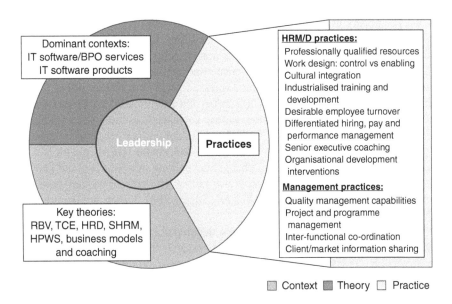

Figure 13.1 Profiting through people: key contexts, theories and practices.

Table 13.1 Key themes and theoretical perspectives

Chapter	Key themes for managing people in the Indian IT industry	Theoretical lens
Part I		
2	HRM shaped by contextual factors, human agency, institutional environment and strategic and entrepreneurial orientation	Institutional theory, strategic choice
	Population ecology approaches also helpful in understanding context	Population ecology
3	Inclusive theoretical approach for human capital exploration and exploitation	HCT, HPWS, MO, QMS
	Incorporates a firm's business development, operations and human capital management practices for developing key organisational capabilities	
4	Further research needed on 'bundles' of HPWS in organisations and how HRM policies and practices play crucial roles in reverse knowledge transfer from Indian settings to global markets	HPWS, RBV, TCE, SHRM
5	Industry evolution from an entrepreneurial-based human capital to a managerial human capital transition supported by SHRM practices and development of individuals with global industry domain and technology skills and delays in moving to a professional and global management culture may have hindered growth of some firms	HCT, SHRM, Institutional theory
6	Key innovative HRM practices for IT services include: job design focusing on excessive control, graduate hiring, industrialised training, high employee turnover, MO and QMS capabilities for efficiency realisation	SHRM, HRD, MO, QMS
7	Key innovative HRM practices for IT product development firms include: empowerment-based work design, long-term HR planning, differentiated recruitment and selection strategy and extensive use of informal and incidental learning	HRD, Work design, RBV
Part II		
8	Tracks temporal changes in skills and development in IT services sector	TCE, SHRM, HRD
	From individual contributors, focusing on investment in generic and technical skills, through bridging technological skills 'gaps' to individuals as strategic 'revenue generators'	
	Training is a strategic business imperative	
9	Key HRM practices for IT product development include: longer-term and proactive HR planning, connected leadership development, talent and skills mix, cultural integration and socialisation, informal and semi-structured learning strategies, rewards and recognition and opportunities for information sharing strategies	RBV, SHRM, MO
10	Reflections from organisational development practices reveal increasing focus of leaders and employees on short-term resource exploitation in IT services market	OD
	Dominant approach still in search of linear coherence and limited focus on innovation due to hard-wired service mindset	
11	Executive coaching can develop behaviours conducive to exploration and exploitation	Self-regulation theory, coaching
12	Framework for managing ideas and innovation in a product development environment by creating value through organisation's employees	Innovation
		SHRM practices for innovation and creativity

Note
HCT = Human capital theory, HPWS = High-performance work systems, HRD = Human resource development, MO = Market orientation, OD = Organisational Development, QMS = Quality management systems, RBV = Resource-based view, SHRM = Strategic HRM, TCE = Transaction-cost economics.

Dominant contexts

As noted previously, in the main the Indian IT industry (services sector) can be broadly classified into two sub-sectors: the ITSS and business process outsourcing (BPO) services market and IT product development and research design and development. While the former sub-sector accounts for more than three-quarters of the industry's revenues, the latter commands about 15% of the overall revenues and is gradually increasing due to a maturing skills ecosystem for product development. People management challenges for services (see, for example, Chapters 6, 8, 10 and 11) and product environments (see for example, Chapters 7, 9, 10, 11 and 12) are very different for both sub-sectors. The underpinning theories informing the SHRM policy choices also differ.

Key theories

Following our review of the chapters in this collection, our own review of the literature on people management in the Indian IT industry and using Swanson's (2007) work focusing on a set of core, contributing and useful theories in building theoretical frameworks, we propose the RBV of a firm and TCE as core theories (Barney, 1991; Williamson, 1975) and theories of HRD, SHRM, HPWS as contributing theories for understanding the dynamics of developing business models and people management in the Indian IT industry (Becker, 1962; Becker and Huselid, 2006; Becker, Ulrich and Huselid, 2001; Delery and Doty, 1996; Huselid, 1995; Paauwe, 2004; Pfeffer, 1998; Schuler and Jackson, 1987; Wright, Dunford and Snell, 2001). Finally, theories of market orientation, quality management, coaching and organisational development are considered useful (Grant, 2001; Du Toit, 2006; Kohli, Jaworski and Kumar, 1993; Reed, Lemak and Mero, 2000; Sinkula, Baker and Noordeweir, 1997; Sitkin, Sutcliffe and Schroeder, 1994; Prajogo and McDermott, 2006).

The IT industry employs a of significant number of knowledge workers and for effectively exploring and exploiting human capital advantages of knowledge workers, RBV and TCE theories serve as a good foundation for understanding differentiation and efficient resource utilisation. The RBV highlights the importance of resource heterogeneity, inimitability and immobility and proposes ways for developing resources that generate human capital and process advantages that are typically needed by product development firms to create new intellectual property and specialist knowledge. Further, for such firms to efficiently manage their unique resources, the TCE lens provides useful theoretical insights. The contributing theories covered in our book have applied SHRM approaches, such as best-practice HRM, context-specific, RBV and configurational SHRM approaches (Pfeffer, 1998; Delery and Doty, 1996; Schuler and Jackson, 1997; Wright et al., 2001) for identifying a key set of HRM practices for exploring and exploiting human capital opportunities. Details of such practices are discussed in the following section.

Leadership, strategy and HRM practices

Leadership approach and a firm's strategic orientation plays a role in shaping the nature and extent of HRM policy choices. Rowley and Ulrich (2012a, 2012b) also emphasise the role and importance of leadership in Asia. For the purposes of this chapter, we have classified HRM practices, in the main, into two groups: those that support an organisation's pursuit to engage in exploitation of existing knowledge and resources, and those that support an organisation's ability to pursue exploration and experimentation to develop new knowledge and learning (see Figure 13.2). These two modes of learning have been noted in March's

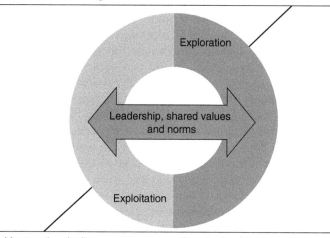

- Extensive HR planning
- Empowerment-based job design
- Flexible work-scheduling
- Embed firm-specific routines
- Unprogrammed learning and development
- Self-directed learning styles
- Differentiated recruitment and selection strategies

- Structured problem-solving
- Reward controlled risk-taking
- Develop university and industry collaboration ecosystem
- Import specialist knowledge
- Increase teamwork and collaboration
- Reward and recognition schemes for innovation

Exploration

Leadership, shared values and norms

Exploitation

- Manage the pipeline (HR planning of secured and forthcoming projects)
- Skill mix forecasts
- Extensive graduate hiring
- Industrialised approach to training and development
- Control-oriented work designs
- Focus on standardisation and reusable work tools and processes

- Standardised business and software development processes
- Strong focus on project and programme management skills
- Quality management capabilities
- Reward execution and process excellence
- Predictive employee turnover for costs and revenue

Figure 13.2 Human capital exploration and exploitation: key HRM and management practices.

(1991) seminal work, wherein exploitation is critical for making efficient use of an organisation's resources and established routines and exploration encourages experimentation and risk-taking behaviour for developing new and innovative products, processes and solutions that addresses either an existing market gap or creates new markets. Recent research on this topic also highlights that ambidextrous leaders need to support both modes of learning for realising a firm's innovation potential (Rosing, Frese and Bausch, 2011).

HRM practices supporting exploration

Case study and ethnographic evidence presented in our book suggests that firms wishing to engage in innovative product or service development must take a longer term view of their human and organisational resources. As such, a medium- to longer-term time horizon for HR planning that incorporates structured innovation management steps and experimentation is evident in IT product development firms. Further attention is needed to the nature of the work design and task scheduling for employees, wherein by creating trust- and empowerment-based designs, employees are allowed some flexibility in the scheduling of their tasks, and undertaking calculated risks and experimentation for developing new product, process or business model innovations (Dovey, 2009; Nooteboom, 2013; Sundbo, 1996; Molina-Morales, Martínez-Fernández and Torlò, 2011).

Most innovative firms develop idiosyncratic routines and knowledge that cannot be easily copied by competitors and thus such firms make conscious efforts to invest in firm-specific routines and practices (Grant, 1996a; Nelson and Winter, 1982; Teece et al., 1997). Such new and idiosyncratic routines can in part be supported by rotating people to develop a range of new skills and by engaging in informal and incidental learning. Most approaches that provide codified modules of knowledge, training and learning can arguably be copied and thus cannot be a source of sustained competitive advantage (Nelson and Winter, 1992; Nonaka, 1994). Allowing employees the space and time for personal reflection supports the generation of new ideas and engaging in the self-directed learning behaviours needed for exploration of new knowledge.

Most high technology products and software applications have a lot of product development history and 'protocol baggage' attached to them. While empowerment-based designs are critical for new product development, it is best if new and existing employees do not tamper with the existing 'protocol baggage', especially those who are tasked with developing synthetic product innovations or product extensions/enhancements. The rationale for such an approach is because any major change in the software product's architecture will most likely have a drastic impact on product functionality and its operational aspects. To overcome this risk, a number of product development firms have adopted a highly disciplined approach in their recruitment, selection and deployment practices.

Quite paradoxically, large product-development firms who plan on deploying new hires on existing product-development teams select people who are least creative and risk-taking. This was borne out in Chapter 7, wherein one case organisation went to the extent of psychometric testing, employing DISC profiling – an instrument that profiles individuals based on their dominance, influence, stability and compliance abilities and styles. Following such an assessment, employees were selected and deployed to product teams. Typically, the preferred profiles of employees included those employees who were good in highly structured problem-solvers, less dominating and influencing and had high levels of stability and compliance behaviours, which allows for structured exploration and risk-taking behaviours.

Another set of critical HRM and management practices for systematic exploration was the organisation's ability to create a favourable skills and resource ecosystem. Collaborating with academia and influencing their curriculum proved extremely valuable as it created industry-ready resources and supported research collaboration between industry and academia. IT product development firms preferred geographic proximity to other organisations in their industry cluster to get a 'pulse' and a sense the emerging technology field. The rationale for this approach is because firms needed access to specialist technical knowledge that was lacking in their ecosystem. Such knowledge can be developed through internal cross-functional team collaboration, or by external clients and product development partner firms. To create a supporting and motivational environment, firms needed to employ intrinsic motivational approaches, such as recognising and rewarding new knowledge, as well as sharing and disseminating success with other peer groups.

HRM practices supporting exploitation

Efficient utilisation of a firm's resources is critical to survival. Firms need to inculcate exploitative routines that are predicated on resource maximisation and efficiency. HRM practices that support exploitation of resources are aptly demonstrated by large IT software service firms. Rahman and Kurien (2007) noted that one of the key HRM tasks IT services firms have to undertake is to forecast and 'manage the pipeline' of contracts in their portfolio. This, along with research covered in our collection, highlights the importance of proactive HR planning. Without careful HR planning and attention to the nature projects in the pipeline, firms will end up having a high percentage of employees 'on the bench' – a term used by the IT industry for the number of employees waiting to be assigned to a billable IT project. Thus, the focus then becomes on increasing resource utilisation and reducing the 'bench-time' for sustained profitability. Firms with a strong order book position can plan for the nature and extent of recruiting and skills. Typically, graduate hiring is the most cost-effective source of hiring and most large IT software service firms hire up to 70% of their annual intake from engineering colleges. Chapters 6 and 8 reinforce the presence of this practice by large IT firms. Further, these firms complement this recruitment practice with extensive provision of in-house, technical and behavioural training. The extent of such training can range from 0 months in duration. This industrialised approach to training has resulted in the establishment of large corporate universities by IT firms and as a consequence producing efficiencies and economies of scale in delivering a range of technical and behavioural training.

Owing to the repetitive nature of most IT or 'technical' work undertaken for multiple clients across multiple industries and geographies, there are opportunities for exploiting efficiencies from a number of reusable components of the technical and business tasks. To fully exploit such opportunities, organisations have developed standard operating processes and protocols. By developing internal best-practice guidelines and process templates, organisations have embedded these into their daily routines. Additionally, by employing quality management frameworks, such as ISO 9000, Capability Maturity Models, Malcolm Baldrige Quality Management and developing strong project and programme skills through PMP (project management professional) certifications, the ability to standardise software development and build operational excellence is greatly increased.

Employee turnover in India's IT and business process outsourcing industry has traditionally been very high and averages between 10% and 70% per annum. The commonly attributed reasons are low salaries, limited career opportunities, stressful working conditions and additional opportunities available in the external labour market. From our review we note that employee turnover also has some other consequences. For example, it helps in reducing the costs associated with annual wage increases of about 14%–20% per annum (which is less than the annual recruitment and training costs) as well as in 'managing the pyramid' of the skills mix and costs associated with such skills mix. Through low employee engagement activities, such as limited career progression opportunities and excessive workflow control, firms can and do achieve predictable and desirable levels of employee turnover. Employee turnover helps firms in reducing the 'bench-time', as well as contributes towards efficiencies from 'managing the pyramid'. The above review highlights the key HRM practices that support exploration and exploitation of human capital. The following section analyses how these HR and management practices support the key elements of IT firms' business models.

Mapping business model elements with HRM and management practices

Firms in the Indian IT industry have constantly reinvented their business models to sustain high levels of growth. Analysing the key elements of a business model (see Figure 13.3), we discuss how certain HR and management practices support the four elements of a firm's business model: customer value proposition; resources architecture; profit formula and robust business process management (Johnson et al., 2008).

Customer value proposition

Firms must continue to solve their customer's expressed and latent problems at an effective cost. To this end, first, firms must possess strong market orientation

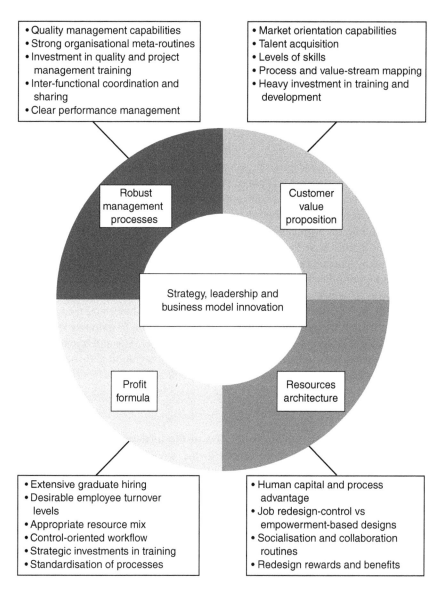

Figure 13.3 Mapping core business model elements with supporting HRM and management practices.

capabilities (Kohli et al., 1993) for accurately sensing customer needs and then disseminate this to development teams who then frame appropriate strategies for responding to their needs. Second, in developing such strategies, firms must be able to generate value through an appropriate number of skilled employees. HRM plays a critical role here by adding value through acquiring and/or developing talent and specific skills. In the case of many large IT firms, significant value was created and realised through higher levels of graduate hiring and efficient use of industrialised approaches to training (see Chapter 8).

Additionally, the presence of strong quality management capabilities, such as Lean and Six Sigma, helped in realising value by reorganising work tasks and accurately estimating the effort required and resource utilisation rates (Malik, Sinha and Blumenfeld, 2012).

Resources architecture

Without the right configuration of resources for undertaking the key tasks of an enterprise, firms run the risk of failure or poor performance. Boxall and Purcell (2011) argued that HR can be a source of sustained competitive advantage if the organisation pays attention to both human capital advantage and human process advantage. While the former relies a lot on talent acquisition and development, the latter focuses on how the HRM function organises these resources in a way that is not only efficient but that also provides opportunities for resource hetero-geneity and immobility through appropriate social capital and routines (Barney, 1991). Since organisations operate in different strategic milieus, they need to align and fit their competitive strategy and HRM policy choices on a continuum of approaches that support the need for control orientation to empowerment ori-entation (Walton, 1985). To embed the above approaches, HR and line managers must ensure employees receive appropriate cultural integration and socialisation support as well as develop reward strategies for embedding these routines.

Profit formula

As noted earlier, by employing up to 70% of the total workforce as graduate engineers, the overall cost of resources in the workforce pyramid is greatly reduced. By leveraging the efficiencies generated through economies of scale in training, firms can generate and realise value through corporate learning univer-sities. Overall, the themes in our book point more towards a control-oriented approach in managing labour and its processes. Large firms in the IT industry break down large and complex tasks into simpler and smaller ones to exercise appropriate management controls through quality management and performance management processes. With increased simplification and standardisation of work tasks and processes though, it becomes easier to deploy the organisation's training and development capabilities much more effectively. Such an approach reduces resource acquisition and development costs, thus contributing to the profit formula of the organisation.

Robust management processes

Once the organisation has developed the right mix of resources through its talent acquisition and development processes, to ensure that these resources engage in efficient modes of development and performance, the organisation needs to develop a strong process backbone and organisational routines. Typically, through well-developed quality management approaches, software development best-practices and process templates can reduce errors and wastage. Further, through controlled workflow and tighter project and programme management approaches, project specifications can be delivered on time. Here again HRM has a significant role to play by outlining clear performance measurement and expectations for employees and appropriate reward structures. Finally, owing to the co-development and interdependent nature of software product development, firms need strong inter-functional coordination skills and capabilities for not only sharing project information between different groups, but also reinforcing organisational routines.

Conclusion

In this chapter we presented an analysis and integration of the key themes in our book. We also identified the key HRM practices that support exploration and exploitation opportunities. This led to a model of human capital development for supporting changes to a firm's business model. The developed model identifies HR practices and opens promising avenues for undertaking further research and exploration by academics as well as highlights implications for practitioners. Our book also points up the challenges and limitations associated with a dispro-portionate reliance on an exploitative mindset in managing human capital. While there are signs of confidence in terms of emerging innovative activity, a lot more remains to be seen and done on the policy and leadership fronts to realise the untapped potential that India as a nation promises in becoming an innovation hub in supporting what has been described as the emergence of an Asian century.

References

Barney, J. (1991). Firm resources and sustained competitive advantage. *Journal of Management, 17*(1), 99–120.

Becker, B.E., and Huselid, M.A. (2006). Strategic human resources management: where do we go from here? *Journal of Management, 32*(6), 898–925.

Becker, B.E., Ulrich, D., and Huselid, M.A. (2001). *The HR scorecard: Linking people, strategy, and performance*. Boston, MA: Harvard Business School Press.

Becker, G. (1962). Investment in human capital: A theoretical analysis Part 2 – Investment in human beings. *Journal of Political Economy, 70*(5), 9–49.

Boxall, P. and Purcell, J. (2011). *Strategy and human resource management* (3rd edn). Basingstoke: Palgrave Macmillan.

Caldwell, R. (2001). Champions, adapters, consultants and synergists: the new change agents in HRM. *Human Resource Management Journal, 11*(3), 39–52.

Delery, J.E., and Doty, D.H. (1996). Modes of theorizing in strategic human resource management: Tests of universalistic, contingency, and configurations. performance predictions. *Academy of Management Journal, 39*(4), 802–835.

Dovey, K. (2009). The role of trust in innovation. *The Learning Organization, 16*(4), 311–325.

Du Toit, A. (2006). Making sense through coaching. *Journal of Management Development, 26*(3), 282.

Grant, A. (2001). Grounded in science or based on hype? An analysis of neuro-associative conditioning? *Australian Psychologist, 36*(3), 232.

Grant, R.M. (1996a). Prospering in dynamically-competitive environments: Organizational capability as knowledge integration. *Organization Science, 7*(4), 375–387.

Grant, R.M. (1996b). Towards a knowledge-based theory of the firm. *Strategic Management Journal, 17*(S2), 109–122.

Huselid, M. (1995). The impact of human resource management practices on turnover, productivity, and corporate financial performance. *Academy of Management Journal, 38*(3), 635–672.

Johnson, M.W., Christensen, C.C., and Kagermann, H. (2008). Reinventing your business model. *Harvard Business Review, 86*(12), 50–59.

Kohli, A.K., Jaworski, B.J., and Kumar, A. (1993). MARKOR: A measure of market orientation. *Journal of Marketing Research, 30*(4), 467–477.

Malik, A., Sinha, A., and Blumenfeld, S. (2012). Role of quality management capabilities in developing market-based organisational learning capabilities: Case study evidence from four Indian business process outsourcing firms. *Industrial Marketing Management, 41*(4), 639–648.

March, J.G. (1991). Exploration and exploitation in organizational learning. *Organization Science, 2*(1), 71–87.

Molina-Morales, F.X., Martínez-Fernández, M.T., and Torlò, V.J. (2011). The dark side of trust: the benefits, costs and optimal levels of trust for innovation performance. *Long Range Planning, 44*(2), 118–133.

Nelson, R., and Winter, S. (1982). *An evolutionary theory of economic change.* Cambridge, MA: Belknap Press.

Nonaka, I. (1994). A dynamic theory of organizational knowledge creation. *Organization Science, 5*(1), 14–37.

Nooteboom, B. (2013). Trust and innovation. In R. Bachmann and A. Zaheer (Eds.), *Handbook of Advances in Trust Research* (pp. 106–124). Cheltenham: Edward Elgar.

O'Reilly, C. III, and Tushman, M.L. (2008). Ambidexterity as a dynamic capability: Resolving the innovator's dilemma. *Research in Organizational Behavior, 28*, 185–206.

Paauwe, J. (2004). *HRM and performance: Achieving long-term viability.* Oxford: Oxford University Press on Demand.

Pfeffer, J. (1998). *The human equation: Building profits by putting people first.* Boston, MA: Harvard Business School Press.

Prajogo, D.I., and McDermott, C.M. (2006). The relationship between total quality management and organizational culture. *International Journal of Operations & Production Management, 25*(11), 1101–1122.

Rahman, W., and Kurien, P. (2007). *Blind men and the elephant: Demystifying the global IT services industry.* New Delhi: Sage.

Reed, R., Lemak, D.J., and Mero, N.P. (2000). Total quality management and sustainable competitive advantage. *Journal of Quality Management, 5*(1), 5–26.

Rosing, K., Frese, M., and Bausch, A. (2011). Explaining the heterogeneity of the leadership-innovation relationship: Ambidextrous leadership. *The Leadership Quarterly, 22*(5), 956–974.

Rowley, C., and Ulrich, D. (2012a). Setting the scene for leadership in Asia. *Asia Pacific Business Review*, *18*(4), 451–464.

Rowley, C., and Ulrich, D. (2012b). Lessons learned and insights derived for leadership in Asia. *Asia Pacific Business Review*, *18*(4), 675–681.

Schuler, R.S., and Jackson, S.E. (1987). Linking competitive strategies with human resource management practices. *Academy of Management Executive*, *1*(3), 207–219.

Sinkula, J.M., Baker, W.E., and Noordeweir, T. (1997). A framework for market-based organisational learning: Linking values, knowledge, and behaviour. *Journal of the Academy of Marketing Science*, *25*(4), 305–318.

Sitkin, S.B., Sutcliffe, K.M., and Schroeder, R.G. (1994). Distinguishing control from learning in total quality management: A contingency perspective. *Academy of Management Review*, *19*(3), 537–564.

Sundbo, J. (1996). The balancing of empowerment. A strategic resource based model of organizing innovation activities in service and low-tech firms. *Technovation*, *16*(8), 397–446.

Swanson, R.A. (2007). Theory framework for applied disciplines: Boundaries, contributing, core, useful, novel, and irrelevant components. *Human Resource Development Review*, *6*(3), 321–339.

Teece, D.J., Pisano, G., and Shuen, A. (1997). Dynamic capabilities and strategic management. *Strategic Management Journal*, *18*(7), 509–533.

Ulrich, D. (1997). *Human resource champions: the next agenda for adding value and delivering results.* Boston, MA: Harvard Business School.

Ulrich, D., and Brockbank, W. (2005). *The HR value proposition.* Boston, MA: Harvard Business School Press.

Walton, R.E. (1985). From control to commitment in the workplace. *Harvard Business Review*, *63*(2), 76–84.

Williamson, O.E. (1975). *Markets and hierarchies: Analysis and antitrust implications.* New York, NY: Free Press.

Wright, P.M., Dunford, B.B., and Snell, S.A. (2001). Human resources and the resource based view of the firm. *Journal of Management*, *27*(6), 701–721.

Zott, C., Amit, R., and Massa, L. (2011). The business model: recent developments and future research. *Journal of Management*, *37*(4), 1019–1042.

Index

Page numbers in *italics* denote tables, those in **bold** denote figures.

For Product Safety Concerns and Information please contact our EU
representative GPSR@taylorandfrancis.com
Taylor & Francis Verlag GmbH, Kaufingerstraße 24, 80331 München, Germany

www.ingramcontent.com/pod-product-compliance
Ingram Content Group UK Ltd.
Pitfield, Milton Keynes, MK11 3LW, UK
UKHW021616240425
457818UK00018B/593